A woodland garden in spring.

WILDFLOWERS
in your GARDEN

Text and Photographs by
VIKI FERRENIEA

Illustrations by
CAROL BOLT

A REGINA **ЯR** RYAN BOOK

RANDOM HOUSE: NEW YORK

Book Producer: Regina Ryan Publishing Enterprises, Inc.

Editor: Regina Ryan

Designer: Murray Belsky

Production Manager: Ellen Kagan

Administrative Editor: Maggie Higgins

Copy Editor: Castle Freeman

Proofreader: Joan Rosenblatt

Indexer: Catherine Dorsey

Typesetting: A & S Graphics, Inc.

Printer: Oceanic Graphic Printing (USA), Inc.

A REGINA RYAN BOOK

Printed in Hong Kong

Library of Congress Cataloging-in-Publication Data:

92-50547

ISBN 0-679-41453-3

This book is dedicated to Dr. Edgar T. Wherry, with whom I shared many a wonderful field trip in search of our native wildflowers. He opened my eyes to their special needs and taught me to interpret their habitats.

To Linc and Timmy Foster, who gave to me so generously and gladly of their time, knowledge and plants, as they did to so many people, enriching all our lives.

And to Sikkim, without whose inquisitive nature and exuberance in life I would have missed many a wildflower and not enjoyed a "walk in the woods" nearly so much!

Sikkim on a boardwalk crossing a fragile bog.

CONTENTS

The bright colors and delicate appearance of the native fire pink (Silene virginica) combine to make it a lovely accent in the spring woodland garden.

The white pasque flower (Anemone patens alba), with its beautiful blossoms in early spring followed by ornamental seed heads and its attractive, heavily dissected foliage, is a striking native wildflower with multiseason interest.

Preface

For love of gardening is a seed that once sown never dies, but always grows and grows to an enduring and ever-increasing source of happiness.

GERTRUDE JEKYLL

WILL CURTIS, THE CREATOR OF Garden in the Woods in Framingham, Massachusetts (see Appendix C), once said, "Growing wildflowers is just common sense and observation." These words, however, came from a man who spent his long life growing wildflowers, and they do not tell the whole story. Gardeners—even experienced ones—need a solid base of knowledge if they can hope to have real success with growing wildflowers.

The word "wildflower" encompasses a broad spectrum of meanings and interpretations. It carries many individual and highly personal definitions, and the question invariably arises concerning the distinction between native and non-native plants.

For the purpose of this book, "wildflower" refers only to those plants that are native to—that is, plants that originated on—the North American continent.

There are also many non-native plants from around the globe that have established themselves throughout this continent, and I do include some of these naturalized "immigrants" in my discussions and garden designs. Although they did not originate here in our woods, fields, deserts, mountains and prairies—and are not considered native wildflowers in the context of this book—the non-native plants are often integral parts of a wildflower area, natural or manmade, and I could in no way create my gardens without them.

Unless you are a purist about origins, the real criterion for accepting a plant should be not whether it is a native, but whether it is the right one for you to grow. Is it suitable for your climate, and does it fit into your garden plan? And do you have a reasonable chance of growing it successfully? Consider these factors, rather than only its heritage.

🌹 🌹 🌹

As an avid gardener and a professional horticulturist specializing in wildflowers for many years, I have traveled and taught extensively in many parts of North America. Through all the years of my gardening, lecturing and teaching, I have found that people repeatedly ask many of the same questions about wildflowers and voice many similar frustrations about their attempts at wildflower gardening. I hope, with this book, to address these common issues and share the knowledge and insights that I have gathered in more than two decades of experience of gardening with wildflowers.

Giving a plant the correct name has always been a complicated and controversial subject, with experts frequently disagreeing among themselves. One reason for the difficulty is that the botanical names of plants are constantly being changed and updated. In this text, I have used the most up-to-date botanical (Latin) names, except when these names are not yet in common usage in the nursery trade or literature. In such cases, the more familiar names have been used in the text; however, the most recent Latin name is listed along with the familiar name in the index.

The common (English) names of plants add even more confusion to this subject, as one plant can have a number of different names. A common name may also refer to several different plants, even ones in a different genus! Again, I have chosen those names that are most frequently used in order to make it easy to recognize and find both familiar and unfamiliar plants. However, because the Latin name is the only certain identification of a plant, I have included it in parentheses after the common name at the first mention of a plant in each chapter. All common and Latin names are also cross-referenced in the index.

Throughout the text, I have used the following reference works for nomenclature: *The New Britton and Brown Illustrated Flora of the Northeastern United States and Adjacent Canada, Hortus Third, A Field Guide to the Ferns* by Boughton Cobb, *Manual of Woody Landscape Plants* by Michael Dirr, *Manual of the Vascular Flora of the Carolinas* by Radford Bell and Ahles Bell, *The Flora of New England* by Frank C. Seymour and *The Flora of Missouri* by Julian Steyermack.

I encourage readers to get to know these plants by their Latin names so there will be no question about which plant is referred to. This will help avoid the disappointment of receiving the wrong wildflower from a nursery or seed house, and it will also help you avoid the possibility of passing a misnamed plant on to someone else.

*The bottlebrush buckeye (*Aesculus parviflora*) is an infrequently seen native shrub of easy culture in full sun or light shade. It grows to 8 to 12 feet high and flowers in summer.*

Introduction

*Let no one be discouraged
by the thought of how
much there is to learn.
For the first steps are
steps into a delightful
Unknown, the first
successes victories, all
the happier for being
scarcely expected.*

GERTRUDE JEKYLL

FOR ME, THE ATTRACTION OF GROWING native plants lies in capturing in my garden something of the beauty and wildness I have seen on forays into unspoilt areas, where these plants grow to perfection. I also enjoy the challenge of growing these truly wonderful plants that I have come to cherish and admire so much.

The very mention of wildflowers, or the suggestion of gardening with them, evokes more emotions and plays more upon the senses than any other group of plants or form of gardening. For some people, it brings to mind a tranquil woodland where the lush greens of foliage are woven together with broad threads of sparkling colors from the flowers. This peaceful and harmonious scene is enhanced by the constantly changing patterns of sunlight so typical of a shady area. Here, also, there is a background of bird song and the underlying smell of rich earth, which add to the appeal of such a place.

Others envision a warm, fragrant summer meadow, ablaze in a vibrant sea of color where the wildflowers sway in the gentlest of breezes and add their rustling sounds to the hum of insects. Butterflies brush the flowers, and birds flash amongst the undergrowth of this haven that is their home.

Perhaps these images are so appealing because wildflowers represent nature's most successful marriage of beauty and resilience, strength and delicacy. The interplay of colors, shapes and textures has developed with no assistance from us, and the very wildness of these plants is a large part of their appeal.

They appear and seem to thrive nearly everywhere: in woods, along hiking trails, in picnic areas and abandoned fields. No one has sown, cultivated, fertilized or propagated these wildlings, so, we conclude, it should be easy to grow them in our gardens. After all, don't we refer to many of them as weeds? We think that by scattering seeds or plopping some wildflowers into a place that is vaguely similar to their natural habitat, the plants will provide us with a beautiful garden where we can enjoy their beauty.

As enticing as it might seem, this approach will not provide us with the lovely, bountiful gardens we are looking for. It's just not that easy. Each wildflower has specific needs that must be met for the plant to grow and flourish. In some cases, these needs can fall within a relatively narrow range of conditions. As gardeners, we are accustomed to think that cultivating plants is simply a question of good soil preparation and proper aftercare. These are vital elements, to be sure, but they are only a small part of the process. To be successful in growing wildflowers, we must shift our focus from creating an excellent "all-purpose" garden bed to establishing one that will meet the particular needs of specific wild plants or groups of them. In effect, we must try to recreate in our garden the wildflowers' natural environment—or the closest facsimile possible.

As gardeners, we are blessed—and our expectations have been raised—by the wealth of good garden plants that have been cultivated for centuries and are readily available to us. We are accustomed to growing plants that have been developed not only for superior characteristics but for their simple and rather uniform culture along with a tolerance for a broad range of environmental conditions.

This is the major difference between growing traditional garden plants and growing wildflowers. The wildlings we treasure have evolved through eons to find their special niche in the world, that singular combination of conditions in the environment where all their needs are in balance and they can flourish.

Once we understand this crucial difference, it is certainly not difficult to change our focus to make the necessary adjustments in our gardens. If we can combine a desire to grow certain plants with a knowledge of their needs and an understanding of our garden environment, we will be amply rewarded.

Sometimes people seem to think that because these plants grow in the wild, it isn't necessary to provide them with all the care we happily lavish on our other plants. In fact the opposite is true. Even though there are few absolutes in gardening—especially in an area as large and varied as the North American continent—good gardening is still good gardening, and all the basic principles of horticulture that we follow for our cultivated garden plants must be applied to our wildflowers as well: thorough soil preparation, conscientious watering and a sound maintenance schedule.

A basic knowledge of each plant's habitat and cultural needs, coupled with practical experience, will enable us to succeed with our initial selections and to gradually expand the number and variety of wildflowers in our garden as our skills and understanding of our property grow. We will also be able to mix wildflowers in our gardens in a manner not seen in nature, because we will be able to monitor and—to some extent—manage the habitat so we can nurture many different species.

Knowing our native plants and their preferred conditions of growth can also demonstrate for us the advantages these plants have over non-natives—in particular, their resilience. Because our native wildflowers originated here, they are well suited to the vagaries of the North American climate and are therefore more likely to flourish here than many of the traditional garden plants we see in cultivation and growing so lushly in other parts of the world. For instance, plants seen in the temperate climate of Britain do not always perform so exuberantly in the severity of the climatic extremes we may experience here. They may not survive, or at the least will do poorly, in the harshness of a Philadelphia summer or a warm humid fall in Atlanta, and will take little joy in a New England winter.

This book is specifically designed to lead a gardener through the steps necessary to create a successful habitat for native plants, whether it is one designed specifically for them or a traditional garden where the wildflowers will be mixed with other, more familiar plants. We'll examine ten different gardens, each with a different setting, environment and selection of plants, and then examine the needs and characteristics of 100 wildflowers and companion plants such as ferns, shrubs and small trees. Following this, I will explain how you can bring wildflowers into your gardens, developing a design that uses them to best advantage. Then I will explain how to build, plant and maintain your own unique wildflower habitat.

To understand a wildflower's environment fully—and to supplement the information in this book—you will need to take the time to observe these plants where they grow well, both in nature and in established, successful wildflower gardens. Over the years, I have found it especially helpful to closely observe wildflowers wherever they are flourishing. The ideal, of course, is to see them where they grow in the wild, but this is not always possible. And so many wildflowers are thriving in gardens throughout North America that it is not difficult to find and study these plants. Seeing them in a contrived setting also offers the opportunity to thoughtfully evaluate the locale, considering everything from soil to sun. An additional advantage of observing wildflowers in gardens is that there will probably be a knowledgeable guide to answer your questions.

I cannot overemphasize the importance of making time to browse through gardens. I'm thinking, not of an eight-gardens-a-day trip with thirty-seven other people, but of a quiet exploration, on your own or with a kindred spirit, in which you can poke around to learn as much as possible and try to match what you see with what you have and what you want to do. When you see something you like, visualize something similar in your own garden—and figure out what you would need to do to duplicate the effect.

Learning these nuances of wildflower gardening is a gradual process. It requires good observations, sound garden sense, perhaps a little detective work along with the inevitable trial and error—and a bit of that happy element so prevalent in gardening: Luck!

As you accumulate bits and pieces of information, you will automatically begin to form a more complete picture of wildflowers and their needs for successful growth. You will then be able to evaluate your information and to decide if what you want is, in fact, feasible: if indeed you can reasonably grow the plants you've selected for your garden. You may want to draw heavily from the garden designs presented in this book; or you may prefer to develop your own scheme based on your sense of what will work on your property, using these gardens as a starting point for ideas.

It's amazing how quickly things fall into place once you have the right focus and know what to look for. Of course, each of us is going to have different experiences with these plants, as happens with all gardening endeavors. You will develop a sense of just where on your property a certain plant or group of plants should grow, and what needs to be done to the site to provide whatever the requirements may be to tip the balance of success in the plant's favor. Although these plants do need special conditions and care, the majority of wildlings will thrive and live for many years when their basic needs are met—and this success can come quite easily. You will also understand why the Turk's-cap lily (*Lilium superbum*) is not found beside the New England aster (*Aster novae-angliae*) or the wood lily (*Lilium philadelphicum*), why the bird's-foot violet (*Viola pedata*) is not found alongside a cool, shady stream with the wood anemone (*Anemone quinquefolia*), and why the goldenrod (*Solidago* species) does not flourish near the rose mallow (*Hibiscus palustris*).

As your powers of observation increase and your skills improve, you may find that some of those wildflowers you once considered beyond your reach may, with special care, flourish. How satisfying it is to accomplish such a goal!

*Blazing star (*Liatris spicata*), black-eyed Susans (*Rudbeckia hirta*) and wild bergamot (*Monarda fistulosa*) form the central theme of this summer meadow that is also home to a multitude of bees and butterflies.*

PART I
The Gardens

There can be few gardeners who at some time or another have not toyed with the idea of a piece of woodland and been beguiled by the thought of making a wild garden therein.

To most of us the term "wild garden" evokes a picture of a piece of woodland, streamside or perhaps an old orchard, an attractive plot of ground which can be made even more delightful by the introduction of suitable plants, native and exotic, which will add to the setting without spoiling it. In such a place the emphasis must always be on the aesthetic. One must take care "not to startle the nightingales."

JUDITH BERRISFORD

EACH OF THE TEN GARDENS in this section presents a wide range of beautiful impressions and gardening opportunities. Because the choice of wildflowers that can be grown in them is so broad, all of these gardens are suitable for the majority of climates in North America. Once you have read through all of them, you can choose the type of garden and the plants that will suit your specific location and will achieve the effects you are looking for.

I have selected both wildflowers and traditional garden plants primarily for their ease of culture and for their ability to establish themselves readily in a broad range of climates and situations. Surprisingly, despite the reputation many wildflowers have for being difficult and challenging, I have found the vast majority to be quite easy to grow, once their requirements for soil, moisture and light are met. How well they do will be affected by your regional weather. Obviously, the plants in a garden in Raleigh, North Carolina, with that area's long growing season, will grow and produce flowers more quickly than those in a garden in Ann Arbor, Michigan, or Ottawa, Ontario, with their shorter growing seasons and harsher winters. Nevertheless, these plants are suitable for almost any climate in North America, all have their own beauty and charm and all will enable you to turn your dreams into reality.

I have also chosen the plants for the special qualities they bring to the garden. Some add color and some provide fragrance; others, such as the ferns and Solomon's seal (*Polygonatum biflorum*), contribute texture and shape. Some are just plain showy, like the bloodroot (*Sanguinaria canadensis*), while others have multiple uses: the colorful foliage and ground-cover effect of the gingers (*Asarum* species), or the bright show of flowers plus good fall color of the blue star (*Amsonia tabernaemontana*). Some bloom very early, like the hepaticas (*Hepatica* species), or for a long period of time, like golden star (*Chrysogonum virginianum*). Still others just give one big splash of breathtaking beauty, after which they recede into a background of green, as with trilliums (*Trillium* species).

❧ ❧ ❧

The gardens I have designed here vary in the amount of effort and involvement they require. Some, like the border gardens, are easy to build and maintain. The Bog Garden, on the other hand, requires a more advanced level of skill and gardening experience. Some gardens are relatively inexpensive to create, while others demand more of a financial investment. To guide you in your choice, I have discussed what is involved in the creation of each one.

Select from these gardens the one or several that best suit your property, resources, level of skill and aspirations, adapting the basic plans as you need to. When you select a wildflower garden, it is important to keep in mind what role your garden will play in your overall landscape plan. It may be the feature planting of your property, or it may be a small corner within a larger garden. Wildflowers may provide the focal display for several weeks, for an entire season, or even for the whole year—including winter.

My recommendation to those who are new to this type of gardening is to select a wildflower garden that will give solid rewards without a lot of aggravation or superhuman effort, so that you will be encouraged to go on after your first successes to the more demanding plants and gardens. More experienced gardeners may find that several of the gardens (perhaps the Rock Garden and certainly the Bog Garden) will present intriguing design possibilities and challenge their horticultural skills. But whatever your choice, remember to keep the size and scope manageable so the whole endeavor is an enjoyable one.

Keep in mind that shade gardens are home primarily to spring-flowering plants and those with ornamental foliage, such as the ferns, while sunny gardens provide summer and fall flower displays. Of the ten gardens presented here, four are shady—the Woodland, the Suburban Woodland, the Fern Garden and the Shady Border—while three are sunny—the Meadow, the Sunny Border, and the Bog Garden—and three could be adapted for either shade or sun with different selections of plants—the Waterside Garden, the Rock Garden and the Container Garden.

Many gardens, however, are neither always in the sun nor always in the shade, and frequently there are "transition zones," areas that receive varying degrees of sun and shade throughout the day and from season to season. These places present the perfect opportunity to introduce plants that will tolerate fluctuating amounts of sun or shade—thus extending the variety of plants that can be grown. (To learn more about sun, shade, and how to determine what a garden site offers, see Chapter 14, "What Kind of Wildflower Garden Is Right for You?")

Before you finally decide on a garden, be sure to read Chapter 15, "Using Wildflowers in Your Garden," which discusses how to use wildflowers as elements of an overall plan, with an emphasis on the all-important task of integrating your garden into the existing landscape.

1

A Woodland Garden

THIS GARDEN PROVIDES THE GARDENER with the opportunity to create a wildflower garden embodying the quintessential North American woodland area that so many gardeners dream of creating, enjoying and caring for.

A woodland garden is at its height of color in the spring, when the majority of our favorite shade-loving plants bloom. This can also be a garden with year-round interest, however, if the plant selection and design are well thought out to bring into play all the ornamental attributes plants offer. The many shades and colors of foliage, the textures and intricate patterns of leaves, the growth habits of the plants themselves: all these features can provide striking displays.

During the summer, the colors of a woodland garden—primarily shades of green, with the creams and silvers of variegated foliage—are subtle, cooling and restful to look upon. They reflect the quietude that is a natural part of a wood at that time of year, providing a refreshing contrast to the busyness and vibrancy of a neighboring sunny garden.

In late summer and autumn, the fruit and seed heads of many plants and the bark of woody plants can also be quite decorative. Fall foliage displays are not limited to a woodland's deciduous trees, either: the full, rich colors of many woodland perennials and shrubs will rival the red maples in their brilliance.

The woodland garden is also a place of fragrance and sound. The aromas change through the seasons, but the most powerful essence of this garden is found in spring, in the dry crisp smell of last year's leaves and in the freshness of the season itself. "You can smell spring in the air," is an often-heard comment of outdoor people. This scent is more than simply the warming of the earth; it is the very essence of spring, a nearly primeval blend of organic fragrances. Along with the rich earth odor, its elements include the scents of vernal witchhazel (*Hamamelis vernalis*), native azaleas, and one of the sweetest and most treasured fragrances of all, that of the trailing arbutus (*Epigaea repens*).

❧ ❧ ❧

Creating a woodland garden requires tall, mature trees. They may be hickories, oaks, maples, or tulip trees, to mention a few. These produce the high shade canopy and diffuse the bright, penetrating sun into a filtered light that is so essential to woodland plants. Beneath the tall trees, there may already be some native understory shrubs or trees; the small trees might be birch (*Betula* species), goosefoot maple (*Acer pensylvanicum*), flowering dogwood (*Cornus florida*), shadbush (*Amelanchier* species), silver bell (*Halesia carolina*), or redbud (*Cercis canadensis*), while the shrubs might include azaleas, mountain laurel (*Kalmia latifolia*), native viburnums (*Viburnum* species) and lowbush blueberry (*Vaccinium*

*Left: A simple grouping of showy trillium (*Trillium grandiflorum*), maidenhair fern (*Adiantum pedatum*) and wood phlox (*Phlox divaricata*) exemplifies the elegant simplicity of our native wildflowers, which is much of their appeal.*

Overleaf: A view of a woodland garden in spring, showing how the flowers, foliage and growth habit of the plants combine to make a diverse and beautiful scene. The garden covers one-quarter of an acre but seems larger because it is surrounded by woods. Shrubs and tall perennials provide a screen that creates an intimate feeling and focuses attention on the plantings close to the paths. A plan view and a key to the plants used in the garden follow the painting.

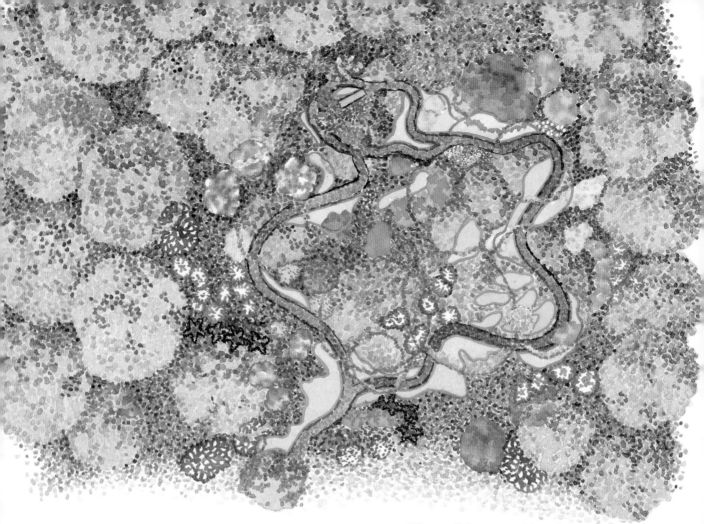

angustifolium). There may also be herbaceous perennials, including ferns, baneberry (*Actaea* species) and false Solomon's seal (*Smilacina racemosa*).

The plants for this woodland garden have been chosen not only for their exceptional beauty, but also for their innate toughness, longevity and apparent readiness to provide gardeners with appealing displays. With careful planning and selection of plants, an existing woodland area can be transformed into a garden that looks very natural, even if it includes non-native plants.

Initially, a woodland garden is best planted with easy-to-grow wildflowers chosen from the rich selection that is available. Some of these should be plants that naturally spread to form a ground cover: foamflower (*Tiarella cordifolia*), crested iris (*Iris cristata*) and creeping phlox (*Phlox stolonifera*) are ideal, as is partridgeberry (*Mitchella repens*), with its snowy white flowers that later develop into bright red berries.

The low-growing plants also offer plenty of choices of color and form, from the many shades of blue and pink found in hepaticas (*Hepatica* species) to the yellow, white or rose flowers of the trout lilies (*Erythronium americanum*) and the sparkling white of the ephemeral Dutchman's-breeches (*Dicentra cucullaria*) and squirrel

The four-foot-wide bark path circles through the garden toward its destination — a rustic bench.

Key to the Planting

1 Allegheny shadbush - *Amelanchier laevis*
2 Baneberry (red) - *Actaea rubra*
3 Blue cohosh - *Caulophyllum thalictroides*
4 Bottlebrush shrub - *Fothergilla major*
5 Carolina rhododendron - *Rhododendron carolinianum*
6 Carolina silverbell - *Halesia carolina*
7 Chokeberry - *Aronia arbutifolia*
8 Christmas fern - *Polystichum acrostichoides*
9 Cinnamon fern - *Osmunda cinnamomea*
10 Double pink-flowered rue anemone - *Anemonella thalictroides* 'Schoaf's Double Pink'
11 European wood anemone - *Anemone nemorosa*
12 Flame azalea - *Rhododendron calendulaceum*
13 Fringe tree - *Chionanthus virginicus*
14 Goatsbeard - *Aruncus dioicus*
15 Japanese columbine - *Aquilegia flabellata* 'Nana'
16 Kamchatka bugbane - *Cimicifuga simplex*
17 Lady fern - *Athyrium filix-femina*
18 Maidenhair fern - *Adiantum pedatum*

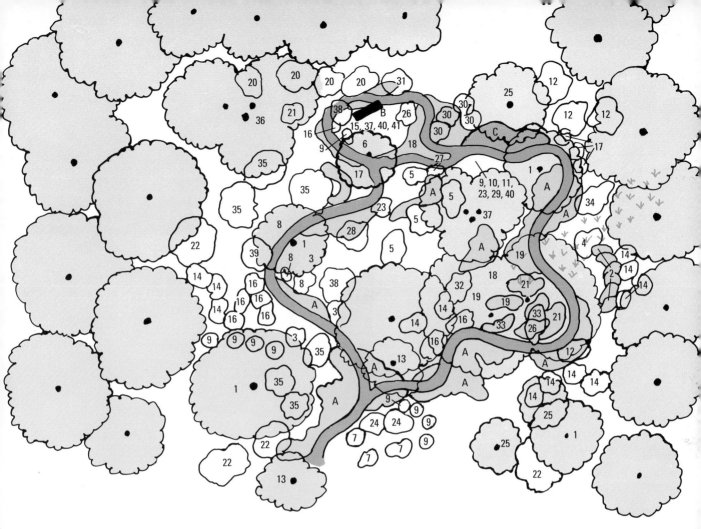

ocation of both introduced and existing plants.

19 Marginal shield fern - *Dryopteris marginalis*
20 Mountain laurel - *Kalmia latifolia*
21 Northern beech fern - *Thelypteris phegopteris*
22 Oak-leaf hydrangea - *Hydrangea quercifolia*
23 Oconee bells - *Shortia galacifolia*
24 Pinxter bloom - *Rhododendron periclymenoides (R. nudiflorum)*
25 Redbud - *Cercis canadensis*
26 Redvein enkianthus - *Enkianthus campanulatus*
27 Rodgersia - *Rodgersia pinnata* 'Superba'
28 Roseshell azalea - *Rododendron roseum (R. prinophyllum)*
29 Showy trillium - *Trillium grandiflorum*
30 Spicebush - *Lindera benzoin*
31 Swamp azalea - *Rhododendron viscosum*
32 Tall bugbane - *Cimicifuga racemosa*
33 Variegated Japanese Solomon's seal - *Polygonatum odoratum* 'Variegatum'
34 Vernal witchhazel - *Hamamelis vernalis*
35 Wayfaring tree - *Viburnum alnifolium*
36 White birch - *Betula papyrifera*
37 Wild columbine - *Aquilegia canadensis*
38 Winterberry - *Ilex verticillata*
39 Winterhazel - *Corylopsis pauciflora*
40 Wood phlox - *Phlox divaricata*
41 Wood poppy - *Stylophorum diphyllum*

A Additional beds
B Bench
C Bed shown in detail

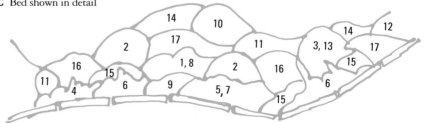

Plan of Bed C (Approximately 20 ft. long)

1 Bloodroot - *Sanguinaria canadensis* interplanted with (8) grape hyacinth - *Muscari armeniacum*
2 Blue cohosh - *Caulophyllum thalictroides*
3 *Cimicifuga dahurica* underplanted with (13) squills - *Scilla sibirica*
4 Creeping phlox - *Phlox stolonifera* 'Blue Ridge'
5 Creeping phlox - *Phlox stolonifera* 'Lavender Lady' interplanted with (7) European wood anemone - *Anemone nemorosa*
6 Crested iris - *Iris cristata*
7 European wood anemone - *Anemone nemorosa*

8 Grape hyacinth - *Muscari armeniacum*
9 Japanese painted fern - *Athyrium nipponicum* 'Pictum'
10 Kamchatka bugbane - *Cimicifuga simplex*
11 Lady fern - *Athyrium filix-femina*
12 Rodgersia - *Rodgersia pinnata* 'Superba'
13 Squills - *Scilla sibirica*
14 Solomon's seal - *Polygonatum biflorum*
15 Wild bleeding heart - *Dicentra eximia*
16 Wood poppy - *Stylophorum diphyllum*
17 Yellow-flowered epimedium - *Epimedium X versicolor* 'Sulphureum'

In spring this mature wildflower garden is carpeted with wood phlox (Phlox divaricata) —both the blue- and white-flowered forms. The phlox swirls around white wild bleeding heart (Dicentra eximia 'Alba'), double showy trillium (Trillium grandiflorum 'Flora Plena') and wood poppy (Stylophorum diphyllum).

corn (*Dicentra canadensis*). (Ephemerals are those plants that go dormant after they have flowered and dispersed their seeds.)

The midsized plants are many, and it is hard to stop at only a few. My choices here include the trilliums (*Trillium* species) in all their pleasing forms and colors, from purest white to maroon and yellow; the brilliant yellow wood poppy (*Stylophorum diphyllum*); clear blue wood phlox (*Phlox divaricata*); and the various shades of pinks, lavenders, blues, purples and white of creeping phlox, which create rivers of color to swirl over the ground and around other plants, much as waves do around rocks.

Taller-growing wildflowers would include the white-flowered baneberries with their bright red or white fruits in late summer; Solomon's seal (*Polygonatum biflorum*), whose graceful arching stems and creamy bells edged in green add an elegant note; or the blue cohosh (*Caulophyllum thalictroides*), with its architectural foliage and clusters of green and brown flowers, followed in late summer with fruits that resemble blueberries.

If the tree and soil preparations are done thoroughly (see Chapter 16, "Building a Wildflower Garden"), this garden will be easy to plant and to care for. The initial effort may require a large investment in time, money and/or labor, but the commitment is necessary to achieve success. Your hard work will not only sustain the plants that you place in a woodland garden, but will also provide an environment that will encourage them to spread and regenerate themselves. This is the hallmark of real success in any established garden.

A group of Trillium discolor *makes a beautiful highlight in the spring woodland garden.*

The pinkshell azalea (Rhododendron vaseyi) *has unusually delicate pink flowers.*

Near a small stream, the expanding fronds of cinnamon fern (Osmunda cinnamomea) *and the bright flowers of daffodils* (Narcissus *species*) *herald spring.*

2
A Suburban Woodland Garden

IT ISN'T NECESSARY TO OWN ACRES of woods to have a fine woodland garden, and in fact, some of the loveliest gardens I've ever seen were created on typically small suburban properties with just a few trees. When space is at a premium, each element of the garden design holds great importance, and each plant needs to be selected very carefully to suit the role it will play. It is the interrelationship of the plants and other design elements that create the atmosphere of a quiet woodland garden—regardless of the amount of space available.

A shady area created by a few trees can provide a starting place for a diverse, intimate and very enjoyable shade garden that can include a number of our loveliest wildflowers and can closely resemble a woodland garden in miniature.

Some people are fortunate to live on a wooded property that has obvious natural potential to become a woodland garden. There may already be a stand of mature trees or a few large shrubs that will suggest the beginnings of such a garden. Many more homeowners, however, have a modest suburban property with few trees. These trees may be leftovers from the time the house was built, or—more likely—they will be part of an earlier landscape plan, and might well include a small clump of birch, a planting of lilacs, maybe an old apple tree or perhaps a few large shade trees, which will always lend a feeling of maturity and permanence.

The garden illustrated here is approximately 21 feet in length and 10 feet in width at its widest point. It was developed around four large hickories. Alone, these trees, although beautiful in their own right, looked rather solitary and uninteresting and appeared to have little relationship to the rest of the property.

Because I have set several of the plantings on the periphery of the shady area, the woodland aspect of this small garden has been drawn outward. The garden and trees then blend unobtrusively into the surrounding landscape without an abrupt transition. This design technique gives a garden the illusion of greater size and privacy, whether the adjoining area is a lawn, a wood margin, a driveway or even a neighbor's garage.

This is not a difficult garden to create, but it requires good planning and careful plant selection to make best use of the limited space and provide year-round interest.

Several shrubs serve as backdrops or screens. These were chosen not only for their floral displays, but for their overall ornamental qualities as well. Japanese andromeda (*Pieris japonica*) and the compact form of inkberry (*Ilex glabra compacta*) (an attractive native holly) have evergreen foliage with winter appeal, while the

*Both creeping phlox (*Phlox stolonifera*) and foamflower (*Tiarella cordifolia*), with their strong flower displays in spring and their ability to make effective ground covers in just a few seasons, are good choices for a woodland garden.*

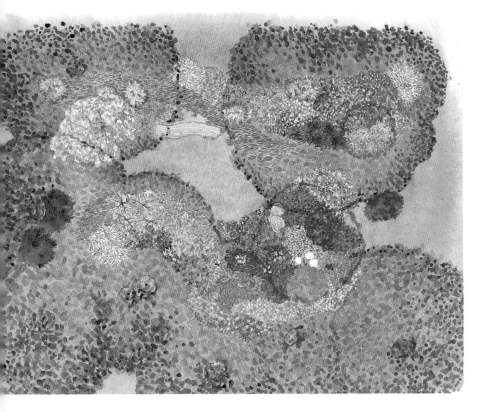

A suburban woodland garden in spring. In the garden illustrated here shagbark hickories (Carya ovata) and white birches (Betula papyrifera) provide ample shade for a small but diverse wildflower garden.

Key to the Planting

1 Alum root—*Heuchera americana*
2 Baneberry (red)—*Actaea rubra*
3 Bloodroot—*Sanguinaria canadensis*
4 Blue cohosh—*Caulophyllum thalictroides*
5 Christmas fern—*Polystichum acrostichoides*
6 Cinnamon fern—*Osmunda cinnamomea*
7 Creeping phlox 'Blue Ridge'—*Phlox stolonifera* 'Blue Ridge'
8 Crested iris—*Iris cristata*
9 Dwarf inkberry—*Ilex glabra compacta*
10 Fall-flowering witchhazel—*Hamamelis virginiana*
11 False Solomon's seal—*Smilacina racemosa*
12 Foamflower—*Tiarella cordifolia*
13 Goatsbeard—*Aruncus dioicus*
14 Golden star—*Chrysogonum virginianum*
15 Highbush blueberry—*Vaccinium corymbosum*
16 Kamchatka bugbane—*Cimicifuga simplex*
17 Jack-in-the-pulpit—*Arisaema triphyllum*
18 Large yellow lady's-slipper—*Cypripedium calceolus* var. *pubescens*
19 Japanese andromeda—*Pieris japonica*
20 *Narcissus* 'February Gold'
21 *Narcissus* 'Thalia'
22 Rodgersia—*Rodgersia aesculifolia*
23 Roseshell azalea—*Rhododendron prinophyllum*
24 Shagbark hickory—*Carya ovata*
25 Shooting-star—*Dodecatheon meadia*
26 Snowdrop—*Galanthus nivalis*
27 Squills—*Scilla sibirica*
28 Tall bugbane—*Cimicifuga racemosa*
29 Variegated Japanese Solomon's seal—*Polygonatum odoratum* 'Variegatum'
30 Variegated Japanese andromeda—*Pieris japonica* 'Variegata'
31 Wake robin—*Trillium erectum*
32 Waldsteinia—*Waldsteinia fragarioides*
33 White birch—*Betula papyrifera*
34 White-flowered epimedium—*Epimedium grandiflorum*
35 Wild columbine—*Aquilegia canadensis*
36 Wild cranesbill—*Geranium maculatum*
37 Winter aconite—*Eranthis hyemalis*
38 Winterhazel—*Corylopsis pauciflora*
39 Wood phlox—*Phlox divaricata*

A Bench
B Tree stump
C End of bed

Plan of the suburban woodland garden.

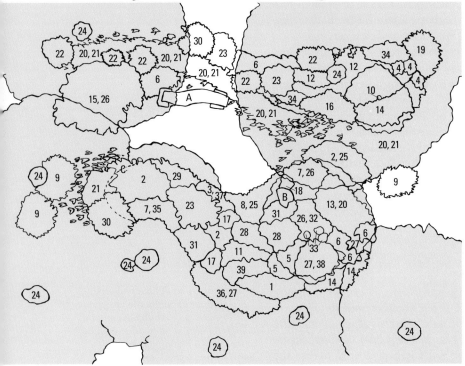

The bold foliage of hosta (Hosta species) and the subtle flower display of the wood phlox (Phlox divaricata) are used here to create a setting that shows off the large yellow lady's-slipper (Cypripedium calceolus var. pubescens).

Variegated Japanese Solomon's seal (Polygonatum odoratum 'Variegatum') and epimedium (Epimedium species) are two outstanding non-native plants that bring great charm to a shady garden, where they can serve as accent plants or as ground covers.

garden season begins with vernal witchhazel (*Hamamelis vernalis*), with its very early fragrant flowers. Another good choice would be the lovely winterhazel (*Corylopsis pauciflora*) from Japan with its soft, fragrant yellow flowers and its elegant shape. Next comes the early-flowering native roseshell azalea (*Rhododendron prinophyllum*), chosen for its high branching habit and its rich pink blossoms, which have a scent reminiscent of cloves.

Highbush blueberry (*Vaccinium corymbosum*) and rodgersia (*Rodgersia aesculifolia*) have been used as a backdrop to scale down the large size of the hickory trees and tie them in to the lower-growing herbaceous wildflowers. Ground covers such as creeping phlox and the golden star lend a fullness to the garden; they also are quick to fill in empty spaces to create the feeling of a mature garden. These can be interplanted with bulbs and spring ephemerals to extend the display time from early to late spring.

Taller plants like baneberry, blue cohosh and goatsbeard (*Aruncus dioicus*) are carefully spotted about the area to give height and accents of interest. These are also planted in the woods behind this garden, thus making the whole area look from a distance like a single, integrated unit.

The trees and shrubs in this garden form the framework, just as they do in a large woodland area, while the perennials are the body of the garden and create the picture itself. Small groups of tall wildflowers (or, in the case of a large plant, a single specimen) and the larger ferns are used to form a sweeping background for the smaller plants and midsized ferns.

Scattered through these are the "carpeters," the mat-forming plants: foamflower, creeping phlox, waldsteinia (*Waldsteinia fragarioides*) and the gingers (*Asarum* species).

In this way, I have created an open and spacious-appearing area. Despite its small size, there is no sense of the garden's being crowded or closed in. Indeed, for me, one of the delights of a lightly shaded garden like this is its airiness: in summer, especially, there is a sense of coolness from the many shades of green and the movement of the plants from the slightest breeze.

Because of its size and close proximity to the house, this garden will be a place to visit often, even on cold winter days.

With proper preparation, the suburban woodland garden is simple and undemanding. It will provide the inexperienced gardener with the perfect introduction to gardening with wildflowers. It can also offer the more experienced gardener the ideal place to watch over some very special plants that might otherwise be lost in a larger area.

*Creeping phlox (*Phlox stolonifera*) and blue cohosh (*Caulophyllum thalictroides*) will fill in the space the ephemeral Virginia bluebells (*Mertensia virginica*) and spring beauty (*Claytonia virginica*) leave when they go dormant.*

*Wild cranesbill (*Geranium maculatum*), cinnamon (*Osmunda cinnamomea*) and maidenhair (*Adiantum pedatum*) fern provide interest from early spring until a hard frost.*

Left: A small, seemingly uninteresting area with a shrub or two and several shade trees is an ideal spot to develop into a small wildflower garden for shade-loving plants.

3
A Shady Border

THIS GARDEN IS BASICALLY a handsome formal bed in the style of a traditional perennial or mixed border, but with wildflowers mixed in among the more familiar perennials. It could be a long rectangular bed next to a building, fence or wall, or a free-form island bed set into a lawn, but whatever shape it takes, the shady border must be in filtered shade for most, if not all, of the day.

The actual amount of shade may vary somewhat. In the morning and evening when the angle of the sun is low, it would do no harm for this garden to receive some direct light. The perimeter of the shade line will also receive some direct light, and your selection of plants will have to take this into consideration.

The height of bloom, as with all shade gardens, is in spring.

The native wildflowers in this garden are particularly well suited to this formal planting because of their ease of culture and freedom of bloom, and because of the impact of their flower display. Plants include the glossy-leaved Ozark phlox (*Phlox pilosa* ssp. *ozarkana*) with its stiff, strong stems that carry numerous pink flowers blushed with lavender, and the golden star, which tolerates light shade, especially in areas with hot summers, and makes a fine foreground or edging plant.

Excellent non-native plants such as the imposing Asian rodgersias and (in warmer climates) the bear's-breeches (*Acanthus spinosus*) from Europe are good choices. The old-fashioned foxglove (*Digitalis purpurea*), with its broad gray-green leaves, is an especially handsome plant even when it is not in bloom, and it adds special interest to a shade garden throughout the growing season.

As this is a formal garden, hostas, with their great variety of foliage colors, sizes and forms, work well. Shade-loving annuals such as impatiens could be included to give a splash of summer color among the greens. People do not often think of rex begonias as companions for wildflowers, but these, with their highly stylized leaves, leaf markings and rich color, can be set into a shady border for the summer, too. They provide a striking contrast to the more typical greens of the season.

During the summer, color and interest come primarily from the colorful foliage of plants such as the rich, burgundy-purple leaves of *Heuchera micrantha* 'Palace Purple' and the very dark green foliage with a rich burgundy cast of astilbe 'Fanal'. With the arrival of cold weather, the foliage of oconee bells (*Shortia galacifolia*) takes on a dark plum-red color, which adds to the year-round interest and appeal of this lovely evergreen wildflower.

Many plants with yellow or silvery variegated foliage give the illusion of exceptional brightness, which makes them particularly useful in darker corners. I have taken advantage of this here by using the variegated wild oats (*Uvularia sessilifolia* 'Variegata') and

*Tall trees that have been limbed up to form a high shade canopy provide the ideal setting beneath which to grow both wildflowers and traditional garden plants. In this border Jacob's ladder (*Polemonium reptans*) and the white crested iris (*Iris cristata alba*) are early performers in a pageant that will go on for many months.*

Plan of the shady border.

A shady border in spring. In a small garden like this, it is especially important to provide several special displays where featured or favorite plants are placed within a setting that puts them in the spotlight. In this garden I used oconee bells (Shortia galacifolia), the white Asian bleeding heart (Dicentra spectabilis 'Alba') and the large yellow lady's-slipper (Cypripedium calceolus var. pubescens) as the featured plants. The old shed is 8 by 15 feet, and the garden (including the shed) is approximately 12 by 42 feet.

Key to the Planting

1. Alum root—*Heuchera americana*
2. Asian bleeding heart—*Dicentra spectabilis*
3. *Astilbe* 'Fanal'
4. *Astilbe* 'Sprite'
5. Baneberry (red)—*Actaea rubra*
6. Bowman's root—*Gillenia trifoliata*
7. Christmas fern—*Polystichum acrostichoides*
8. Creeping phlox 'Blue Ridge'—*Phlox stolonifera* 'Blue Ridge'
9. Creeping phlox 'Lavender Lady'— *Phlox stolonifera* 'Lavender Lady'
10. Crested iris—*Iris cristata*
11. Dutchman's-breeches—*Dicentra cucullaria*
12. Dwarf epimedium—*Epimedium* X *Youngianum* 'Niveum'
13. False rue anemone—*Isopyrum biternatum*
14. Galax—*Galax aphylla*
15. Giant Solomon's seal—*Polygonatum canaliculatum*
16. Golden star—*Chrysogonum virginianum*
17. Large yellow lady's-slipper— *Cypripedium calceolus* var. *pubescens*
18. Lenten rose—*Helleborus orientalis*
19. Mountain laurel—*Kalmia latifolia*
20. Oconee bells—*Shortia galacifolia*

21. Pinxter bloom—*Rhododendron periclymenoides*
22. Purple-leaved coral bells—*Heuchera micrantha* 'Palace Purple'
23. Rodgersia—*Rodgersia aesculifolia*
24. Rosy twisted-stalk—*Streptopus roseus*
25. Round-lobed hepatica—*Hepatica americana*
26. Spinulose wood fern—*Dryopteris spinulosa*
27. Sweet woodruff—*Asperula odorata*
28. Toad lily—*Tricyrtus hirta*
29. Trumpet honeysuckle 'Cedar Lane'— *Lonicera sempervirens* 'Cedar Lane'

30. Variegated Japanese Solomon's seal— *Polygonatum odoratum* 'Variegatum'
31. Vernal witchhazel—*Hamamelis vernalis*
32. Virginia bluebells—*Mertensia virginica*
33. White Asian bleeding heart—*Dicentra spectabilis* 'Alba'
34. Wood phlox—*Phlox divaricata*
35. Yellow-flowered epimedium— *Epimedium* X *versicolor* 'Sulphureum'

A. Tool shed

*Right: A stone wall or hedge in a shady area can provide the ideal background for a wildflower garden. Here, in early spring, creeping phlox (*Phlox stolonifera*) forms a ground cover amongst rhododendron, showy trillium (*Trillium grandiflorum*), Solomon's seal (*Polygonatum biflorum*) and goatsbeard (*Aruncus dioicus*).*

*Many shade-loving plants have extraordinarily attractive foliage that provides interest and color throughout the growing season. Here, alum root (*Heuchera americana*), with its striking silver-mottled leaves, makes a handsome companion for wood phlox (*Phlox divaricata*).*

the evergreen Virginia ginger (*Asarum virginicum*).

And do not overlook the summer-flowering bulbs that will grow well in light shade, such as naked ladies (*Lycoris squamigera*), with their tall (30 inches or more) stems and terminal clusters of pink flowers, which add a wonderful splash of color scattered among the lush greens of summer.

Several shrubs are tolerant of light shade in the North, and require it in the South. These include the native summer-flowering oak-leaf hydrangea (*Hydrangea quercifolia*), the plumleaf azalea (*Rhododendron prunifolium*), and the non-native Robin Hill azaleas.

In the warmer zones, the evergreen vine *Clematis armandii* is a fine choice with its glossy, dark green foliage, covered with flowers in the spring, and it seems happy in shade or sun. For a vine with more restrained growth, use the native trumpet honeysuckle (*Lonicera sempervirens*), of which 'Cedar Lane' is a distinctive and lovely selection with scarlet-orange flowers that form a cascade of bright color.

Later, in early fall, the blue mist shrub (*Caryopteris* X *clandonensis*) and the toad lilies (*Tricyrtis* species) (both from China and Japan, and so infrequently seen in gardens) flower, putting on an exotic display while sweet autumn clematis (*Clematis maximowicziana*) spices the air with its lovely fragrance.

In autumn, the yellow flowers and foliage of the native fall-flowering witchhazel (*Hamamelis virginiana*) are always welcome, as is the deep-red-to-plum foliage of the wayfaring tree (*Viburnum alnifolium*) and redvein enkianthus (*Enkianthus campanulatus*). And for a lovely autumn display, remember the fall fruit of the many viburnums and the winterberry (*Ilex verticillata*), or the subtler displays of berries on blue cohosh and Indian cucumber root (*Medeola virginiana*). In this season, many of the colors are soft, mellow tones that are no less engaging than the fiery brilliance of the woody plants' fall foliage.

🌿 🌿 🌿

The old garden shed in the garden shown here has been made into an important design element and also provides a backdrop for the plantings. In this example, the wood of the shed is aged and blends in beautifully with the natural look of the plantings. If you have a new wooden structure, plants and weather will soon soften its harsh appearance, or the wood can be stained a pleasing shade to hasten the process.

Tall oaks provide the shade here, but there is plenty of reflected light from the surrounding areas, as the landscape is in full sun away from the oaks. These oaks have been limbed up and a few branches have been thinned out to produce a light, filtered shade.

An old planting of mountain laurel forms the backdrop on slightly elevated ground beside the shed, and this gives additional height for the screen. The azaleas and witchhazel were added to provide some early color and fragrance, and to soften the solid green of the mountain laurel foliage. The back line formed by the mountain laurel balances the shed and draws the overall dimensions of the border outward, thus reducing the prominence of the shed and settling it into the plantings.

The old tree stump and log not only add interest but also provide a setting and a haven for favorite plants, especially the smaller ones whose roots can tuck themselves down into the cool, damp earth that is mixed with the decaying wood. The native ferns, baneberries, Virginia bluebells (*Mertensia virginica*) and Solomon's seal create a secondary frame and provide strong vertical accents for the lower-growing plants such as the crested iris and false rue anemone (*Isopyrum biternatum*). The ground covers—foamflower and creeping phlox—tie the whole area together, giving it unity and fluidity, while the large yellow lady's-slipper (*Cypripedium calceolus* var. *pubescens*), oconee bells and wild bleeding heart (*Dicentra eximia*) are beautiful features that heighten the visual impact and interest of this garden.

The shady border should appeal to those gardeners who have an existing bed in which they would like to include some favorite native plants without becoming totally immersed in wildflowers. It is an easy garden to create and maintain. If it does replace an earlier planting, it is an even easier undertaking because you can take advantage of the previously prepared bed and soil work.

*Color in a garden comes from both flowers and foliage. This lovely purple-leaved bugbane (*Cimicifuga ramosa atropurpurea*) makes a spectacular specimen plant, adding a dramatic splash of color before, during and after the flower display.*

*Below left: The intense sky-blue flowers of the native Jacob's ladder (*Polemonium reptans*) combine with the elegant white Asian bleeding heart (*Dicentra spectabilis 'Alba'*) to create a beautiful spring picture.*

Bottom: Native and non-native plants blend together beneath a crab apple in this small courtyard to give many months of interest in an easily cared for garden.

4
A Fern Garden

THERE ARE MANY PLACES IN THE WILD where ferns can be seen growing under optimum conditions, and in these places they make an enviable display. Simply taking the time to stop and look at them should convince any gardener of the merits of these plants for a shade garden.

Ferns, like the ornamental grasses, are all too conspicuous by their absence in most garden landscapes. It is sad that primarily green or nonflowering plants are so often overlooked when gardens are planned.

A fern garden provides the opportunity to create one of the most delightful and subtle of gardens, and the ferns themselves are always an essential component of any woodland wildflower garden. Most are easy to grow, require relatively little care, and with a minimum of effort will provide a varied and fascinating display throughout the growing season.

In early spring, the curled croziers of the ferns snuggle close to the ground and hold the promise of spring before expanding to their full gracefulness. In the summer months, ferns give the impression of a cool, restful retreat. And in the crisp autumn air, they form a kaleidoscope of yellows, golds, oranges and beiges that make a superb show to end the season. Their colorful tints and hues will rival the more vibrant displays from the trees.

A fern garden can be as small as a narrow border set along the shady side of a tiny cottage (as shown here), or as large as several hundred square feet within a woodland.

In a cool northern climate this garden may be grown in partial to full sun, especially if the soil is kept constantly moist from a nearby source of water such as a stream or the overflow from an artificial pond. Generally, however, the fern garden will flourish best in the shade of large trees or on the northern side of a protective building.

The wonderfully diverse patterns and textures of the different ferns provide variety and contrast in a planting. Many are almost architectural in appearance, producing a form of living sculpture with endless variation. This sculptural effect is further heightened by the splashes of sunlight that filter through the tree cover and dance on the fronds, changing the entire scene—according to the time of day and the way the tree canopy moves in the breeze.

With a fern garden, you do not have to think about color schemes and seasonal displays in the same way that you do when you develop a design with flowering plants. Except for early spring, when ferns are beginning their growth, and in fall, when they are developing their many autumn colors, the visual perspective remains very much the same throughout the growing season. Therefore, the design of the garden is especially important and should take full advantage of the individual growth habits and subtle colorations that make each kind of fern special.

The royal fern (Osmunda regalis) forms a beautiful accent from the moment its coppery fronds emerge in spring. They mature into a rich green in summer and turn a soft yellow in the fall. The royal fern is perhaps the most elegant of all ferns.

Plan of the fern garden.

A fern garden in spring. With their diverse shapes and subtle colors, ferns are a delight in a shady area. They can be used as specimens, ground covers or as part of a group with other ferns or shade-loving flowering plants.

Key to the Planting

1 Autumn fern — *Dryopteris erythrosora*
2 Christmas fern — *Polystichum acrostichoides*
3 Cinnamon fern — *Osmunda cinnamomea*
4 Japanese painted fern — *Athyrium nipponicum* 'Pictum'
5 Lady fern — *Athyrium filix-femina*
6 Maidenhair fern — *Adiantum pedatum*

7 Marginal shield fern — *Dryopteris marginalis*
8 Northern beech fern — *Thelypteris phegopteris*
9 Redvein enkianthus — *Enkianthus campanulatus*

A Bird bath

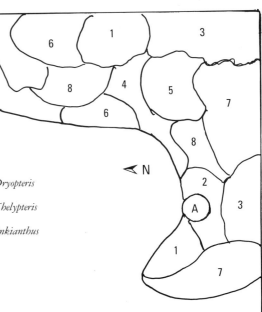

Top left: A group of stately ostrich fern (Matteuccia struthiopteris) *makes a wonderful accent, especially amongst spring ephemerals. In summer the spreading fronds fill in the space left by the early dormancy of the virginia bluebells* (Mertensia virginica) *shown here.*

Top right: The tall ferns have many uses in the informal and naturalistic garden. Here cinnamon fern (Osmunda cinnamomea) *is used to edge a shady driveway.*

Below: The attractive foliage and flowers of merrybells (Uvularia perfoliata) *and foamflower* (Tiarella cordifolia) *and the unusual mottled foliage of Shuttleworth's ginger* (Asarum shuttleworthii) *contrast with the pale green of the southern maidenhair fern* (Adiantum capillus-veneris).

For instance, the tall species like goldie's fern (*Dryopteris goldiana*) and ostrich fern (*Matteuccia struthiopteris*) make wonderful background plantings. They can also be used as edging along a shady driveway (provided enough room is left for their full summer proportions, which can be quite large). They can be ground covers, specimens or companion plants—in fact, they fill just about any role. And these tall ferns certainly add the final touch of beauty when set beside a bench or garden ornament.

The fern garden I have designed does have some large specimen shade trees giving it cover, but as it is on the north side of the house, it gets most of its shade from the building.

The native ferns in this garden inclue the dark, glossy Christmas fern (*Polystichum acrostichoides*) and picturesque marginal shield fern (*Dryopteris marginalis*) (both of which are evergreen), the graceful lady fern (*Athyrium felix-femina*), the refined, filigreed maidenhair (*Adiantum pedatum*), the stately cinnamon fern (*Osmunda cinnamomea*) (used here as a background plant) and the northern beech fern (*Thelypteris phegopteris*). These plants are quite distinct from each other and offer ample diversity in color, foliage pattern and growth habit.

With ferns, you can use both native and non-native varieties to create a color display that will come primarily from shades of green such as that seen in the beautiful bright green fronds of the native oak fern (*Gymnocarpium dryopteris*). The autumn fern (*Dryopteris erythrosora*) from Japan is spectacular, bearing new copper-colored foliage in spring that changes to a dark, glistening green in summer. You can enhance this effect by selecting those varieties with other color nuances, like the Japanese painted fern (*Athyrium nipponicum* 'Pictum') with its silver variegation, the red-stemmed form of lady fern (*Athyrium filix-femina* forma *rubellum*), or the ebony-stemmed maidenhair fern (certainly one of the loveliest and most refined of all). In wet places, the elegant royal fern (*Osmunda regalis*) begins its display in coppery tones that change into a bright green for summer, completing the cycle in fall with a cascade of yellow.

Some of the smaller and more challenging ferns, such as the ebony spleenwort (*Asplenium platyneuron*) and the purple cliff brake (*Pellaea atropurpurea*), are best used singly to feature their diminutive proportions. Both prosper in tight crevices of limestone rocks; the cliff brake, in fact, prefers this location.

Many wildflowers mix well with ferns and provide additional color and variety in the spring. Consider, for instance, some of the spring ephemerals like Virginia bluebells, toothwort (*Dentaria diphylla*) and Dutchman's-breeches. Or you might include the blue wood phlox, wild columbine (*Aquilegia canadensis*) and the cheerful yellow wood poppy. One of the loveliest spring memories I have is of a spacious planting of ostrich fern, around which swirled an ocean of deep sky-blue forget-me-nots (*Myosotis alpestris*). Other good companions for ferns are primroses, as they also favor cool, moist soils with plenty of organic matter.

I also like to use Johnny-jump-ups (*Viola tricolor*) as a ground cover around the larger ferns—much to my friends' surprise, as these plants are considered invasive. In a fern garden, however, these cheerful and prolific wildflowers do not become a problem as they do among lower-growing wildflowers, where they have a tendency in their exuberance to smother the more delicate plants.

In sunny areas, colorful natives like cardinal flower (*Lobelia cardinalis*), sneezeweed (*Helenium autumnale*) and pink turtle-head (*Chelone lyonii*) will add extra sparkle to a planting of ferns.

For late color, think of any of the several species of toad lily or fall-flowering crocus (*Crocus speciosus*) to give bright splashes of lavender or white. These mix particularly well with the golds and yellows of ferns in the fall.

All in all, this is a very satisfying, attractive and easy to maintain garden. Once the plants are established, it requires little maintenance but must always be kept well watered, as ferns do poorly in dry soils. It is a good garden for people who have little time, and it is ideal for those who travel a great deal because it is such a peaceful place to return to.

*Above: The forget-me-nots (*Myosotis alpestris*) scattered around the ostrich ferns (*Matteuccia struthiopteris*) add a special sparkle to this spring display.*

*Left: In a fern garden you can take advantage of the distinctive foliage of the plants, their growth habit and their many shades of green—all of which create an engaging scene. The delicate appearance of the maidenhair (*Adiantum pedatum*) and lady fern (*Athyrium filix-femina*) is enhanced by the bold leaves of the skunk cabbage (*Symplocarpus foetidus*) growing behind them.*

5

A Waterside Garden

THIS REFRESHING AND PEACEFUL garden is designed to nestle alongside a stream and wrap around a small pool. It is a beautiful place that attracts wildlife and birds as well as people.

You can create the features of a waterside garden artificially, or you can work with an existing wet area on your property. (See the section on constructing waterside gardens in Chapter 16, "Building a Wildflower Garden.") The latter may be a wild area, full of unsightly weeds and rank growth, difficult to do much with and impossible to maintain. This is a place that contains an abundance of the wet, oozing muck that seems to have a proclivity for sucking in garden machinery down to the axles!

But it is also a place that can (with some hard work and imagination) be transformed into a delightful garden, a special place of great charm. Moisture-loving ferns and wildflowers will flourish here, with the right preparation and care. The careful management of such an area—which includes controlling the growth of the invasive weeds—will allow many desirable native plants with less-aggressive tendencies to appear, sprouting from dormant seeds or from those fortuitously brought in by wind, animals or birds. These will add their unexpected display to the design you have intentionally created.

Whether you develop your waterside garden from a naturally wet place (as was done in our illustrated garden) or create it artificially, this habitat provides not only constant soil moisture, but also—because of its proximity to water and the cooling effects of evaporation—a comparatively lower air temperature in summer. Here you can capitalize on the tempered environment and various microclimates afforded by a waterside location, and you may well be able to grow many plants that favor cool growing conditions and that could not otherwise be considered in a warm climate. Additional factors, including variations in sun and shade and protection from wind, make it possible to grow many different plants in a waterside environment, and this garden is therefore well suited to most regions of North America.

A waterside garden is suitable for a large area which can accommodate sizable plants, especially those with dramatic foliage. Over time you can establish sweeps of a favorite plant, using bold colors to draw the eye to different areas.

Striking effects can be created with variegated iris, a carpet of primroses (*Primula* species)—especially the Japanese primrose (*Primula japonica*)—or perhaps a shrub, like the mature highbush blueberry, that is given special emphasis by being pruned into a highly ornamental shape, as shown in the illustrated garden. This plant naturally has a rather Oriental form which, with some careful pruning, can become as distinctive as any Japanese maple.

A waterside garden can also be quite small and still be very

*Top left: Japanese primrose (*Primula japonica*), marsh marigold (*Caltha palustris*) and later in the season cardinal flower (*Lobelia cardinalis*) are colorful additions to a moist shady area that never completely dries out. In such a location they will self-sow and form sizable colonies.*

*Bottom left: The coast azalea (*Rhododendron atlanticum*) prefers to grow in full sun and moist to wet soils, where it will cover itself in late spring in brilliant and strongly fragrant white flowers brushed in pink.*

*Bottom right: In areas beside water where the soils are cool and moist, Christmas (*Polystichum acrostichoides*) and cinnamon fern (*Osmunda cinnamomea*) will grow lushly and add a cool, restful appearance to a summer landscape.*

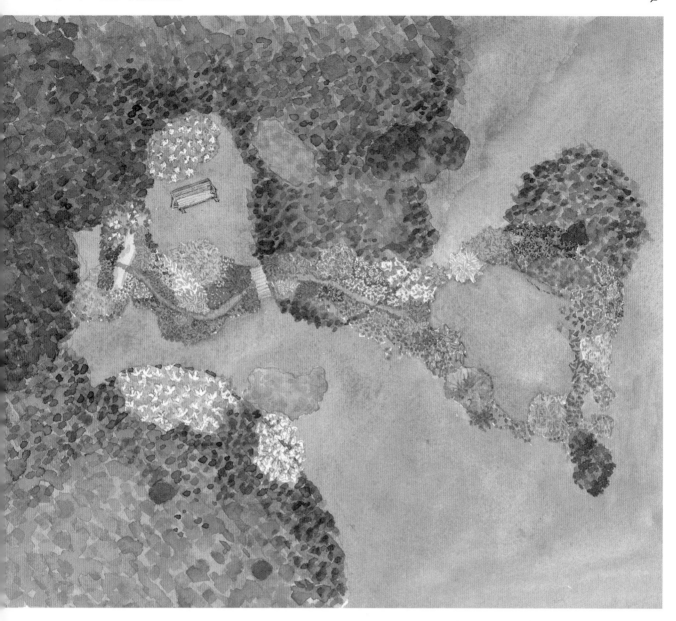

This waterside garden, shown here in spring, has been created around a natural spring that emerges in the shade of the woods; the garden continues along the small stream that meanders down the hill, and circles around the sunny, shallow pond at the stream's end. The tempered environment and microclimates found in the vicinity of water allow gardeners to succeed with a broader range of plants than they would normally.

effective. You might have just one corner of your larger garden (perhaps a natural low spot, even at the edge of a marsh or swamp) planted with moisture-loving plants to bring a unique element to your garden. Or you might create a secluded place of quiet retreat with a small artificial pool or stream.

🌿 🌿 🌿

The waterside garden's display begins early, often when ice is still to be found along the water's edge. First to come are the warming golden flowers of marsh marigold (*Caltha palustris*) (the kingcups of England, where it is also found), whose sparkling

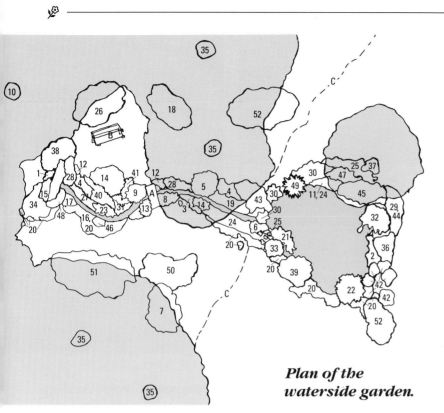

Plan of the waterside garden.

beauty contrasts with the somber green and brown hoods of the skunk cabbage (*Symplocarpus foetidus*). These are soon followed by the pleated leaves of false hellebore (*Veratrum viride*) and the soft green croziers of ferns. After these come the delicate white blossoms of wood anemone (*Anemone quinquefolia*) and the soft pink flowers of the ephemeral spring beauty (*Claytonia virginica*), which will easily form sizable colonies to carpet a moist area.

After these earliest harbingers of spring, the creamy white flowers of the native bottlebrush shrub (*Fothergilla major*) open and add their subtle, honeylike fragrance to the other aromas of this season. The display moves toward summer with multicolored Japanese primroses and astilbes, the blue of camas lily (*Camassia cusickii*), and the various colors of the water-loving iris. Summer's bright scarlet cardinal flower, so loved by hummingbirds, is one of the next to show, along with the rich blue of the great blue lobelia (*Lobelia siphilitica*). Next to arrive are the pink or white turtleheads (*Chelone lyonii* and *C. glabra*) and the many golden flowers of mid- to late summer that include sneezeweed, Indian-cup (*Silphium perfoliatum*) and goldenrod (*Solidago* species) that make such a lovely display with the dusty rose pink of Joe-pye-weed (*Eupatorium purpureum*).

The show of color finally draws to a close in fall with the deep blue of bottle gentian (*Gentiana andrewsii*) and the rich hues of autumn foliage as the plants move toward senescence: there are

Top left: Golden club (Orontium aquaticum) thrives in the shallow water at the edge of a pond, while the swamp pink (Helonias bullata) creates a splash of color on the marshy bank.

Top right: In summer, providing the soil remains damp, moisture-loving plants will flourish even if water is not visible.

Bottom: The variegated yellow flag iris (Iris pseudacorus 'Variegata') forms a focal point throughout the growing season.

the soft yellows of the native sweet pepperbush (*Clethra alnifolia*), the scarlet of chokeberry (*Aronia arbutifolia*) and sourwood (*Oxydendrum arboreum*), and the dark plum colors of Virginia sweetspire (*Itea virginica*). Seed heads and fruits, which are especially plentiful in wet areas, often share the last moments of the season with splashes of purple from the lingering flowers of ironweed (*Vernonia noveboracensis* and *V. altissima*) and the lavenders, whites and pinks of asters.

Wherever your waterside garden is located, there is a great array of plants to choose from to match a garden's climate and the gardener's enthusiasm and taste.

Native ground covers like partridgeberry and Labrador violet (*Viola labradorica*), for instance, can tumble over the edges of the artificial streamside and pool and give a natural, settled look to the manmade structure. This can be further enhanced by including ferns and other plants with foliage that has a mounding form to it, such as Bowles golden sedge (*Carex stricta* 'Bowles Golden'), Allegheny spurge (*Pachysandra procumbens*), oconee bells, golden Alexander (*Zizia aurea*), and vancouveria (*Vancouveria hexandra*).

In the sunny location, golden club (*Orontium aquaticum*), pickerel weed (*Pontederia cordata*) and arrowhead (*Sagittaria latifolia*) thrive in the shallow water they prefer. Small trees and shrubs such as goosefoot maple, birch, spicebush (*Lindera benzoin*), swamp azalea (*Rhododendron viscosum*) and sweet pepperbush screen out the rest of the world, creating a quiet haven. They also shelter the area from drying winds, preserving the cool, moist air of the waterside.

Some of the more unusual plants, especially those with imposing growth habits, can be grown as specimens in a waterside garden to accentuate their unique charm. These include the almost prehistoric-looking gunnera (*Gunnera chilensis*) from South America, the imposing goldie's fern, and the tall, stately (but rarely seen) featherfleece (*Stenanthium gramineum* var. *robustum*).

A wonderful side benefit of a waterside garden is the wildlife it can attract. Many birds will gather near a shallow pool to drink and bathe, especially in winter, when they need access to open water. In warm weather, there will also be a plentiful supply of insects near the water for the birds to feed on, and they will be particularly attracted to this area when they have young to raise.

In the garden illustrated here, a natural spring emerges in the woods and meanders down a gentle slope to a sunny depression where the water table is high and a wet, marshy area has formed. Previously, weeds and sedges abounded, giving it an unkempt look, and the area was impossible to mow. The natural course of the trickle of water was excavated with a hoe and spade to make a stream, and the low spot was scooped out with a backhoe into a small, shallow pond measuring about 15 by 20 feet and approximately 6 to 8 feet deep.

Some gardening expertise is needed with this type of garden. It's important that you know enough about the requirements and tolerances of each plant so you can site them in places that are the most suitable for them. Too much moisture, and some may rot—too little, and some will do poorly. Some wildflowers do not mind periodic immersion in water; others must have their crowns above water but will thrive if their roots are down in really soggy wet soil; still others need standing water; and there are those that prefer to grow in running water. Others will take winter wetness or spring flooding, and some will surprise you by surviving an unexpectedly dry summer. It's a lot to know about!

*Above: The margin of a small stream of crystal-clear water provides the perfect setting for the marsh marigold (*Caltha palustris*), which thrives in soils that are permanently wet. Bishop's cap (*Mitella diphylla*) will form extensive colonies from self-sown seeds in the damp soils in this streamside location.*

*Below: The architectural foliage of maidenhair fern (*Adiantum pedatum*) and rodgersia (*Rodgersia aesculifolia*) makes a strong counterbalance to the intense rosy pink of the Japanese primroses (*Primula japonica*) in this small damp corner beside a quiet pond.*

*Left: A stream that tumbles into a pool, whether it's natural or artificial, makes a wonderful spot in which to grow a variety of plants. The globe flower (*Trollius laxus*), marsh marigold (*Caltha palustris*), pink and white mossy phlox (*Phlox subulata*) and bird's-eye primrose (*Primula frondosa*) surround this small pool.*

6
A Container Garden

As a method of growing and enjoying plants, container gardening has been greatly over-looked by the majority of gardeners. It is a form of gardening almost never considered for the display and enjoyment of wildflowers, perhaps because it seems completely contradictory to the nature of wildflowers to grow them in the confines of a container.

Yet a container planting can evoke, in minia-ture, the remembered delights of almost any wildflower habitat—including an alpine envi-ronment. Through the use of carefully prepared soil, a gardener can provide highly specialized plants with the exact soil mixture they require—without having to make soil improvements to a large garden space.

A number of very beautiful wildflowers (and even some rare ones) will do surprisingly well in containers of various sorts for a few years, making this a wonderful way to bring these plants into close view so they can be enjoyed for their individual effects. The most minute details of the flower can be appreciated and the true intricacies of nature seen, perhaps for the first time.

Through the use of containers, it is possible to grow and display a number of wildflowers on terraces, decks, balconies and even on windowsills. In this way, people with limited space can bring a piece of the woods and meadows into their daily lives.

A group of individual plants in containers will make a small garden to give the handicapped a chance to enjoy wildflowers without the barriers imposed by natural terrain. This method also provides a simple way to introduce children to the wonders of our native flora, while impressing upon them the importance of con-servation and protection of our country's wild things.

A container garden can present a subtle display, or it can offer a bright, splashy accent. These displays can feature just one type of plant per container, perhaps with several different kinds of plants grouped together to simulate the diversity of a garden planting; or a large container, with appropriately sized plants arranged together, can become a miniature garden. Hepaticas, wood anemones, bluets (*Houstonia caerulea*), goldthread (*Coptis groen-landica*) and the tiny oak fern are all good candidates for a small-scale shade planting. A sizable clay pot or wood planter can hold the large crested iris, wood poppy, shooting-star (*Dodecatheon mea-dia*) and delicate wild columbine. And very large containers will be perfectly satisfactory for a wide selection of plants that can range from the blue cohosh to a favorite shrub.

A wide variety of containers can be used for growing wildflow-ers, from pots to troughs, wooden tubs and even the ubiquitous whiskey barrel. Containers can be the plants' permanent home for a few years, after which time the plants probably will need trans-planting into the garden. Or container-grown plants can be recy-

*Growing wildflowers in a container is a wonderful way to see them close at hand and enjoy their variety. Pots holding individual plants can be massed together, as was done here with evening primrose (*Oenothera fruticosa*), wood poppy (*Stylophorum diphyllum*), wild bleeding heart (*Dicentra eximia*) and ferns. The result is a wildflower garden in miniature.*

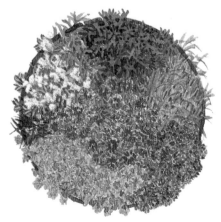

Key to Container A (large circular tub, 30 in. diameter by 20 in. high)

1 Dwarf blue star—*Amsonia montana*
2 Mossy phlox 'Millstream Jupiter'—*Phlox subulata* 'Millstream Jupiter'
3 Northern sea oats—*Chasmanthium latifolium*
4 Prairie smoke—*Geum triflorum*
5 Stokes' aster—*Stokesia laevis*
6 Summer squill—*Scilla chinensis*
7 Ragged robin—*Lychnis flos-cuculi*
8 Variegated queen-of-the-meadow—*Filipendula ulmaria* 'Aurea-variegata'
9 Yellow star grass—*Hypoxis hirsuta*

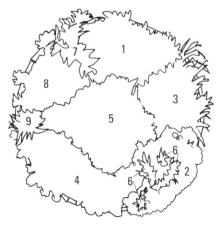

Plan of the container garden.

Individual Pots

1 Climbing hydrangea—*Hydrangea petiolaris*
2 Dwarf blazing star—*Liatris spicata* 'Kobold'
3 *Geranium* X *cantabrigiense* 'Biokovo'
4 Morrow's variegated sedge—*Carex morrowii* 'Aurea Variegata'
5 Pasque flower—*Anemone patens* and (7) wild pink—*Silene caroliniana*
6 Three-toothed cinquefoil—*Potentilla tridentata*
7 Wild pink—*Silene caroliniana*
8 Chokeberry—*Aronia arbutifolia*
9 Baneberry (red)—*Actaea rubra* and (18) waldsteinia—*Waldsteinia fragarioides*
10 Bishop's cap—*Mitella diphylla*
11 Cliff-green—*Paxistima canbyi*
12 Dewdrop—*Dalibarda repens* with (15) Kamchatka bugbane—*Cimicifuga simplex* and (16) shooting-star—*Dodecatheon meadia*
13 Double bloodroot—*Sanguinaria canadensis* 'Multiplex'
14 Japanese painted fern—*Athyrium nipponicum* 'Pictum'
15 Kamchatka bugbane—*Cimicifuga simplex*
16 Shooting-star—*Dodecatheon meadia*
17 Twinleaf—*Jeffersonia diphylla*
18 Waldsteinia—*Waldsteinia fragarioides*

Key to the Plantings

Container A—See page 52
Container B—See page 54
Container C—See page 55
Container D—See page 54
Container E—See page 55

Several microclimates occur on this terrace, permitting a variety of wildflowers that need quite different growing conditions to thrive here. On the south side, a large shagbark hickory (Carya ovata) provides filtered light for shade-loving plants. Sunny warm spots occur alongside the house for summer-flowering sun-lovers. The area along the western side of the terrace is shaded in the morning but receives good sun in the afternoon, creating a transition area for plants that typically grow in sunny situations but will flourish in this partly shaded area. The result is a terrace with attractive, ever-changing displays that continue for many months.

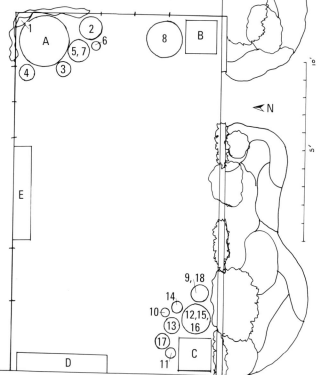

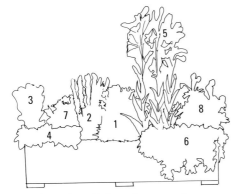

Key to Container D (wooden trough, 5 ft. by 1 ft. by 10 in. high)

1 Bristly aster—*Aster linearifolius*
2 Dwarf blazing star—*Liatris spicata* 'Kobold'
3 Golden ragwort—*Senecio aureus*
4 Golden star—*Chrysogonum virginianum*
5 Hairy beard-tongue—*Penstemon digitalis* 'Husker Red'
6 Verbena 'Lavender'—*Verbena canadensis* 'Lavender'
7 Wild columbine—*Aquilegia canadensis*
8 Wild cranesbill—*Geranium maculatum*

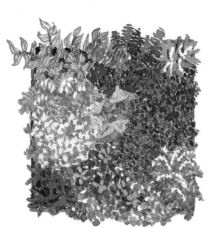

Key to Container B (wooden planter, 20 in. square by 15 in. high)

1 Barbara's buttons—*Marshallia grandiflora*
2 Christmas fern—*Polystichum acrostichoides*
3 Devil's bit—*Chamaelirium luteum*
4 Dewdrop—*Dalibarda repens*
5 Large yellow lady's-slipper—
   Cypripedium calceolus var. *pubescens*
6 Shooting-star—*Dodecatheon meadia*
7 Squirrel corn—*Dicentra canadensis*
8 Variegated Japanese Solomon's seal—
   Polygonatum odoratum 'Variegatum'
9 Virginia ginger—*Asarum virginicum*
10 Wild bleeding heart—*Dicentra eximia*
   'Alba'

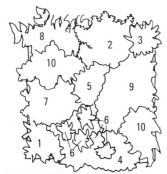

cled through the garden on a yearly or seasonal basis: after flowering in their pots, they can be replanted in the garden and new ones selected for the next container display, which may be the following spring or the next season.

Since most containers are movable, those that hold wildflowers grown just for their flowers can be placed in the background when their display is finished, while different ones are moved up into a prominent position as they approach flowering time. And because the containers are portable, you aren't as limited by a plant's requirements for sun or shade as you are in a garden; you can move the pots around to take full advantage of optimum light or shade during the course of a season.

Containers also provide a way to grow nonhardy wildflowers, if an appropriate winter storage area for them is available. (This is discussed further in Chapter 17, "Garden Maintenance.") Also, because the soil in the individual containers can be tailored to the specific needs of each wildling, plants may be brought together in a grouping that would never be seen in nature or in a small garden area.

The illustrated container garden has several different exposures. The southeast side of this terrace receives shade from two large oak trees, while the northwest side receives sun from late morning until late in the afternoon. Planters B and C, each containing several different kinds of plants, are in shade and have a rich, humusy woodland soil mix. For these containers, I have chosen easy-to-grow wildflowers that have some special merit such as small, intricate flowers, or that are among my favorites that I simply enjoy having close at hand.

In Planter C, for example, is a native alum root (*Heuchera americana*) with exceptionally fine mottled foliage. Wherry's foam-

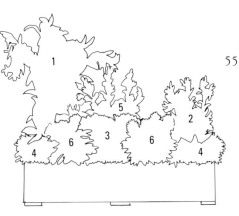

Key to Container E (wooden trough, 5 ft. by 1 ft. by 10 in. high)

1 Bowman's root—*Gillenia trifoliata*
2 Cardinal flower—*Lobelia cardinalis*
3 *Coreopsis* X 'Moonbeam'
4 Dwarf coreopsis—*Coreopsis auriculata* 'Nana'
5 Pink turtle-head—*Chelone lyonii*
6 Stokes' aster—*Stokesia laevis*

Key to Container C (wooden planter, 20 in. square by 15 in. high)

1 Alum root—*Heuchera americana*, interplanted with (7) Snowdrop—*Galanthus nivalis*
2 Double pink-flowered rue anemone—*Anemonella thalictroides* 'Schoaf's Double Pink'
3 Jack-in-the-pulpit—*Arisaema triphyllum*
4 Lady fern—*Athyrium filix-femina*
5 Merrybells—*Uvularia grandiflora*
6 Partridgeberry—*Mitchella repens*, interplanted with (10) winter aconite—*Eranthis hyemalis*
7 Snowdrop—*Galanthus nivalis*
8 Wherry's foamflower—*Tiarella wherryi*
9 Wild bleeding heart—*Dicentra eximia* 'Alba'
10 Winter aconite—*Eranthis hyemalis*
11 Yellow trillium—*Trillium luteum*

flower (*Tiarella wherryi*), another plant in this container, has masses of tiny flowers that are a marvel under a magnifying glass, while its overall habit of growth is so trim and pleasing that I never tire of it. And the flowers of partridgeberry are unsurpassed for beauty, a fact that is often overlooked because they are small and, in nature, trail over the ground. I also included one of my most favorite plants, the white native bleeding heart (*Dicentra eximia* 'Alba').

In Planter B I planted the variegated Japanese Solomon's seal (*Polygonatum odoratum* 'Variegatum') for the many months of color it affords in its cream-and-green foliage patterns, and for its graceful growth habit. Whenever I look at it, I have to believe someone painstakingly brushed on the cream markings that edge the leaves. Beside it the resilient native vancouveria forms as beautiful a ground cover as I have ever seen.

I chose to grow the yellow trillium (*Trillium luteum*) as a container plant for its attractive mottled foliage, and because the flowers are so sweetly fragrant—though you have to be quite close to be aware of their perfume. For me, it carries many memories of hiking in the Blue Ridge and Smoky mountains, where I first saw it in the wild along with so many of our other native plants.

In the shaded pots holding single plants, I chose mostly those wildflowers that have particularly good and distinctive growth habits, because I wanted each one to be well suited as a specimen plant. These often have multiseasonal interest from buds, flowers, fruit and foliage displays. I especially enjoy the Japanese painted fern with its graceful mounds of lacy fronds and the delicate cliffgreen (*Paxistima canbyi*) with its small, shiny evergreen leaves. The flowers of the double bloodroot (*Sanguinaria canadensis* 'Multi-

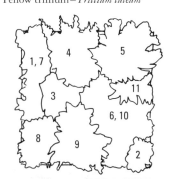

Right: In this shady site, wooden troughs have been filled with Christmas fern (Polystichum acrostichoides) *and foamflower* (Tiarella cordifolia) *to provide a long and easily maintained show.*

Spring ephemerals like the Dutchman's-breeches (Dicentra cucullaria) *shown here do well in containers, where they can be enjoyed for their early spring flowers.*

plex') are outstanding and deserve to be singled out for display.

In the planters for the sunny locations (A, D and E), I have selected not only favorite wildflowers, but combinations of them to give a long season of interest.

Planter A is a circular barrel with a good general soil mix, one you would typically find in a well-maintained sunny perennial border that had some extra drainage material added. (Planters D and E have the same mix.) Here, I have put the dwarf blue star (*Amsonia montana*), just 15 inches high but with all the attributes the taller species offers. The distinctive foliage of the variegated queen-of-the-meadow (*Filipendula ulmaria* 'Aureo-variegata') displays patterns of rich, deep yellow that give interest throughout the growing season; next to this is the delicate yellow star grass (*Hypoxis hirsuta*). Threaded through both of these is the European ragged robin (*Lychnis flos-cuculi*), which brings additional color in spring.

At the other side of the dwarf blue star are the appealing wild oats (*Uvularia sessilifolia*), the northern sea oats (*Chasmanthium latifolium*) with ornamental seed heads and soft yellow fall foliage. Stokes' aster (*Stokesia laevis*) displays its abundant lavender flowers all summer long, often reblooming in mild, moist autumns. The late spring flowering mossy phlox (*Phlox subulata*) and prairie smoke (*Geum triflorum*) with its deep pink flowers act as ground covers and tumble over the edge of the container. To give added summer color to this planter, I have tucked in the tiny bulbs of the pink-flowering summer squill (*Scilla chinensis*).

For added color around Planter A, I have grouped several individual pots of other sun-loving plants. These create an impression of greater space and interest in that corner. *Geranium* X *cantabrigiense* 'Biokovo', a hybrid between the European *Geranium macrorrhizum* and *Geranium dalmaticum*, occupies one of these pots.

In another pot is Morrow's variegated sedge (*Carex morrowii* 'Aurea Variegata'), a lovely sedge wth grasslike cream-and-green-striped leaves. For early spring flowers, attractive foliage and interesting seed heads, I chose the pasque flower (*Anemone patens*), which will be followed by the bright flower displays of the wild pink (*Silene caroliniana*). And for summer, I have added the tiny bluets.

The last container in this corner holds evergreen mats of three-toothed cinquefoil (*Potentilla tridentata*). In spring, the small white flowers make a bright contrast with the shiny dark leaves which, in fall, turn scarlet.

Bowman's root (*Gillenia trifoliata*) (in Planter E), with its neat appearance, myriad white flowers and finely toothed foliage, is an ideal choice for a highly visible container. And I never tire of seeing the big lavender flowers of Stokes' aster, especially when they are surrounded by a sea of green and pale yellow created by its companion plant, Coreopsis X 'Moonbeam'. Wild verbena (*Verbena canadensis*) has wonderfully dissected foliage, and it is an ideal ground cover for a planter, where it soon spreads, spilling over the edges. The form 'Lavender', which is used here, is sweetly scented and seems never to be out of flower. It also lasts a long time as a cut flower. In warmer climates, it is evergreen with occasional flushes of winter flowers.

By selecting appropriate plants, you can adapt the ideas from this container garden to suit all but the most severe of environments.

Container gardening is special because here, more than in the other gardens, each gardener sets the parameters. Whether the effect is simple or complex, this is usually one of the easiest forms of gardening.

Maintenance—especially regular watering—is a major consideration with a container garden, particularly if you live in a hot, dry climate or travel often or live in an area with extremely cold winters and have no suitable winter storage for your plants. (Winter storage is discussed in Chapter 17, "Garden Maintenance.")

A container garden not only adds another dimension to growing wildflowers, it makes this a very intimate form of gardening—allowing you to enjoy wildflowers in a way that is rarely achieved in the relative spaciousness of a garden proper.

Unusual native plants, especially those with such captivating flowers as the infrequently seen Phlox X *'Chattahoochee', can be enjoyed all the more when grown in containers.*

*The double pink-flowered rue anemone (*Anemonella thalictroides *'Schoaf's Double Pink') is an excellent choice to grow in a container, where its exquisite flowers and intricate foliage can be admired close at hand.*

7

A Sunny Border

THIS GARDEN IS SIMILAR to the shady border in that it is designed in a rather formal and traditional style and mixes native and non-native wildflowers with cultivated garden plants. A sunny border can be placed either in front of a building, wall or fence, or run along a driveway. It can also form a partition between different sections of the property or, as is the case with the garden shown here, it may be a freestanding island bed set in a grassy area that can be viewed from all sides. Because a sunny border is so adaptable, it can be sited just about anywhere on a property, so long as it receives no less than eight hours of sunlight a day.

The sunny border starts its show subtly in late spring and early summer, building to a peak in midsummer and gradually fading into the mellow tones of fall. It is designed so that robust, vividly colored flowering plants are balanced by bold foliage effects, along with some cooler colors for summer.

The display begins in spring with bulbs. If the border is sizable, then the large-flowered hybrids of daffodils and tulips can be used. I feel they are most effectively displayed in a border if used in several small groups of five to seven plants, rather than set out in the bold sweeps that are best suited for naturalizing. Any more than a handful of bulbs and the effect will be heavy and overwhelming. There will also be a lot of unattractive foliage left that will spoil the display of the other plants as the season advances.

In a small border, miniature and species bulbs will give the best effect. In the garden illustrated here, I have used four different varieties of dwarf narcissus—'Jack Snipe', 'Thalia' and 'April Tears'—and, for very early color, 'February Gold'. In areas that have cool summers, the ephemeral woodland wildflowers of spring can also be used. These will be dormant by summer, when their foliage disappears, and their underground portions will be protected from the heat of the summer sun by the foliage of other plants.

Early flowering plants for the sunny border include blue star with a multitude of blossoms in a rich shade of light blue; leopard's-bane (*Doronicum caucasicum*), from Europe, with rich yellow flowers that will bloom (with cool weather and ample moisture) for up to eight weeks before going dormant, and wild indigo (*Baptisia australis*), with its attractive glaucous foliage and its spires of blue so reminiscent of lupines. These combine nicely with the familiar red and yellow flowers of the wild columbine and the deep yellow of golden ragwort (*Senecio aureus*)—a greatly overlooked plant of quiet charm and easy culture.

Low plants for the foreground include the dwarf coreopsis (*Coreopsis auriculata* 'Nana'), purple-leaved stonecrop (*Sedum sieboldii*), wild verbena, and—if the soil is light and well

*In a sunny border native and non-native plants can be grown in many combinations to form colorful, bright patterns. Here the intense yellow of the sweet sunflower (*Heliopsis helianthoides*) is a wonderful accent against the bright purple of blazing star (*Liatris spicata*) and the strong red of the beebalm (*Monarda didyma*). The white flowers of Phlox 'Miss Lingard' soften these strong colors that are such a familiar part of the summer landscape.*

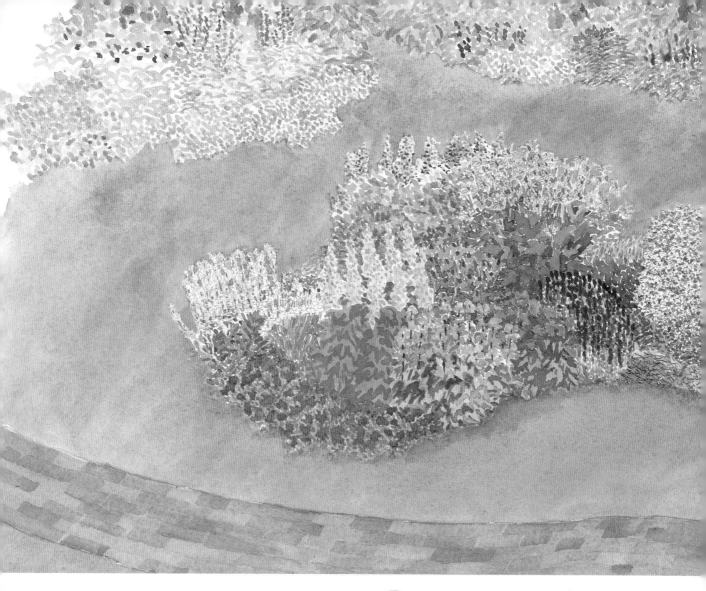

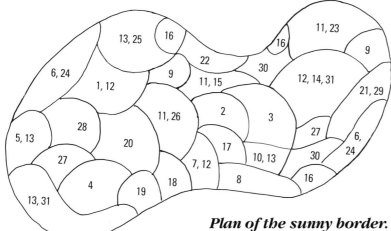

Plan of the sunny border.

Key to the Planting

1 *Artemisia* 'Powis Castle' interplanted with (12) *Narcissus* 'Thalia'

2 Blue star—*Amsonia tabernaemontana*

3 Boltonia 'Snowbank'—*Boltonia asteroides* 'Snowbank'

4 Bush pea—*Thermopsis caroliniana*

5 Canadian burnet—*Sanguisorba canadensis* interplanted with (13) *Narcissus triandrus* 'April Tears'

6 *Coreopsis* X 'Moonbeam' interplanted with (24) Stokes' aster—*Stokesia laevis*

7 Dwarf blazing star 'Kobold'—*Liatris spicata* 'Kobold' interplanted with (12) *Narcissus* 'Thalia'

8 Dwarf coreopsis—*Coreopsis auriculata* 'Nana'

9 False dragonhead 'Vivid'—*Physostegia virginiana* 'Vivid'

10 Leopard's-bane 'Madam Mason'— *Doronicum caucasicum* 'Madam Mason' interplanted with (13) *Narcissus triandus* 'April Tears'

11 *Narcissus* 'Jack Snipe'

12 *Narcissus* 'Thalia'

13 *Narcissus triandrus* 'April Tears'

14 New England aster—*Aster novae-angliae* interplanted with (12) *Narcissus* 'Thalia' and (31) wild verbena—*Verbena canadensis*

15 Northern sea oats—*Chasmanthium latifolium* interplanted with (11) *Narcissus* 'Jack Snipe'

16 Pasque flower—*Anemone patens*

An island bed provides a wonderful opportunity to work with color, form, shape and texture in bold displays. The individual groups of plants are more prominent when woven amongst the greens and grays of foliage as I've done here.

drained—the exquisitely beautiful pasque flower, which is as pretty when the fluffy clematis-like seed heads are present as it is when in flower. In the right location, it is a tough, long-lived plant, increasing each year in size and the number of flowers it produces. Other low-growing plants include the lovely wild bleeding heart and the wild cranesbill (*Geranium maculatum*) with its attractive foliage and soft pink flowers. All these wildflowers mix well with the whites and many shades of blue found in Siberian iris (*Iris sibirica*), which I have found to be extremely tolerant of intense summer heat and which will always look in prime condition if given a deeply dug, well-prepared soil.

There are a great number of perennials to choose from for a sunny border. For early summer flowers, I have included bush pea (*Thermopsis caroliniana*) with its strong yellow blooms, the early phloxes (including the *P. maculata* types and 'Miss Lingard'), hairy beard-tongue (*Penstemon hirsutus*), and the pink-flowered, low-growing species of evening primrose (*Oenothera speciosa* 'Rosea'). Although I have not used it here, another good choice would be the mossy phlox—with its rainbow colors of pink, blue, lavender and white—that carpets the ground in a sea of color.

When summer is at its full strength, so is the wildflower display in the sunny border. The tall, virtually indestructible purple coneflower (*Echinacea purpurea*) harmonizes well with the 16-inch tall phlox 'Pinafore Pink'. Beebalm (*Monarda didyma*), false dragonhead (*Physostegia virginiana*), blazing star (*Liatris spicata*) and the threadleaf coreopsis (*Coreopsis verticillata*) are just some of the plants that fill out the pageant.

A softening touch to all this color comes from the gray foliage and, later, from the mass of white, daisylike fall flowers of boltonia

17 *Phlox* 'Miss Lingard'
18 *Phlox* 'Pinafore Pink'—*Phlox paniculata* 'Pinafore Pink'
19 Pink turtle-head—*Chelone lyonii*
20 Purple coneflower—*Echinacea purpurea*
21 Ragwort—*Senecio aureus* interplanted with (29) wild columbine—*Aquilegia canadensis*
22 *Sedum* 'Vera Jameson'
23 Sneezeweed—*Helenium autumnale* interplanted with (11) *Narcissus* 'Jack Snipe'
24 Stokes' aster—*Stokesia laevis*
25 *Thalictrum rochebrunianum* interplanted with (13) *Narcissus triandus* 'April Tears'
26 Three-lobed coneflower—*Rudbeckia triloba* interplanted with (11) *Narcissus* 'Jack Snipe'
27 White Siberian iris—*Iris sibirica* 'White Swirl'
28 Wild bergamot—*Monarda fistulosa*
29 Wild columbine—*Aquilegia canadensis*
30 Wild cranesbill—*Geranium maculatum*
31 Wild verbena—*Verbena canadensis* interplanted with (13) *Narcissus triandus* 'April Tears'

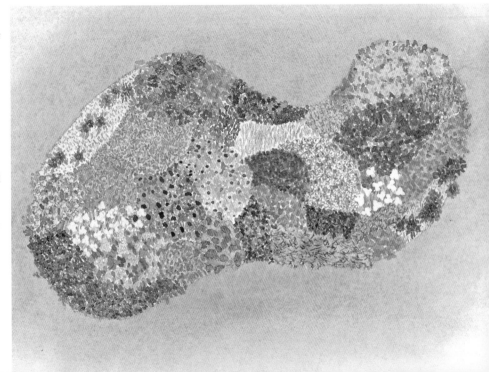

Top: Many plants, like the blue star (Amsonia tabernaemontana) shown here, have quite a significant secondary display in the fall created by their colorful foliage.

Bottom: Boltonia (Boltonia asteroides), with its billowing cascade of snowy white flowers from summer until killing frost, makes a good background. It is also a good choice to fill in a space left by a plant that goes dormant in late spring or early summer.

(*Boltonia asteroides* 'Snowbank') and from the gray of artemisia's foliage. My favorite artemisia is 'Powis Castle' with its finely dissected leaves and total indifference to heat, humidity and generally unfavorable weather; it is far less demanding than most of the artemisias. (This cultivar is questionably hardy in northern areas with severe winters.) Add to this the purple foliage and pink flowers of *Sedum* 'Vera Jameson' for a special and cooling display. All forms of meadow-rue (*Thalictrum* species) are also perfect for this garden, bringing delicacy and a soft vertical accent.

As the season moves into fall, more muted flower tones take over the sunny border. The rich lavenders, pinks and whites of asters, the deep purple of ironweed, the yellows of goldenrod and sneezeweed combine with the gold and sandy tones of grass foliage, now approaching dormancy. Fall-blooming bulbs, such as the lavender, pink (and rarely, white) of colchicums (*Colchicum autumnale*) and the smaller fall-flowering crocus, are a pleasure to see. In warmer climates spider (*Lycoris radiata*) and rain lilies (*Zephyranthes candida*) make their display at this time, giving a bright accent of autumn color. In the North, their counterpart is the summer-flowering naked ladies. To soften the rather stark appearance of the latter plant's bare stems, I like to mix them among plants with good foliage like queen-of-the-prairie (*Filipendula rubra*), Japanese burnet (*Sanguisorba obtusa*) and bear's-breeches.

You can also design seasonal pictures by using the different aspects plants have during other times of the year, such as the intricate seed heads of the pasque flower that develop in early summer or the buds of the fall-flowering Japanese anemone (*Anemone japonica*), which look like plush pale green pearls and are especially noticeable against this plant's dark green foliage. Then there are the displays of early fall that might include the colored foliage of *Geranium macrorrhizum* and *Geranium* X *cantabrigiense* 'Biokovo'.

Along the back of a border set against a building, wall or hedge, will go tall, prominent wildflowers and other more traditional plants with a strong presence. These plants could include the queen-of-the-prairie, Joe-pye-weed and narrow-leaved sunflower (*Helianthus angustifolius*). Even a shrub or two can be used to good effect. Occasionally one or two of these taller plants can be placed in the very front section to add a visual counterbalance and provide interest among the lower-growing plants set in the foreground.

In a border like this I like to use a small group or two of plants (or a single plant if it is large) with variegated, intricately designed or heavily textured foliage to add emphasis and sparkle. A favorite shrub of mine is the native *Cornus sericea* 'Silver and Gold', with its cream and green variegated leaves. It has the added attraction of bright golden-colored stems that are very noticeable in winter. Another good choice would be the form of queen-of-the-meadow that has yellow variegated foliage. The tall, stately meadow-rues with their delicate filigreed leaves in shades of blue-green brushed with gray are also good accent plants, especially in borders of small proportions.

The midsized plants such as dwarf blue star, pink turtle-heads and wild columbine add fullness and bold accents of color, while many of the lower-growing ones such as golden star, moss verbena (*Verbena tenuisecta*) and wild cranesbill can be used to make distinctive edges.

Throughout all sunny borders, no matter what their size, I use a generous sprinkling of bulbs to extend the various seasons. Some of my favorites include dogtooth violet (*Erythronium tuolumnense*) (especially the creamy white-flowered hybrid 'Pagoda') for spring, the camas lily with its prominent spires of blue for early summer and the tender crinums and dwarf winter-hardy gladioli (*Gladiolus nanus*) of midsummer, with fall-flowering crocus and colchicums to end the growing season in autumn.

The island border I have designed here is 20 feet long by 12 feet wide at its widest part. Tall plants with bold flower displays and strong foliage patterns, like wild indigo and three-lobed coneflower (*Rudbeckia triloba*), form a curving line along the central section to provide height and a background for the foreground plants. As a foil to this bold look, I've added a few tall plants with a more delicate appearance, like *Boltonia* 'Snowbank', golden ragwort and the lavender-flowered meadow-rue *Thalictrum rochebrunianum*.

This is an undemanding garden to create and maintain. All of these plants are easy to find and grow and—once established—are quite self-sufficient, requiring no more than the regular maintenance one would give to any sunny border garden.

*The white wild indigo (*Baptisia pendula*), with its distinctive habit of growth and glaucous foliage, makes an eye-catching accent plant for the sunny garden.*

*Below: An impressive summer display comes from massing native and non-native plants together to form a colorful and long-lasting picture. The native threadleaf coreopsis (*Coreopsis verticillata*), Coreopsis X 'Moonbeam', and Stokes' aster (*Stokesia laevis*) are woven together here with traditional garden favorites.*

8

A Rock Garden

THIS IS GENERALLY A GARDEN of small treasures displayed among rocks and tucked into crevices. Such a garden can be reminiscent of a rugged mountain setting or the rocky ledges found in so many areas throughout the world, and it is a place where—in the wild or in the garden—rocks and plants are combined to enhance their beauty.

A true rock garden is made up of mostly small (sometimes diminutive), low-growing plants, many of which come from mountainous regions or desert areas. Ours is not this purist's rock garden, reserved only for alpines and specialized rock-garden plants that are too demanding for anyone except ardent rock gardeners. Instead, I have included wildflowers and other plants that look appropriate and in scale with the surroundings. These all grow happily in an open, sandy soil that is lower in organic matter than the average garden soil. They also tend to prefer a setting where there is little competition.

With the right choice of plants, a rock garden containing wildflowers can be created just about anywhere in North America. It can also be adapted to become a very specialized desert garden.

The rock garden illustrated here has a broad range of color and plant forms. Some of the plants included, however, do require classic rock-garden conditions: a cool root zone, rapid drainage and a lean soil low in organic matter. The leanness of the soil is particularly important, because many of the plants that would naturally grow in mountain or desert environments are quite susceptible to soil-borne diseases that are associated with soils rich in organic matter and warmer climates.

I have included native wildflowers such as the golden-flowered dwarf coreopsis, wild pink, lavender bird's-foot violet (_Viola pedata_) and the dainty yellow star grass, along with the greatly admired pasque flower. Non-native plants include miniature variegated sedge (_Carex conica_ 'Variegata'), candytuft (_Iberis sempervirens_), the Siberian draba (_Draba sibirica_) and smaller grasses like hair grass (_Deschampsia caespitosa_).

Even cactus and the small aloes (which must be kept in a frost-free place over the winter) can be tucked into sunny corners and tight crevices to add to the seasonal display. The rock garden's height of interest and color is in late spring and early summer, although there is also an appreciable display in both early spring and fall.

A gray granite ledge clothed in lichens provides the perfect setting for the little harebells (_Campanula rotundifolia_); and, in shade, what better way is there to display the native early saxifrage (_Saxifraga virginiensis_) or the rock polypody fern (_Polypodium virginianum_)? These plants and others of similar stature would be lost if grown at ground level surrounded by other plants.

_The often austere appearance of rocks can be softened and their natural beauty seen when they are combined with plants. White crested iris (_Iris cristata alba_), dwarf Japanese twinleaf (_Jeffersonia dubia_), Gartrell azaleas,_ Aruncus aethusifolius _and wood phlox (_Phlox divaricata_) have been used in this garden to create a beautiful and varied scene around a granite ledge._

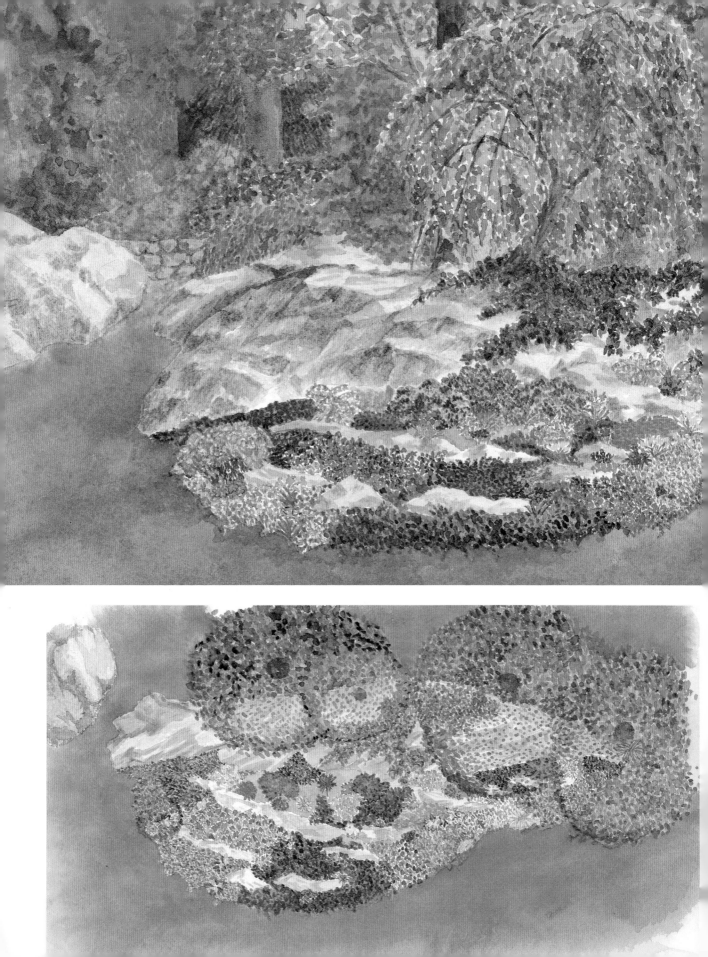

The garden illustrated here was developed from a large naturally occurring rock outcropping. It was further enhanced by building a rock garden in front of the outcrop to tie it smoothly into the surrounding landscape. The added garden space also provides a large area in which to grow an abundance of wildflowers and other plants suitable for this habitat.

Key to the Planting

1 *Allium pulchellum*
2 Bird's-foot violet—*Viola pedata*
3 Blue-eyed grass—*Sisyrinchium angustifolium*
4 Bog rosemary—*Andromeda polifolia*
5 Bowles golden sedge—*Carex stricta* 'Bowles Golden'
6 Candytuft—*Iberis sempervirens*
7 *Clematis montana rubens*
8 Dwarf coreopsis—*Coreopsis auriculata* 'Nana'
9 *Geranium dalmaticum*
10 Harebell—*Campanula rotundifolia*
11 Hair grass—*Deschampsia caespitosa*
12 Hoop petticoat daffodil—*Narcissus cyclamineus*
13 Japanese columbine—*Aquilegia flabellata* 'Nana'
14 Japanese spirea—*Spirea japonica* var. *alpina*
15 Lemperg's soapwort—*Saponaria lempergii*
16 Mossy phlox 'Millstream Jupiter'— *Phlox subulata* 'Millstream Jupiter'
17 *Narcissus asturiensis*
18 Prairie phlox 'Betty Blake'—*Phlox bifida* 'Betty Blake'
19 Prairie smoke—*Geum triflorum*
20 Shagbark hickory—*Carya ovata*
21 Summer squill—*Scilla chinensis*
22 *Veronica incana*
23 Weeping Canadian hemlock—*Tsuga canadensis* 'Pendula'
24 Weeping crab apple 'Red Jade'—*Malus* 'Red Jade'
25 White pasque flower—*Anemone patens alba*
26 Wild bleeding heart—*Dicentra eximia*
27 Wild pink—*Silene caroliniana*
28 Wild verbena—*Verbena canadensis*
29 Yellow star grass—*Hypoxis hirsuta*

Plan of the rock garden.

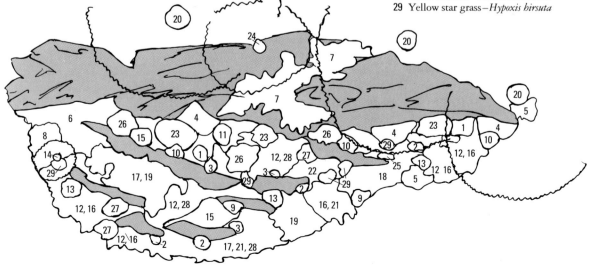

*Top: Large granite rocks are surrounded by a garden of many different plants, including creeping phlox (*Phlox stolonifera), *foamflower (*Tiarella cordifolia) *and spring bulbs.*

*Bottom: Unusual annuals like the California poppy (*Eschscholzia californica) *shown here are perfect to use in the rock garden, where they can cascade over rocks or form a thick ground cover.*

The dainty blue-and-white Japanese columbine (*Aquilegia flabellata* 'Nana') is also ideal for this location, as is the soft pink *Geranium dalmaticum* (which has the added advantage of foliage that turns a rich plum and red in the fall). Tumbling over rocks are the rich pink-flowered soapwort (*Saponaria ocymoides*) and the bright lavender flowers of the mossy phlox 'Millstream Jupiter'. A particular favorite of mine for a rock garden is prairie smoke, a delightful low-growing plant from the western mountains of North America. In the wild, it grows so thickly and flowers so prolifically that the seed heads give the effect of a smoky haze—hence the plant's name.

Miniature bulbs can be included to add their cheerful colors. In spring, the tiny *Narcissus asturiensis* and *cyclamineus*, followed by snowdrop (*Galanthus nivalis*) and species crocus, happily poke up through the snow, and a little later, species tulips such as the apricot-flowered *Tulipa batalinii* 'Bright Gem' and *Tulipa tarda*, whose yellow-and-white flowers glisten in the sun and cheer the chilly, overcast days of early spring. Then, in fall, *Crocus goulimyi* and *speciosus* put on a pretty display along with colchicums.

Slow-growing and naturally dwarf shrubs are included to give balance to the design, while small evergreens add to the winter interest of the rock garden. These include the bog rosemary (*Andromeda polifolia*) and the lovely weeping form of Canadian hemlock (*Tsuga canadensis* 'Pendula') along with the woody ground covers bearberry (*Arctostaphylos uva-ursi*) and three-toothed cinquefoil, all of which provide a year-round display.

The rock garden described here is primarily sunny, although it does get some afternoon shade along the back. However, if you have rocky outcroppings in a shady area, you can certainly create a beautiful garden with a rich variety of plants, including ferns. After all, many lovely rock gardens occur naturally throughout this country (and abroad) in shady woods—and few of those need to be improved upon. Simply apply the same principles of preparation and design outlined in Chapter 16 and select the appropriate shade-loving plants: some of the smaller ferns, early saxifrage, trillium, the various bleeding hearts, dwarf iris (*Iris verna*) and epimediums (*Epimedium* species) are all good selections. Trailing woodland wildflowers like dewdrop (*Dalibarda repens*) and creeping phlox also lend themselves to a rocky habitat, where they can weave among the rocks and trail along the crevices.

There are many plants found at lower elevations that are well suited to a garden such as this and will grow in a more typical garden soil.

Building a rock garden from scratch requires skill and some experience. The degree of difficulty can vary greatly, depending on the existing features of your property and your ambitions. The goal should be to simulate a natural rock outcropping with ledges, pockets of soil and small crevices for the plants. (See Chapter 16, "Building a Wildflower Garden," for a discussion of what is involved in the construction of a rock garden.)

Once the garden is built or a natural rock outcropping has been cleared, you should have good success with this type of garden, providing you prepare the site properly and select the plants carefully to suit the specific growing conditions and your degree of experience.

*Mossy phlox (*Phlox subulata*) comes in an array of colors and forms large mounds that cascade over walls and rocks, where its roots will find a home in the smallest of crevices.*

*Below: "Interplanting" is a way to protect plants that are dormant during part of the growing season and to extend seasonal interest in a certain spot. Here the windflower (*Anemone blanda*) carries its large, graceful flowers above those of the mossy phlox (*Phlox subulata*), which continues to flower well after the windflower has disappeared.*

Left: Rocks that were a nuisance jutting out of a lawn become beautiful features in the miniature rock garden developed around them.

9
A Meadow Garden

THIS GARDEN IS A BRIGHT SEA of color and movement, and it is also a prime butterfly and wildlife habitat. Although a meadow garden should look completely natural and spontaneous, it is, in fact, artfully contrived; it requires a clever design, careful planning, proper preparation and a good deal of effort to sustain it, at least for the first few years.

A meadow is at its height of color in summer with a good secondary display in the fall. Indeed, many people favor it in autumn because the colors are softer and more restful than in summer. A meadow garden is suitable for most climates in North America, with displays composed of plants adapted to the particular climatic conditions found in temperate regions.

In the garden illustrated here, the show begins in late spring and early summer with wild indigo, blue star, the nodding onion (*Allium cernuum*) and camas lily. The display can include a few low-growing plants like the dwarf coreopsis and wild cranesbill around the edges or along paths, where the vegetation is thinner. These plants will also appreciate the summer shade from the later-appearing, taller perennials typically used in a meadow.

Gradually the tempo of bloom picks up as the season moves into the fullness of summer with an amazing, almost endless selection of plants. The natives include the rich lavender of the blazing star, the cheerful yellow countenance of the familiar black-eyed Susans (*Rudbeckia hirta*), and the bright orange blossoms of butterfly weed, which stand out like beacons to humans and insects alike. There are goldenrod, sunflowers, and Indian-cups with their multitude of yellows, coneflowers in a bright purple, queen-of-the-prairie and rose mallow (*Hibiscus palustris*) displaying their pink flowers. And would any natural planting be complete without the delicate feathery clusters of the naturalized Queen-Anne's-lace (*Daucus carota*)?

An area that tends to be somewhat damp or that can easily be given extra moisture can provide a good home for the tall, native Turk's-cap (*Lilium superbum*) and Canada lily (*Lilium canadense*). In late spring and early summer, both will fill such a place with myriad orange flowers handsomely speckled with deep purple and held in full loose clusters atop tall, strong stems.

If you have plenty of room, plant the giant cow parsnip (*Heracleum mantegazzianum*) for its sheer impressiveness: its mass of green foliage adds a wonderful focus and provides shade for other plants that do not necessarily like full, piercing sun all day. It also softens the hot colors of the summer. (Note that although I have used this plant in gardens for years without ill effect, it has been reported to cause dermatitis.)

Along the path where there is less competition, the low-growing *Aster* X *frikartii* (a hybrid developed in Europe), with its pro-

Ratibida pinnata, *a tall, bold, native wildflower with buttery yellow flowers, forms a prominent blaze of color in the summer meadow where it is surrounded by wild bergamot* (Monarda fistulosa). *They are perfect companions for the native grasses.*

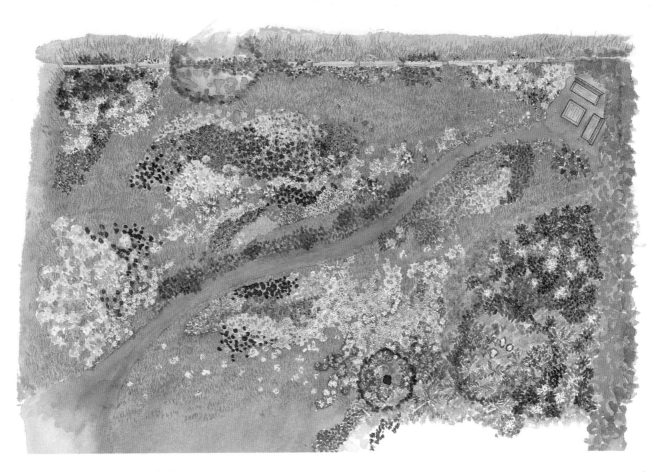

By midsummer a meadow is resplendent with bright colors. The display begins subtly in spring and continues to a killing frost.

Plan of the meadow garden.

Key to the Planting

1 American larch—*Larix americana*
2 Apple tree—*Malus hybrida*
3 Black-eyed Susan—*Rudbeckia hirta*
4 Blazing star—*Liatris spicata*
5 Bluets—*Houstonia caerulea*
6 Blue flag iris—*Iris versicolor*
7 Blue star—*Amsonia tabernaemontana*
8 Butterfly weed—*Asclepias tuberosa*
9 *Camassia leichtlinii*
10 Canadian goldenrod—*Solidago canadensis*
11 Cosmos—*Cosmos bipinnatus*
12 Dwarf coreopsis—*Coreopsis auriculata* 'Nana'
13 Indian-cup—*Silphium perfoliatum*
14 Ironweed—*Vernonia noveboracensis*
15 Joe-pye-weed—*Eupatorium purpureum*
16 Narrow-leaved sunflower—*Helianthus angustifolius*
17 New England aster—*Aster novae-angliae*
18 Nodding onion—*Allium cernuum*
19 Ox-eyed daisy—*Chrysanthemum leucanthemum*
20 Pink turtle-head—*Chelone lyonii*
21 Purple coneflower—*Echinacea purpurea*
22 Queen-Anne's-lace—*Daucus carota*
23 Queen-of-the-prairie—*Filipendula rubra*
24 Sensitive fern—*Onoclea sensibilis*

25 Sneezeweed—*Helenium autumnale*
26 Swamp milkweed—*Asclepias incarnata*
27 Sweet autumn clematis—*Clematis maximowicziana*
28 Tall hedge—*Rhamnus frangula*
29 Tall meadow-rue—*Thalictrum polygamum*
30 Three-lobed coneflower—*Rudbeckia triloba*

31 Turk's-cap lily—*Lilium superbum*
32 White birch—*Betula papyrifera*
33 Wild bergamot—*Monarda fistulosa*
34 Wild cranesbill—*Geranium maculatum*
35 Wild indigo—*Baptisia australis*
36 Wild senna—*Cassia hebecarpa*
37 Wild swamp mallow—*Hibiscus moscheutos*

A Seating group

Above: Meadowsweet (Spiraea latifolia) is an easily grown and attractive native shrub found in grassy meadows and along wood margins.

Below: Joe-pye-weed (Eupatorium purpureum), ironweed (Vernonia noveboracensis) and rose mallow (Hibiscus palustris) are three sizable native wildflowers that thrive in damp meadows. The rose mallow shown here is a rare, red-flowered hybrid that is as yet unnamed. It provides a strong focal point in a sea of dark purple and lavender.

lific mounds of lavender, plays a significant part in this cast of many. In warmer climates, where it needs light afternoon shade, it carries its flower display longer than any other perennial I can think of. Added to all this are the bright accents of the annual spider flower (*Cleome spinosa*) and, of course, cosmos (*Cosmos bipinnatus*). Cosmos is one of my favorites, and it's hard for me to think of a prettier flower!

As summer moves toward fall, we look for the pinks, lavenders and blues of the asters, the white of boltonia and the yellow of Patrinia (*Patrinia scabiosifolia*) (a tall, billowy Queen-Anne's-lace look-alike from Asia). With these as companions, the grasses take over center stage with their highly ornamental and colorful plumed seed heads. Gradually they turn from green to soft reds, russets, yellows and honey browns—all the colors of an old tapestry—and they are perhaps at their most beautiful in a mantle of snow.

Growing over a nearby wall or fence could be vines such as the fragrant sweet autumn clematis, virgin's bower (*Clematis virginiana*), or the trumpet vine (*Campsis radicans*), with its familiar large red flowers that are a favorite of hummingbirds. The flowers of both the virgin's bower and sweet autumn clematis are followed by an equally prolific show of fluffy seed heads, and the plants themselves are a marvelous haven for birds. In warm climates Carolina jessamine (*Gelsemium sempervirens*), an evergreen vine, gives a welcome spring note of yellow. (The species *G. rankinii* reblooms in fall.)

🌺 🌺 🌺

The creation of meadow gardens has been a hotly debated topic in gardening circles for a number of years, with many different approaches achieving a variety of results. In Chapter 16, "Build-

ing a Wildflower Garden," I have described two methods of creating a meadow garden that have worked well for me. Both contain native and non-native wildflowers, grasses and some familiar garden plants. Whatever method or combination of methods you use to create your meadow, it can be an area of outstanding beauty — a place that is a pleasure to walk through, explore, work in and just plain enjoy.

You will need to give some serious thought to the location of this garden. For one thing, it will need full sun all day long. A varied terrain will be a bonus, as it adds an element of interest to the landscape, but it is certainly not a prerequisite. Meadows are, by nature, informal places, and some people consider them untidy — which is another reason to carefully consider your garden's location. You may want to site it at the back of the property, rather than in the middle of a formal landscape or the front lawn.

Your meadow should blend into the surrounding landscape, either by being set in an informal location (near a pasture, by an old orchard or in front of a wooded area, for example) or by its use as a transition zone in the form of a broad swath separating formal from informal areas, or woods from lawn. Perhaps the meadow can be set apart from the more traditional part of the garden by an old stone wall, fence or outbuilding.

A meadow garden is not really difficult to establish, but it does require time, patience and labor to build, plant and maintain. It is not a simple undertaking, despite all the colorful and seductive advertising of recent years. Nor does it occur by "letting nature take over" after you have simply scattered wildflower seeds in an open area. Your vision of a thriving meadow will only come about through careful, realistic planning, the thoughtful selection of plants, and hard work.

Top left: The three-lobed coneflower (Rudbeckia triloba), *great blue lobelia* (Lobelia siphilitica) *and pink turtle-head* (Chelone lyonii) *are colorful denizens of the summer meadow. Each has a slightly different flowering time, and as these overlap, the planting creates a strong focal point during the summer weeks.*

Top right: In late summer and fall Aster tataricus, *with its soft lavender flowers and dark green foliage, makes quite a spectacle.*

Bottom: The narrow-leaved sunflower (Helianthus angustifolius) *is a tall, conspicuous native which in late summer and fall is covered in brilliant yellow flowers of great beauty.*

10
A Bog Garden

THERE IS A WILD BEAUTY to a natural bog, whether it covers a large area stretching over several acres or occupies a relatively small pocket in a sunny glade, perhaps surrounded by tall, imposing spruce trees.

The larger, more open bogs are most notable for their swaths of cotton grass (*Eriophorum* species), but a closer inspection of this fascinating habitat reveals bright patches of color. The fringed orchids (*Habenaria* species) offer shades of deep lavender, orange and greenish white, and the purple pitcher plant (*Sarracenia purpurea*) presents rich maroon hues in flowers and foliage. An even closer look reveals a wonderland of plants tucked down in the covering mat of sphagnum. There are the white flowers of wren's-egg cranberry (*Vaccinium oxycoccus*) and creeping snowberry (*Chiogenes hispidula*) and the pale pinks of the sundews (*Drosera* species) amid the many shades of green from the different kinds of foliage.

Other plants, like the enchanting rose pogonia (*Pogonia ophioglossoides*) and nodding ladies' tresses (*Spiranthes cernua*), prefer to grow with their crowns below the sphagnum and their roots down in the wet, acid humus beneath it. Still others like to make their homes on low hummocks, where they can keep their crowns or tubers above any standing water and the general wetness of a bog. This is a favorite place for the lovely showy lady's-slipper (*Cypripedium reginae*) with its large white and pink slipper-shaped flowers carried on strong stems that, in cultivation, usually reach 12 to 24 inches high (in the wild they can be found at heights of up to 36 inches).

The fringed orchids also flourish on hummocks. I have used the purple fringed orchid (*Habenaria psycodes*) with its large lavender-purple flowers, and the yellow fringed orchid (*Habenaria ciliaris*) with its intensely colored flowers, long spurs and heavily fringed lower petal. The prairie fringed orchid (*Habenaria leucophaea*), with its smaller white flowers overlaid with green and displaying a delicate filigreed lip, is another plant that thrives on the hummocks. I have also included the grass pink (*Calopogon pulchellus*) because of the exquisite beauty of its large, showy flowers of lavender-pink, its 6- to 8-inch height, and its eagerness to grow in a well-made bog. This has long been a favorite of mine since I first saw natural bogs in Maine pink with it in early summer.

A number of beautiful shrubs, including Labrador tea (*Ledum groenlandicum*), bog rosemary, bog laurel (*Kalmia polifolia*) and leatherleaf (*Chamaedaphne calyculata*), can be grown on large hummocks and at the edges of the bog. With their height and form, they add an important dimension to the general flatness of the bog itself.

Labrador tea, with its small, narrow, leathery foliage, is typical of many of the shrubs found in and around a bog and is well

While the overall aspect of a bog is generally subtle, as seen here in this natural bog, a close look at the individual plants finds them exceptionally intricate and colorful.

A bog garden in early summer. A bog garden can be one of the most challenging gardens to create, but at the same time it can be one of the most rewarding. It contains mostly rare plants that are difficult to grow but are extremely beautiful and not hard to maintain once established.

Key to the Planting

1 Bog rosemary—*Andromeda polifolia*
2 Dwarf birch—*Betula nana*
3 Highbush blueberry—*Vaccinium corymbosum*
4 Large cranberry—*Vaccinium macrocarpon*
5 Purple fringed orchid—*Habenaria psycodes*
6 Purple pitcher plant—*Sarracenia purpurea*
7 Rose pogonia—*Pogonia ophioglossoides*
8 Sheep laurel—*Kalmia angustifolia*
9 Showy lady's-slipper—*Cypripedium reginae*
10 Sphagnum moss—*Sphagnum* species

11 Staggerbush—*Lyonia mariana*
12 Threadleaved sundew—*Drosera filiformis*
13 Winterberry—*Ilex verticillata*
14 Yellow fringed orchid—*Habenaria ciliaris*

A Hummock
B Pond

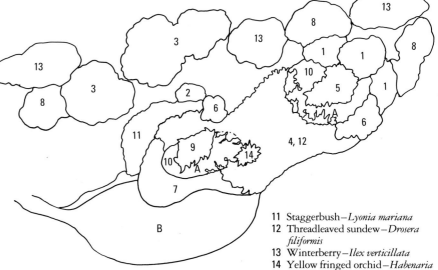

Plan of the bog garden.

*Above: In summer the bright, clear purple flowers of the grass pink (*Calopogon pulchellus*) create an intense spotlight of color in the bog garden.*

*Below: Labrador tea (*Ledum groenlandicum*) is an attractive summer-flowering shrub that thrives in moist acid soils and sun. It is well suited to growing either on a hummock in a bog garden or along the edges of the garden, where it can be used to blend this specialized habitat into the surrounding landscape.*

adapted to this unusual environment. In late spring, delicate clusters of white flowers—with just a hint of yellow in their centers—cover the plant. Bog gardens are typically quite small, because of the complexity of creating and maintaining them, and only one (or, at most, two) of these shrubs is enough to draw attention to this garden.

Bog rosemary, one of the most ornamental of bog plants with gray-green, slender foliage, forms a compact, low mound of 12 to 24 inches in height. In late spring, dainty rosy pink, bell-shaped flowers appear, providing a perfect accent for the glaucous foliage. (Its cousin, the European bog rosemary (*Andromeda glaucophylla*), is the one most frequently found in nurseries, and is just as pretty.)

The well-known and greatly loved mountain laurel has a small relative that grows here, the swamp or bog laurel. It is closer in appearance and size to the bog rosemary than to its better known cousin, but its miniature flowers of intense pink mirror those of the familiar mountain laurel and are produced in great abundance in summer.

For the plants that typically grow in and around a bog, the prime flowering time is in late spring and early summer, with an impressive secondary display of rich colors from foliage and fruit in the fall.

In the bog garden illustrated here, I have used staggerbush (*Lyonia mariana*), along with several other shrubs associated with acid soils that remain moist year-round. These add structure and height to this rather flat world and can also be used outside the bog itself to integrate it into the surrounding landscape. To provide the correct growing conditions, the soil for these transition plants will need to be amended with sand and acid humus to help

their fine roots get established. And, since they will not actually be in the very wet soil of the bog, they may need extra water in dry spells. Shrubs that can be used in the transition zones include staggerbush (*Lyonia mariana*), highbush blueberry, witherod (*Viburnum cassinoides*) and sand myrtle (*Leiophyllum buxifolium*).

With few exceptions, a bog garden is a totally artificial place. It should be set in a sunny location, although some light shade along the edges would not be a problem. Through careful design and construction, it is possible to duplicate the unique conditions of a natural bog and create a home for a number of highly specialized and wonderful plants, including some of our loveliest native orchids.

In this exacting environment, the plants have very specific needs, and most have little tolerance for deviation from the narrow range of conditions they require. The success of this garden, therefore, depends on a careful balance: You must create the right overall environment and the various specialty locations, select the right plants for each place and watch over them to meet their needs and adjust the habitat when necessary. (See Chapter 16, "Building a Wildflower Garden," for the creation of bog gardens.)

Most plants that grow in this habitat are not only very exacting in their cultural needs, they are also quite rare and often hard to find. Some can be found in specialty wildflower nurseries, but for the most part, these plants will have to come from friends, contacts made through plant societies, or plant rescues.

An advanced level of horticultural skill and knowledge is needed to grow the plants that live in a bog garden successfully. Locating and acquiring the plants for a bog can be time-consuming, and you will also need a source for the live sphagnum moss needed to cover the prepared soil mix and hummocks.

When a bog garden is done properly, it is a treasure trove of rare and beautiful plants and is not difficult to maintain. Although this is a highly specialized garden, built to grow a relatively small range of choice and demanding plants, it is one of the most enjoyable gardens, both because of the delicate beauty of the plants themselves, and because of the satisfaction gained from having succeeded in creating a habitat that is just right for these plants. The typically small size of a bog garden makes it quite manageable, and I think that this aspect also holds appeal for many gardeners.

*Top left: The berries of large cranberry (*Vaccinium macrocarpon*), an easily grown plant in this habitat, add a bright aspect to the fall landscape of a bog garden.*

*Top right: The distinctive yellow leaves of the trumpet pitcher plant (*Sarracenia flava*) are a colorful addition to a bog garden.*

*Bottom: Rose pogonia (*Pogonia ophioglossoides*) can form thick colonies in a bog garden. In early summer the multitude of flowers creates a soft pink haze.*

PART II
The Wildflowers

Flowers are the wealth, glory and delight of a garden. But in an overall garden design they are the last to go in.

JOHN REA

THERE IS TREMENDOUS GARDEN POTENTIAL in our rich and diverse native flora. Those gardeners who are more familiar with conventional horticultural garden forms become aware that the natives (especially the woodlanders) often have smaller, narrower or thinner leaves and often significantly smaller flowers and inflorescences, and that they are not as aggressive in their growth as are the typical garden plants. In character, the natives have a balance between flowers, foliage and form—a delicacy that many of the highly ornamental selections have lost.

Wild species, with their refined beauty, exert a special charm. There are so many kinds of wildflowers that they can be used to create virtually any landscape effect, color combination, or mood in a garden. They encompass all plant forms, foliage patterns, fruit and seed head displays, colors and degrees of ease in culture.

Although the plants portrayed here are native to North America, some also occur on other continents. The harebell (*Campanula rotundifolia*), for instance, can be found in many different parts of the world. I also mention those species with wild cousins from abroad that have made themselves at home here in our woods and fields.

The array extends from the woodlanders, whose subtle but often breathtakingly beautiful spring displays begin the garden year, to the residents of the meadows and watersides that bring brilliant color to the spectrum of summer, to the fall-flowering plants of the fields with their softer tones that offer a counterpoint to the often brilliant foliage colors of autumn. With so much to choose from, it's often hard to know where to begin.

To simplify the process and help you select plants that are suitable for your particular garden and your specific degree of skill and interest, I have for this section selected wildflowers that, in my experience, do particularly well in cultivation. I have also taken into consideration how the plants grow, as certain ones—some of those with a trailing habit of growth, for instance—can be challenging to get established, although once they are growing strongly, most are undemanding and easy to maintain.

These plants are divided into three main groups, primarily according to their ease of culture and availability: the Stalwarts, the Intermediates and the Specialty Plants. Each group is further separated into shade-loving and sun-loving plants. In the Stalwarts chapter, I have also included sixteen native trees and shrubs of particular garden merit, not only for their ornamental value and ease of culture, but also because they form an integral part of a garden design. These are grouped under the subheading "Woody Plants."

The Stalwarts are the easiest to find and grow; the Intermediates are somewhat more demanding to cultivate and often more difficult to find; and the Specialty Plants require a good deal of horticultural skill to be grown successfully and are hard to come by. I have not, however, included any plants that are what the English refer to as "miffy"—those demanding eccentrics that challenge not only one's gardening skill but also one's tolerance for perversity. I recommend that for your initial efforts at wildflower gardening you choose plants primarily from the first group—the Stalwarts. Then, as your confidence, skill and interest grow, you can add others from different categories.

In each plant portrait, I discuss the acquisition and care of the wildflowers and suggest other plants that may be grown as companions. I also mention special selections that have unique or unusual features.

The choice of wildflowers for each group is based on my own experience and on how I feel they would be best approached by someone who has not grown them before, or has had difficulty with them.

Using these observations as a guide, you can begin to develop a foundation of information and experience upon which to build your own wildflower collection—which I hope will ultimately be extensive and include not only the easily grown wildflowers, but the more challenging ones as well.

❧ ❧ ❧

Although "Stalwarts" isn't a particularly pretty term, it is an apt one. This first group includes woody and herbaceous plants of easy culture that are not as specific in their needs as those in the other two groups. They are readily available and easy to handle and transplant. With the herbaceous plants, simple division will generally provide ample quantities of new plants to expand existing plantings or begin new ones—often with a plant or two left over to provide you with the satisfaction of giving a favorite wildflower to a friend.

The Stalwarts are wildflowers both for the beginner who has little knowledge of gardening and for the more experienced gardener who knows little of growing wildflowers. At the same time, they are wonderful plants for the seasoned gardener because they are the mainstay of a garden.

This group contains a number of fine ground covers that will soon spread to provide rich carpets of color, plus many vigorous clump-formers that quickly increase in size from small beginnings to bold, showy displays.

As you gain experience with growing wildflowers and your understanding of your garden environment increases, try some of the plants in the next group, the Intermediates, to find new companions for the Stalwarts. The wildflowers in this second group generally demand more attention to their particular needs for site, habitat or culture. However, some may be as easy to grow as the Stalwarts, and may be included in the Intermediates because they don't create enough of a presence in a garden in terms of size or numbers. Other wildflowers in the Intermediate class are there because they are difficult to get established or to propagate. Finally, some Intermediates are simply difficult to find.

I have also put the spring ephemerals in this group because they go dormant and disappear so early in the year that they can be forgotten, and so there is always the possibility that they will be planted over, dug up or lost in some way. In addition, some of the spring ephemerals are often initially difficult to get going and quite delicate to handle.

For the most part, the Intermediates are most effective when they are woven in among the Stalwarts to create more intricate and interesting displays. Some, however, like the double pink-flowered rue anemone (*Anemonella thalictroides* 'Schoaf's Double Pink'), make beautiful specimen plants to highlight a special place. Because of their uniqueness, others—such as the large yellow lady's-slipper (*Cypripedium calceolus* var. *pubescens*)—should not be grown in large groups but in twos or threes to further emphasize their exceptional beauty.

Most of the wildflowers in the Intermediates group are found only in nurseries specializing in wildflowers. And not all wildflower nurseries will carry all the plants listed here, for no other reason than that these plants are not well known and thus there is, sadly, little demand for them.

The last group contains the Specialty Plants. Most of the wildflowers in this group are hard to come by, slow and difficult to propagate and generally challenging to grow and get established. They are best tried only by experienced gardeners, people who have acquired a sound understanding of the specific wildflower's habitat and have some skill in horticulture. For these plants to prosper, the gardener must understand the nuances of how to provide, in a contrived garden setting, the environment that they enjoy in the wild. Many are extremely specialized in their requirements and will not survive under general cultivation. Specialty plants are frequently seen only in small numbers in the wild— even singly, in some cases. Just the same, they are beautiful, garden-worthy plants. Mastering their cultivation is well worth the perseverance required. They can be used as individual focal points and conversation pieces, creating excitement by their rarity. More important, a gardener can take pride in growing these difficult plants successfully.

❧ ❧ ❧

Only a sampling of the vast number of wildflowers available to gardeners is discussed here. Of the 100 wildflowers covered, some of my favorites (and yours too, perhaps) are absent, although not because they are any less worthy or desirable than those that have been included.

Of the plants that are included, I have chosen some because of their beauty and some because they fill my garden with interest or provide a particular effect I am looking for. Some plants may elicit

_A simple yet striking picture can be created by planting low-growing ground covers such as crested iris (_Iris cristata_) and creeping phlox (_Phlox stolonifera_) beneath shrubs. Here they are used as a carpet around the white-flowered form of Catawba rhododendron (_Rhododendron catawbiense 'Album'_). The delicate rue anemone (_Anemonella thalictroides_) nestles amongst the crested iris to provide the finishing touch to this spring display._

nostalgia, and others have simply withstood my benign ineptness—especially in my early gardening years. Many of these treasures have been transplanted to different parts of the country, reestablishing themselves, flourishing and giving me years of pleasure and satisfaction. They have proved to be willing additions to my gardening schemes, and I have come to know and rely on them time and again to provide the essential elements of color, form and the harmonious interrelationship of plants with each other and with their environment. It is these factors that make a group of wildflowers evolve into a distinctive, cohesive garden, one that flows together and forms the very soul of the outdoor world I cherish.

The wildflowers discussed here, like all garden plants, need good soil preparation, even those that are happiest in the lean soil of a meadow garden. (See Chapter 16, "Building a Wildflower Garden.") Careful site selection and occasional deep waterings in long dry spells are also essential parts of a well-nurtured wildflower garden. Sometimes it is not possible to water during dry spells, and the better the soil preparation is, the better the plants can withstand these adverse conditions. Good horticultural practices will make all the difference between a flourishing garden that can withstand occasional spells of inclement weather and one that will go downhill quite rapidly during the inevitable harsh periods.

The wildflowers portrayed here are the threads of a special tapestry you can weave as you wish, choosing patterns to achieve an effect that is uniquely yours and that will, with good care, last for as long as you like.

11

The Stalwarts

Woody Plants (Shade)

❦ *Amelanchier* species
Shadbush

One of our most charming native woody plants, the shadbush forms a small tree or large shrub depending on the species. In spring, its myriad small flowers create fluffy white clouds against the somber grays and browns of the other, still-dormant trees along a wooded roadside and in sunny woodland glades. Everything about this plant is engaging, from the purple-and-bronze color of the new foliage, to the striking gray bark and abundant fruit, which is a favorite of many birds. It is easily grown and does equally well in full sun or light shade; the latter is preferable in areas

with long hot summers.

Allegheny shadbush (*A. laevis*), shown here, forms a tree 15 to 25 feet

high with a broad, upright growth habit that makes it well suited to be grown as a specimen tree or in small groups where it will provide shade for other plants. Beneath its branches, a small wildflower area can be developed with the blues of Virginia bluebells (*Mertensia virginica*), the white of rue anemone (*Anemonella thalictroides*) and bloodroot (*Sanguinaria canadensis*) and the bright yellows of miniature daffodils.

Shadbush (*A. canadensis*) has a shrubby growth habit and ranges in height from 6 to 15 feet. This makes it an ideal background or screening plant, especially when spotted throughout a woodland area. Although the flowers are small, they are produced so prolifically that they rival the display of an ornamental crabapple. *A. canadensis* makes a good companion for native azaleas, spicebush (*Lindera benzoin*) and stoloniferous dogwoods such as *Cornus alba* 'Sibirica', and the flowers stand out particularly well against the dark foliage of evergreens.

Shadbushes are easily grown plants with multiseasonal interest that have been overlooked for too long in our gardens and deserve to be used far more extensively. Like so many of our native trees, they are rarely troubled by disease or pest problems.

❦ *Aronia arbutifolia*
Chokeberry

A somber, overcast day in fall is cheered and warmed by the bright scarlet foliage covering this bushy shrub. When the sun shines, the effect is quite spectacular.

In spring, a multitude of small white flowers put on a fine display; by summer, they have developed into bright scarlet berries. These displays continue over many months and make this a good choice for the gardener

who is looking for a multiseasonal plant.

Chokeberry grows 6 to 10 feet high and can be used equally effectively along the edges of a meadow or wood margin, or in a more formal sunny border. It works well as a background for early summer wildflowers like the wild columbine (*Aquilegia canadensis*), golden star (*Chrysogonum virginianum*) and nodding onion (*Allium cernuum*), or it can be set beside water where bog rosemary (*Andromeda polifolia*), staggerbush (*Lyonia mariana*) and sweet pepperbush (*Clethra alnifolia*) might be its companions along with the bright colors of iris, cardinal flower (*Lobelia cardinalis*) and turtleheads (*Chelone* species).

To accentuate the fall display of brilliant scarlet foliage, I use gray-foliaged plants such as boltonia (*Boltonia asteroides*) and artemisia and the soft yellow foliage of blue star (*Amsonia tabernaemontana*).

This plant is easy to grow in full sun or light to part shade, and is tolerant of quite wet soils. It should be well watered during times of little rain.

❦ *Cercis canadensis*
Redbud

Redbud is one of the earliest plants to flower, producing masses of tightly bunched pealike blooms along its branches before there is any sign of foliage. The flowers are a bright, intense lavender-pink, and are most appealing against a background of dark green. Conifers are an especially good foil, softening the brightness of the flowers while emphasizing the beauty of this lovely small tree.

Later, large, delicate heart-shaped leaves in bright green create a delightfully light and airy display that gives a wonderful feeling of coolness to a garden in summer. Because of its small size (18–25 feet), redbud is well suited for use as a specimen tree in a small garden or courtyard, or as a transition plant between shaded and sunny areas. In the wild, redbud often grows along a wood margin or hedgerow as an understory tree, where it flowers heavily in filtered shade. It will also thrive in full sun if it is given a good soil and deep summer watering.

I like to underplant redbud with spring flowers and bulbs in pastel shades, using the dark foliage of waldsteinia (*Waldsteinia fragarioides*) or Allegheny spurge (*Pachysandra procumbens*) as a ground cover for the spring flowers to grow through; the dark color of the ground covers contrasts so well with them and with the redbud itself.

While *C. canadensis,* shown here, is the most widely available species, there are several others of great charm, and several fine forms including a white-flowered one ('Alba') that is not quite as hardy as the straight species. 'Forest Pansy' is a form with rich,

deep purple foliage that makes a striking highlight of color in a garden, especially in the spring months when the color is most intense. Also look for 'Oklahoma', with its shiny polished

foliage and wavy margins.

I found southern New Hampshire to be the northern edge of this plant's winter hardiness, and my experience has been that trees planted as seedlings seem better able to adapt to the cold than those that have been planted as more mature specimens in areas where they are marginally winter-hardy.

Chionanthus virginicus
Fringe Tree

Why this lovely native tree is not more widely grown is a mystery. It is exceptionally beautiful and easy to grow.

In late spring, the whole plant is clothed with flowers formed from clusters of the delicate white ribbons that so aptly give it its common name. It grows well in full sun but also flowers prolifically in part shade or in the shade on the north side of a building. In hot climates, the fringe tree prefers a location where it is sheltered from intense heat.

Although initially slow to put on growth, it flowers at a very early age; I have seen plants only 15 inches high covered with fragrant white streamers. Because of the fringe tree's overall grace, refined appearance and sweetly fragrant flowers, it makes a wonderful specimen tree, especially for a lawn or small garden area. It is a good "lead-in" plant for a woodland garden, and also provides an attractive setting for small plantings of wildflowers under its branches.

When it is not pruned, the fringe tree's lower-growing branches start almost at ground level. A low ground cover interplanted with early spring bulbs, therefore, suits it well. Even a carpet of soft pink impatiens for summer color is pretty. I have also used the

black foliage of mondo grass (*Ophiopogor planiscapus* 'Nigrescens') as a ground cover, interplanted with spring and fall crocus.

Pruning the lower branches is a simple task and will allow you to grow taller wildflowers under it. In a shady location, these might include hepaticas (*Hepatica* species), crested iris (*Iris cristata*), Jack-in-the-pulpits (*Arisaema triphyllum*), trillium (*Trillium* species) and wild gingers (*Asarum* species), along with ferns. In a sunny location the wild cranesbill (*Geranium maculatum*), columbine (*Aquilegia* species), Stokes' aster (*Stokesia laevis*) and bowman's root (*Gillenia trifoliata*) are all ideal companions, to name only a few.

Look also for this tree's lovely Asian cousin, *C. retusus.* It forms a very broad shrub that in early summer is covered in flowers similar to those of the native fringe tree, except they are a little shorter and form tighter clusters.

Clethra alnifolia
Sweet Pepperbush

The scent from just one plant of sweet pepperbush will permeate the summer garden with a sweet fragrance that attracts hummingbirds and all kinds of butterflies. The multi-

tude of small flowers form upright candles of creamy white that cover this medium-height shrub for many weeks. It is suited to growing in wet places in sun or light shade, although it will also grow well in a typical garden situation if it is kept watered during dry spells.

Sweet pepperbush spreads by stolons which can be easily separated from the parent plant, providing a simple way to start this attractive shrub in other areas of the garden.

When it is happy, it will spread to form handsome, full clumps.

Although this is considered a plant for sunny areas, in the wild I have seen sweet pepperbush form colonies in wet, shady woodlands, where it flowers well. Another favorite spot is around brackish ponds, where it grows in impenetrable thickets that are especially beautiful in summer, when it is in full bloom, and in fall, when the foliage turns a rich yellow.

This shrub makes a good background for a garden. It is also effective when set at the side of a pool or stream as a companion plant to perennials that like damp places, such as the native lilies (*Lilium* species), cardinal flower and the shrublike rose mallow (*Hibiscus palustris*). Or it may be grown in a moist spot beside a clump of white birch (*Betula papyrifera*), beneath which primroses (*Primula* species) and spring beauty (*Claytonia virginica*) can be planted for an early spring display, with a carpet of bluets (*Houstonia caerulea*) providing color for the early summer season. The bottle gentians (*Gentiana andrewsii*) end the year's display with their intense blue flowers. A planting such as this looks particularly lovely when mixed with cinnamon ferns (*Osmunda cinnamomea*) with their soft yellow and beige fall foliage—the same colors as those of the sweet pepperbush in autumn.

There are several other species well worth growing, especially *C. barbinervis* from Asia, with its wonderful brown and gray mottled bark and long, semipendulous racemes of creamy white flowers.

Like so many of our native trees and shrubs, sweet pepperbush is easy to grow and trouble-free.

Fothergilla species
Bottlebrush Shrub

My early spring walks on crisp, bracing days to visit nearby marsh marigolds (*Caltha palustris*) always contain an added pleasure when I come across the tall, graceful form of the bottlebrush shrub (*Fothergilla major*), shown here, which likes the same kind of wet, swampy places.

Its clusters of ivory-white flowers, sheathing every branch tip and scenting the air with their honey fragrance, are produced well before the leaves are in evidence. Later, the foliage, which is very similar to that of witchhazel (*Hamamelis* species), expands to provide a soft, green, textured display on upright branches. In fall these leaves turn a bright fiery red that will set a quiet corner ablaze.

The bottlebrush shrub grows to a height of approximately 12 feet and is more readily available than the dwarf species (*F. gardenii*), which is more compact and ranges from 3 to 4 feet tall.

There is a form of this dwarf species called 'Blue Mist' with lovely, glaucous-blue foliage that is well worth looking for. It will, however, lose this coloring if it is planted in sun.

Because of a natural love of moisture around its roots, bottlebrush shrub is a good choice to plant near water or in wet, marshy places, but it will grow in a typical garden situation as long as extra humus is added to the soil and additional water is given during dry spells. It grows well in full sun or light shade (the latter is preferable in a hot climate), and thus is a good plant for the transition area along a woods' edge.

If grown in a group with a couple of tall trees, the bottlebrush shrub can become the frame for a small shade garden. Add an azalea or two to the group, and you will have a delightful wildflower area waiting to be filled with colorful herbaceous plants. The bottlebrush shrub also makes a marvelous specimen plant.

Halesia carolina
Silver-Bell Tree

A small, often multistemmed woodland tree growing about 30 feet high, the silver-bell tree is breathtakingly ornate during the early spring when it is covered in pristine white bell-shaped flowers. When this abundance of flowers drops to the ground, the effect is reminiscent of a late spring snowfall—and it lasts as brief a time. What a treat to come across it in full flower beside a driveway, along a wood

margin, as a specimen in a shady area or—best of all—beside a winding path in a woodland garden. Walking beneath the clouds of flowers is an experience rivaling a scene from a Hans Christian Andersen fairy tale.

The silver-bell tree provides a canopy for a multitude of wildflowers and serves as a companion for other woody plants such as azaleas and magnolias. I like to grow oconee bells (*Shortia galacifolia*) and galax (*Galax aphylla*) beneath it, as their dark shiny evergreen foliage adds an extra intensity to the whiteness of silver-bell's flowers. This woodlander is best grown in a deep, acid, humusy soil in light shade.

Two-winged silver-bell tree (*H. diptera*), just 20–30 feet tall, is a little-known relative, with larger flowers. It is hard to find, but well worth trying to locate.

Silver-bell tree seems to be more available at garden centers and nurseries now than it was several years ago, which I hope is a sign of a growing appreciation for its lovely display and ease of culture.

Hamamelis virginiana
Fall-flowering Witchhazel

One of my greatest pleasures when walking along a brook in late fall is to find the rich yellow blossoms of the fall-flowering witchhazel. Even though it is a reminder that winter is near at hand, this plant's flowers and soft yellow foliage, shown here, perfectly complement this gentle time of year. It blends into a woodland setting, adding a warmth and vitality to the days of late fall.

The vernal witchhazel (*H. vernalis*), on the other hand, heralds the spring with its bright yellow flowers long before any foliage is showing. In the wild it will be a companion to skunk

cabbage (*Symplocarpus foetidus*) and false hellebore (*Veratrum viride*), with which they provide a wonderful array of textures and early interest, especially if a large clump of marsh marigold is growing close by.

In the wild, both are most often found along a brook, and both prefer summer shade and moisture-retentive soils. In a garden, they are perfect for lightly shaded corners and sunny glades, and they also do well in full sun where the summers are temperate. The witchhazel's canopy of foliage provides a sheltered haven for many wildflowers, especially those that favor damp soils. These companions would include Virginia bluebells and the Christmas (*Polystichum acrostichoides*), interrupted (*Osmunda claytoniana*) and cinnamon ferns, with a scattering of wood anemone (*Anemone quinquefolia*) and spring beauty in the foreground.

During the growing season, the open habit of growth and textured light green foliage of witchhazel set off companion plants with heavier dark leaves such as rhododendrons and fetterbush (*Leucothoe fontanesiana*).

Although our two native witchhazels are not as showy as their Asian cousins or the hybrids, they add their own quiet charm to a garden and provide a pleasing counterbalance to the more flamboyant plants.

Hydrangea quercifolia
Oak-Leaf Hydrangea

Seeing this plant in full bloom in a woodland garden is the only encouragement anyone needs to go right out and get a couple for one's own garden.

The oak-leaf hydrangea is a sturdy shrub, 4 to 6 feet high, with year-round appeal. In early spring, the leaf and flower buds are so heavily covered in hairs as to have a felty feel and look to them. The beige buds are set against cinnamon-colored bark that exfoliates in ribbons of gray. The expanding leaf buds are miniature works of art, alluding to the beauty to come when the heavily textured leaves are fully expanded.

These leaves, and the highly ornamental buds, would be enough to give oak-leaf hydrangea a place in my garden, but when the flower display begins in summer, this becomes an even more engaging plant. The typical hydrangea flowers are carried on large, upright cones that cover the plant and look like giant candles of creamy white amongst the greens and dappled light of a shade garden. With the onset of cool weather, the foliage, always dramatic, turns a wonderful dark red and plum color. The plant's year-round show continues magnificently into winter, as its cinnamon and gray bark warms the snowy landscape.

The oak-leaf hydrangea will grow

in sun or shade (the latter is preferable in areas with hot summers), and needs a rich, moisture-retentive soil for best results. The cultivar 'Snow Queen' is a superior form with strong stems that easily hold the large, heavy flower panicles upright, while the plant itself has an overall vigor that is a noticeable improvement over the species and other cultivars.

Ilex verticillata
Winterberry

One winter day many years ago, I was driving by a swampy area in New Hampshire when I noticed a scarlet haze. It was an especially welcome sight amongst the grays and browns of other plants on a cold, bleak day, and it came from the fat scarlet fruit of the winterberry, one of our greatly overlooked native North American hollies.

For most of the growing season, winterberry is just a green plant that blends into the landscape. Then, in fall, the leaves and fruits turn a brilliant red. Long after the leaves have disappeared, the tight clusters of berries continue to sparkle, and they look especially pretty against a background of snow.

In the wild, this shrub, which reaches a height of 6 to 10 feet, prefers full sun and wet, swampy places. It will also fare well in a good garden soil that is on the acid side and receives regular deep watering. In any of these locations, it is an undemanding, easily grown plant.

There are now several cultivars, such as 'Sparkleberry' and 'Harvest Red', that sport larger and more abundant fruit than the original wild variety. I, for one, am glad to see these signs of this plant's growing popularity.

Another native holly to look for is the inkberry (*Ilex glabra*), especially the cultivar 'Nordic', which grows slowly to a height of only 3 to 4 feet, as opposed to the 5- to 6-foot height of the straight species. The foliage bears little resemblance to that of traditional hollies except that it has a shiny dark evergreen leaf. It's a compact, rounded shrub of easy culture when grown in a sunny situation and is ideal for the winter landscape. In the wild it is frequently found in swampy places where the soil is acid, but, like the winterberry, it does not require these conditions in a garden situation.

Itea virginica
Virginia Sweetspire

This is a small, well-proportioned shrub of great appeal, either for a mixed planting with perennials and other shrubs, or as a specimen. In summer, its panicles of lightly fragrant flowers form long, graceful,

creamy fountains. In fall, sweetspire's deep red and plum foliage makes a wonderful splash of intense color that is particularly welcome because it is always the very last plant to drop its leaves. In the south, the leaves persist well into winter.

Virginia Sweetspire can attain a height of 5 feet in temperate climates, but in northern areas with severe winters, it is usually killed down to ground level in winter and does not grow much above 3 feet tall annually. It should be covered with a thick winter mulch over the crown, from which it will resprout the following spring with great vigor. I have seen clumps 8 to 10 feet high edging rivers in Tennessee and Georgia, where the flower and foliage displays provide an unexpected splash of color amongst the greens that dominate the woodland. It spreads by stolons and, in a mild climate, it will form an unusual and striking ground cover.

The form 'Henry's Garnet' is even more handsome in its fall foliage display than the straight species. It is aptly named, as the fall color of the leaves is a rich, sumptuous garnet red.

Nyssa sylvatica
Black Tupelo

A greatly underused native tree, the black tupelo puts on one of the most brilliant of fall displays. Its shimmering scarlet leaves combine with full clusters of black fruit to create a show that is unsurpassed for sheer loveliness and makes this a perfect specimen plant. The tree's pyramid shape and horizontal branching habit give it an appealing countenance in summer and a distinctive silhouette in the winter landscape.

The most impressive use of this plant I have ever seen was at an approach to a home where it lined both sides of a long driveway. In fall, it was hard to tear one's gaze from this glorious sight. On a smaller scale, planting a tupelo on either side of the entrance to a driveway or broad walk can also be impressive.

Because black tupelos have deep taproots that make it hard to establish them any later, I recommend transplanting them when they are relatively small—6 to 7 feet high at most. They will grow in full sun or part shade (even all-day shade, if it is light) to a height of 30 to 40 feet at maturity. Although I have seen them growing in a wide variety of places and soils—in lawns, in quite wet soils at the edge of a swamp and occasionally in the impoverished soils of an abandoned

field—they will do best in rich, organic soils. Because they tolerate such a broad range of conditions, black tupelos can be used in a great number of ways in the garden landscape.

Oxydendrum arboreum
Sourwood

Truly one of the most beautiful and graceful of all trees, sourwood has a

slender, upright form that is unique and useful in many garden situations. In early summer, the whole tree is outlined by a cascade of long, pendulous panicles of milk-white flowers not unlike those of the Japanese andromeda (*Pieris japonica*). The long, creamy central stems that carry these flowers remain on the plant until late fall, giving the impression that the tree is always in bloom. These stems are especially noticeable in fall when the foliage turns scarlet; the contrast creates a spectacular effect in the landscape. During the winter, the elegant growth habit is accentuated by sourwood's heavily ribbed bark.

Sourwood can be found growing in a wide variety of places—in full sun and impoverished soils, and in shady mountain woods in rich, humusy leaf mold. It looks and performs at its best, however, when it is grown in good soils and not allowed to dry out in the summer months. I have found it does poorly in cultivation if it is subjected to dry summers and poor soils.

In the wild, sourwood is most often seen as a forest tree, and filtered light does not seem to diminish its heavy flowering. It establishes easily in a garden, but it is slow to reach its mature height of approximately 30 feet.

Sourwood is an exceptional tree grown in any situation, but it is especially dramatic with a backdrop of pines or hemlocks. The narrow, upright growth habit makes it one of the finest specimen trees for small or narrow areas, and it is truly lovely in a woodland wildflower garden.

As a member of the Heath family, sourwood naturally requires an acid soil; it should be cared for in the same way as are its cousins, azaleas and mountain laurel (*Kalmia latifolia*).

Vaccinium corymbosum
Highbush Blueberry

While the highbush blueberry has long been esteemed for its fruit, it should not be overlooked for its great ornamental value in the garden landscape.

This shrub adds a great deal of beauty to a sunny wildflower garden. In early spring, a multitude of creamy flowers decorate the bare, twiggy stems. Familiar blue berries accompany the soft green foliage of summer, which changes to a brilliant scarlet in fall. And in winter, the distinctive character of the blueberry's intricate branching habit stands out in the somber landscape.

It will grow in light shade or full sun, in a typical garden soil or a wet swampy place (where it is most frequently found in the wild). As long as the soil is acid and rich in organic matter, and never bakes dry during a drought, the highbush blueberry is an easy, care-free plant of great garden value. It will take quite a few years to reach its mature height, which will be in the range of 8 to 12 feet, depending on where and how it is grown. All that is needed to create an exceptional specimen is a little judicious pruning to accentuate its unique natural form.

Viburnum alnifolium
Wayfaring Tree

There are so many wonderful viburnums to choose from, both native and non-native, that it's almost impossible to select one or two. This diverse group of shrubs is noted for its blossoms (which are often fragrant), colorful fruit, striking fall color and good architectural lines. Of the native species, a favorite of mine is the wayfaring tree, shown here, which has a rather open, loose habit of growth that I find particularly appealing. The large, thick, heavily textured leaves are particularly distinctive, especially in the midst of all the sameness of a green summer shade garden.

The buds of the wayfaring tree are

covered in a creamy white fur that is attractive in the late winter garden, while in spring the white flowers form large flat clusters 3 to 5 inches across. This ornamental display is followed in summer with bright scarlet berries that ultimately turn a purple-black and are much favored by birds.

In fall, the leaves, shown at right, become a rich, rosy claret color with a purple overlay that is extremely handsome and reminds me of the muted colors in an old taspestry. In its autumn foliage, the wayfaring tree stands out among the woodland greens, browns, golds and grays, bringing a look of substance to the woods at a time of year when so much seems fleeting and tentative. It is perhaps loveliest at this time of year, especially late in the day when it is backlit by the sun.

The wayfaring tree is a large shrub with an asymmetrical shape that I feel

is part of its charm. I use it to reinforce the unstructured, natural feel of a wildflower area. Plant it among heavily textured dark evergreens such as Christmas fern and wintergreen (*Gaultheria procumbens*), then add the charm of trilliums, bloodroot and Asian epimediums (*Epimedium* species), the tall baneberries (*Actaea* species) and Solomon's seal (*Polygonatum biflorum*) to create a very pretty woodland scene.

The wayfaring tree is extremely hardy and will grow in sun in cool northern climates. It is also well suited to damp, shady places, as well as locations with partial shade. It is a plant to grow along a brook or path, either set back to act as a natural light screen, or placed near the path itself to frame a vista.

Give this shrub a humusy soil that is moisture-retentive, as it prefers extra moisture, and do a little pruning once in a while to keep it more compact and bushy, and it will give you year-round interest.

A selection called 'Mohican', a recent introduction of the National Arboretum, has a more compact growth habit than the species and is a good choice for smaller areas. Both are extremely hardy.

Witherod (*V. cassinoides*) is another very garden-worthy viburnum. It is an attractive shrub that grows 5 to 6 feet tall in the garden, although I have seen it as high as 12 feet in the wild. Witherod has a dense, compact growth habit with glossy foliage. In summer, the clusters of creamy white flowers are borne in great profusion and last for a long time. These develop into outstanding berries that turn from pink to blue and finally to black; sometimes berries in all three color

stages are present on the same shrub at the same time and make a strikingly beautiful picture. In the fall, the foliage presents a colorful display that can range from orange to crimson and purple.

This shrub is suitable for a number of situations, from light shade under deciduous trees to open, sunny places near a swamp or bog.

It is unfortunate that such a wonderful plant is so little used in gardens and rarely offered by nurseries.

The nannyberry or blackhaw (*V. prunifolium*) is usually seen as a large, multistemmed shrub, but it can ultimately grow into a small tree, 15 to 20 feet tall. In spring, the multitude of small, creamy white flowers form large flat clusters that can reach 4 inches across. These are followed by berries that begin pink and mature to a dark blue dusted with white. In fall, the handsome dark foliage turns a variety of colors from deep red to a bronze purple.

🌸 🌸 🌸

All viburnums are easy, long-lived, hardy and trouble-free plants, and all are good choices for a wildflower garden in sun or shade. Nannyberry will also tolerate quite dry soils.

The viburnums are good companions for native azalea, witchhazels and the ferns. A patchwork carpet of spring wildflowers grown in the shelter beneath a viburnum is always a pretty sight.

🌸 *Xanthorhiza simplicissima* Yellowroot

Yellowroot forms an attractive ground cover that grows 20 to 24 inches high in a rich moist soil in shade. The woody stems arise from stolons, and the plant has a light, airy quality about it, making it an excel-

lent cover around tall wildflowers or shrubs and trees. It can also be an appealing backdrop behind lower-growing wildflowers like Jack-in-the-pulpit, wood poppy (*Stylophorum diphyllum*), trillium and the ferns. Mixed with other ground covers to form bands of foliage at varying heights, it will create an effective and unusual display. Waldsteinia might be used in the foreground, then vancouveria (*Vancouveria hexandra*), followed by yellowroot behind it, with several plants of blue cohosh (*Caulophyllum thalictroides*) in the background.

In northern areas, yellowroot can be grown in full sun, where it will be lower and denser. The purplish-green flowers that are produced in spring are not particularly showy, but this is a wildflower well worth including in all but the smallest of gardens for the light, flowing aspect it brings to any planting, and it should be used more often.

Bulbs and Herbaceous Plants (Shade)

🌸 *Actaea rubra* Baneberry

Whether one is more attracted by baneberry's flowers or by its large clusters of sparkling red fruit (which are white in the species *A. pachypoda*), this is a delightful plant for the woodland or shade garden.

In spring, this midsized perennial (20 to 24 inches tall) produces many terminal clusters of delicate white flowers. These are carried above the dark green foliage that provides an ideal stage for the blossoms and, in late summer, the fruiting displays.

Baneberry is an easily grown, trouble-free plant that mixes well with giant Solomon's seal (*Polygonatum canaliculatum*), Virginia bluebells, bugbane (*Cimicifuga* species) and ferns. As baneberry's foliage begins well above ground level, it makes an effective display when used with an under-

planting of taller ground covers such as vancouveria, wild oats (*Uvularia sessilifolia*), golden seal (*Hydrastis canadensis*) or Japanese painted fern (*Athyrium niponicum* 'Pictum'). Another lovely planting is one featuring waldsteinia, interplanted with Dutchman's-breeches (*Dicentra cucullaria*) and toothwort (*Dentaria*

diphylla). I also like to grow the two species of baneberry with their different colored berries together.

This trim plant is perfectly suited to a position in front of a border, and is equally appropriate when used as a specimen planting in a terrace garden—perhaps in a shady corner or a large container. In the spaciousness of a woodland garden, baneberry can be used in small groups to provide a background for smaller foreground plants.

🌸 *Aruncus dioicus* Goatsbeard

I first saw this billowy but stately plant growing in large colonies along a bank beside the southern section of the Blue Ridge Parkway. The display and general growth habit made such a favorable impression on me that I have used it extensively in many plantings ever since.

Because of its size and full habit of growth, goatsbeard creates a bold display, even when viewed from a distance. In early summer it produces a mass of full plumes comprised of many creamy white flowers, and looks rather like a giant astilbe. Goatsbeard brings a light, feathery accent to a woodland garden or a shady border. Because of its height (4 to 5 feet), it is well suited for use as a background planting or screen, and can fill the role played by a shrub in a garden landscape. In a large garden, several can be planted as a highlight; in a smaller area, a single plant creates a pleasing accent.

Where summers are not too hot—or are hot only for a short time—goatsbeard will grow in full sun or in morning sun with afternoon shade, but take care to see that it is watered well in hot spells. Otherwise, it is best grown in filtered shade.

In a shaded spot, the natural companions for goatsbeard are native flowering shrubs such as wayfaring tree, the graceful redvein enkianthus (*Enkianthus campanulatus*) from Asia, and tall herbaceous wildflowers that have equally impressive forms, like blue cohosh, autumn fern (*Dryopteris erythrosora*) and rodgersia (*Rodgersia aesculifolia*). Ground covers such as golden seal, mayapple (*Podophyllum peltatum*) and alum root (*Heuchera americana*) are also excellent complements to goatsbeard and—in sunnier places—wild cranesbill and golden aster (*Chrysopsis mariana*) present a good counterpoint to its size.

Asarum species
The Wild Gingers

Although all parts of these attractive wildflowers smell strongly of ginger, they are not the culinary ginger of commerce. All the wild species of asarum form dense ground covers in shady areas, where they create graceful sweeps along a path or beneath taller-growing plants. Many wildflowers can easily push up through their leaves, and the ephemeral Dutchman's-breeches and squirrel corn (*Dicentra canadensis*), with their white flowers and gray foliage, make an especially pretty picture. The ginger's foliage also protects the roots of the ephemerals once they go dormant.

All the gingers have strange brown flowers that appear right at ground level, tucked under the leaves. Each species has a slightly different flower. The deciduous wild ginger (*A. canadense*), shown here, with its furry gray-green leaves, is probably the best known and most widely available of the group. The evergreen species are preferred by most gardeners for their handsome, shiny foliage, often beautifully mottled in silver, which adds an interesting note to the garden.

Look for Virginia ginger (*A. virginicum*), with its silvery gray mottled leaves, and Shuttleworth's ginger 'Callaway' form (*A. shuttleworthii* forma 'Callaway')—the smallest of all, but by far the most beautiful, with sparkling dark green foliage heavily marbled in silver. 'Callaway' is most effective as a specimen plant, as it does not spread like the others and will always invite comments on

its striking appearance. Plant this cultivar near bloodroot, bleeding heart (*Dicentra eximia*), or vancouveria, whose lighter green and gray foliage contrasts with 'Callaway's dark color.

There are other native species from the southern and western states worth looking for, and the European ginger (*A. europaeum*) is also a well-known member of this genus. It mixes in with other shade-loving plants, where its glossy foliage (evergreen in mild areas) brings a bright accent to planting.

All of the gingers are well worth a place in the wildflower garden. They are all easy to grow and divide, but division must be done carefully, as the roots and stems are rather brittle.

Caulophyllum thalictroides
Blue Cohosh

This lovely plant is unsurpassed for its elegant growth habit. The blue cohosh's strong, upright stems (24 to 30 inches high) carry glaucous foliage that creates a distinctive airiness which is accentuated by a woodland's constantly changing patterns of dappled light and shade. In spring, the stem tips carry clusters of attractive greenish-yellow flowers brushed in

brown—perhaps not everyone's idea of a pretty flower, but they are so beautifully formed and delicate that I find them very appealing.

In a woods area, several plants can be used as a light screen to form a background for a wealth of spring flowers. A single specimen makes an ideal accent plant, perhaps in a bed of creeping phlox (*Phlox stolonifera*), northern beech fern (*Thelypteris phegopteris*), or epimedium. It also makes a wonderful companion for evergreen rhododenrons, as its bright, glaucous foliage lightens their dark, often somber, appearance. Or it can be planted for contrast in front of the dark, heavily textured foliage of the tall bugbane (*Cimicifuga racemosa*).

Give blue cohosh a rich, moisture-retentive soil and light shade, and for the whole growing season it will grace your garden, finishing its display with clusters of blue berries in late summer.

 *Cimicifuga* species
Bugbane

What a delightful airy display the bugbanes make in the woodland, with their tall spikes of ivory-white flowers casting wands of light in the early summer shade. I love to see them in small groups set back from a path where the flowers appear to float in the air, seemingly unconnected to the earth. Bugbanes can just as easily be used as specimen plants near a walkway, beside a bench or set against the pale green foliage of spicebush and the rarely grown leatherwood (*Dirca palustris*).

The tallest form is the tall bugbane (*C. racemosa*), shown here, which can grow upwards of 5 feet high—but, like so many of the taller wildflowers—requires no staking. The rarely seen dwarf bugbane (*C. americana*) is only about 3 feet tall when in flower, which makes it an ideal choice for an area where the taller one would be out of scale. In summer, the Asian *C. dahurica* and, in early fall, the Kamchatka bugbane (*C. sim-*

plex) from Siberia provide similarly beautiful displays. Both are 24 to 30 inches tall and have the same lovely

elegance as our native species.

All bugbanes are excellent companions for a wide variety of shade-loving plants, including ferns and a number of flowering perennials such as vancouveria, whose pale green foliage contrasts well with the dark leaves of the bugbane, or the low-growing golden Alexander (*Zizia aurea*) and variegated wild oats (*Uvularia sessilifolia* 'Variegata'), which balance the height and grace of the bugbanes. In the fall, the Asian toad lilies (*Tricyrtis* species) add color in purple and white, while the tall Japanese anemones (*Anemone japonica*) contribute the white and pink of their flowers. The large-leaved hostas, especially those with blue foliage like *Hosta plantaginea* 'Grandiflora' or the golden splashes of *H. sieboldiana* 'Frances Williams', also go well with bugbane.

Bugbanes are so undemanding that they should be used much more in small and large shade gardens alike.

 *Dicentra* species
Bleeding Heart

Every member of this genus is a delight in a shady garden, and as pretty a plant as can be grown.

There are a number of native American bleeding hearts and a well-known non-native—the Asian bleeding heart (*D. spectabilis*)—available to North American gardeners. The deep-pink-flowered wild bleeding heart (*D. eximia*) is the one most often seen, but the prize of all the bleeding hearts, for me, is the white-flowered form, *D. eximia* 'Alba', shown here. Its mound of finely dissected, soft gray foliage would make this a choice plant for the shade garden even if it never flowered. It does flower, of course—in spring, with cascades of flowers lasting many weeks. They are so intricate in their design that I never tire of admiring them, and I often put one into a container so I can look at it frequently and closely. A lovelier plant is hard to imagine.

For an especially beautiful effect, plant a white bleeding heart in front of white birch. *D.e.* 'Alba' also looks good in front of a dark evergreen, or

amid an array of other spring wildflowers. If the white form is kept separated from the pink, it will come true from seed.

Wild bleeding heart grows and readily self-sows in sunny spots as well as in the shady garden, but *D. formosa* (a western species) is the true sun-lover of this group in all climates except those where the summers are

long and hot. There is hardly a place it will not be found flowering happily, even in tight rock crevices. Although both have their primary display in spring, they will flower through the summer into fall, an unusual characteristic in a perennial. The cooler and moister the climate and soil are, the better the display.

Look for the various selections and hybrids now available. These offer a variety of hues that range from very dark reds to pinks.

The well-known Asian bleeding heart is the one so often seen in old-fashioned cottage gardens. It's a graceful, statuesque plant that goes dormant with the onset of summer, a process that can be slowed by keeping the soil well watered. The Asian bleeding heart also has a beautiful white-flowered form (*D. spectabilis* 'Alba') that is exceptionally handsome. Both need companion plantings that will fill in the space left by them, perhaps astilbes (*Astilbe* species) or Japanese anemones.

Two other members of the dicentra group, squirrel corn (*D. canadensis*) and Dutchman's-breeches (*D. cucullaria*), tend to prefer soils that are slightly on the alkaline side and, because of their delicacy and ephemeral nature, are best tucked into safe niches. Once their seeds have been disseminated, the plants die back and go dormant, so care must be taken not to disturb the resting underground portions. Squirrel corn grows from corms that look like tiny kernels of corn—hence the name—and Dutchman's-breeches grows from tiny pink tubers. Since both are found either just at or just below ground level, they are vulnerable to damage or disturbance, which is why I prefer to interplant them among a ground cover. The successful culture of these two members of the genus *Dicentra* requires more skill and care than the others.

Ferns

All of the ferns have long been favorites of mine, and I cannot imagine a woodland or shade garden without the many shapes of their colorful fronds and diverse growth habits. They bring grace and an architectural quality to any planting, whether they are small, like the ebony spleenwort (*Asplenium platyneuron*) and rattlesnake fern (*Botrychium virginianum*), or giants, like goldie's (*Dryopteris goldiana*), ostrich (*Matteuccia struthiopteris*) interrupted fern (*Osmunda claytoniana*) and cinnamon fern (*Osmunda cinnamomea*) shown above, right.

Some ferns require alkaline soils, and others prefer those that are acid, but most—like the flowering plants—do not seem too particular as long as the soil preparation and culture are good.

A small group of ferns, including the purple cliff brake (*Pellaea atropurpurea*) and rock polypody (*Polypodium virginianum*), are happiest when tucked into rocky crevices or narrow vertical cracks. Here they can get their roots down into the cool dampness while their crowns remain dry, as any moisture that does not seep down into the root run will drain off. These ferns do require some gardening expertise to provide them with the right place and help them get established.

In general, the woodland ferns, like the lady (*Athyrium filix-femina*), shown at right, Christmas, marginal shield (*Dryopteris marginalis*) and maidenhair (*Adiantum pedatum*), and those that favor moist or wet soil, like interrupted, royal (*Osmunda regalis*),

marsh (*Thelypteris palustris*) and goldie's ferns, are generally not difficult to grow. They will grow in sun also if the soil is very moist and the summers are not too hot. Establishing them is mostly a question of selecting the correct site and setting the rhizomes (rootstock) firmly into the soil at the right depth. If they are set too shallow, the roots will be exposed and become desiccated; too deep, and the tender new growth may rot or be unable to push up through the soil. For the most part, however, ferns are tough, forgiving plants that respond well to good care.

The next time you are out in the woods or browsing in a friend's garden, take a good close look at the rootstock of the ferns you find and observe closely how they are formed and set in the soil. This is the best way to understand what you will need to do with the ferns that you plant. If you are moving them from a garden or your own woods—or if you are on a plant rescue—take the extra time and effort to dig a big rootball, so most of the roots remain undisturbed. Set this large ball into a generous hole so the soil of the rootball is level with the surrounding ground. If you use this simple transplanting method and keep them well watered, ferns will quickly adjust to their new environment.

As it takes a while for the existing roots to become established and for new roots to grow out into the soil, it is imperative that the soil not be

allowed to dry out. It should not be kept soggy, either—just nice and moist. And, as the fronds are brittle and easily broken when handled, ferns are best transplanted in late fall when they are dormant or almost so, or very early in the year before they have started to grow.

There are even some species that thrive in dry, impoverished soils, including the hay-scented (*Dennstaedtia punctilobula*) and New York (*Thelypteris noveboracensis*) ferns. They will form thick ground covers and in good soils quickly become invasive. In these conditions, they are therefore best used in areas around shrubs and trees or in association with some of the taller perennials such as bugbane and umbrella leaf (*Diphylleia cymosa*), where they can be appreciated for the beauty of the thick colonies they form. The sensitive fern (*Onoclea sensibilis*), which loves wet places, will also spread quickly to form a thick cover. All three will grow in shade or in sun, except in

the hottest of climates. The extremely rare climbing fern (*Lygodium palmatum*) deserves mention because of its attractive growth habit. It is quite challenging to grow and demands just the right site, with an acid, humusy soil that is always moist if not wet. It seems to prosper in shade (and, in northern climates, partial sun) and, once the right place is found, the evergreen foliage will form a dense ground cover. The young stems twine up or over surrounding vegetation.

Hepatica species
Liverleafs

Early in the year, when the air is still cold and crisp, it is the hepaticas that signal the beginning of spring. I eagerly search for their tiny spotlights of color among the foliage of dark evergreens and the brown remains of autumn and winter. They are soon joined by the colorful flowers of spicebush, bloodroot and Virginia bluebells, and by the new croziers of ferns.

There are two native American species of hepatica: the round-lobed (*H. americana*), shown here, and the sharp-lobed (*H. acutiloba*). The buds of both are covered in silky hair which opens to reveal flowers that range in color from rich pink to deepest blue to white. These bright flowers stand out even more clearly because of the dark foliage. The sharp-lobed hepatica has the added appeal of mottled leaves. I have seen this species growing as a thick ground cover in cool, moist, humusy soils in the Smoky Mountains.

An interesting — if brief — show is seen in both species when the contrasting bright apple-green new leaves appear through the old dark evergreen ones.

Hepaticas mix well with many shade-loving plants, but because of their relatively small size, they should not be planted near vigorous ground covers such as the gingers and foamflowers (*Tiarella cordifolia*) or the European sweet woodruff (*Asperula odorata*); any of these could quickly smother this much daintier plant. Hepaticas will do best in a foreground planting where they can

be combined with partridgeberry (*Mitchella repens*), toothwort and starflower (*Trientalis americana*), with the lower-growing ferns used as a background. Or they can be left alone with some unplanted space around them to emphasize their own special beauty and leaf form. For an especially early display, set these little wildlings on a south-facing slope that will warm quickly and stir them into growth even sooner.

In the wild, the round-lobed hepatica is most often found in rather acid soils, while the sharp-lobed species occurs most often in alkaline ones. In the garden, however, I have found they are not fussy about pH, and it is more important that they be given a rich, humusy soil that does not become dried out in summer.

Iris **species**

All the native iris are good plants to include in wildflower gardens, with the different species growing easily in a variety of locations ranging from rich woodlands to open watersides.

What shady garden is complete without the lovely crested iris (*I. cristata*), shown here, tracing a path's winding outline with cheery springtime flowers and arching leaves? Crested iris also looks lovely at the corner of a stone step, along a rocky ledge or tucked in at the edge of a container.

Crested iris is an ideal ground cover: the flowers, on stems 4 to 6 inches high, form clouds of blue that can range from the palest sky blue to a deep, rich hue. There is also a white form that sparkles in the sun as if minuscule diamonds were embedded in the petals. The small rue anemone often self-sows amongst it and looks perfectly at home nestled into the iris foliage or peering out amongst the flowers. The wild bleeding hearts, with their fernlike foliage and deep pink flowers, create a delightful color and foliage combination when grown behind the iris. The delicate vertical lines of rosy twisted-stalk (*Streptopus roseus*), the graceful arching habit of Solomon's seal, and the dark green foliage of oconee bells complete a simple but enchanting display.

I. cristata is a tough and accommodating little plant that needs a good soil and regular division (usually every few years) to keep it vigorous and encourage it to maintain the masses of flowers it is known for. It is one of the most restrained of ground covers, never spreading too much or romping over other plants. Its welcoming flowers make it ideal for the entrance to a shady walk.

Another iris, probably the least known of our natives, is *I. missouriensis*, which produces flowers in the prettiest shade of pale blue. It should be planted in a sunny wet place, where it will be quite long-lived. Sadly, it is often hard to find, which is surprising as it is easy to grow and raise from seed.

Blue flag iris (*I. versicolor*) grows well in low, wet places in full sun near streams and ponds, while *I. verna* enjoys fertile, well-drained soils with plenty of sand or gravel but little organic matter. It prefers light shade or shade in the afternoon to protect it from the searing heat of the summer sun. Of all the irises, this is the most challenging to grow.

Jeffersonia diphylla **Twinleaf**

Providing an elegant accent in a shady place, twinleaf gives many months of interest beginning in early spring with the appearence of stems and expanding foliage in a strong purple brushed with gray. Soon these are joined by the fleeting and beautiful white flower cups, which must be looked for daily so their brief display is not missed.

As spring advances, the gray-green, softly textured leaves mature into one of the finest and most unusual of foliage displays. Standing only 12 to 15 inches high, the plant carries a distinctively crisp, clean outline.

When twinleaf is mixed with the autumn fern and a sweep of Japanese painted fern, an even lovelier picture is created. Add some early-flowering wood phlox (*Phlox divaricata*) and the pastel colors of primroses to create an especially enchanting spot.

The dwarf Japanese species, *J. dubia*, is as beautiful as a plant can be. It is no more than 4 to 6 inches high, with purple foliage identical to the color found in the early foliage of *J. diphylla*. In *J. dubia*, the foliage never loses this purple hue, which is also repeated in the lavender-purple flowers. To see this beguiling plant set against weathered granite is breathtaking, and a picture never to be forgotten.

Both species of twinleaf are easy to grow but hard to find, which is surprising as seedlings abound around the base of the parent plants, and they transplant easily into a rich woodsy soil. Below the surface, twinleaf develops a large, tenacious root system that helps the plant recover and get reestablished quickly after it is divided.

🌹 *Phlox* species

This is strictly a North American genus, with a wealth of wonderful plants suitable for just about all locations and effects in a garden. From ground covers in a sunny rock garden to stately varieties for a sunny border to denizens of a shady woodland, all the phloxes are beautiful and bring much to the wildflower garden.

In the spring shade, creeping phlox (*P. stolonifera*) creates rivers of color in white, pinks, lavenders and blues; its prostrate leafy stems run over the ground and are covered by the 6- to 8-inch-high flowering stems. In contrast, the flowers of the clump-forming wood phlox (*P. divaricata*) produce spotlights of soft blue. Standing about 10 inches high, it has a delicacy seldom seen in any plant that has so many flowers and creates such a presence in a garden.

For a display with less impact—but no less beauty—there is downy phlox (*P. pilosa*), or its close relative, smooth phlox (*P. glaberrima*), shown here. The primary difference is in the habitat: downy phlox likes dry woods, while smooth phlox is best set in high shade in a woodsy soil that is kept well watered. Both flower late in the spring, with full heads of pink flowers atop 12- to 15-inch stems clothed in dark foliage.

In a sunny spot (and especially a rock garden with open, well-drained soil) the mossy phloxes billow around rocks and tumble over ledges in a rainbow of colors—blues, pinks, lavenders and white. Many of the flowers have distinct eye markings. *P. subulata* is the best known and most easily found of these, but others such as *P. amoena* and *P. bifida* are well worth looking for. All the mossy phloxes have a multitude of named varieties, and it becomes a question of selecting the species or varieties that do best in your climate and the colors that you prefer.

Among the other sun-lovers are the tall perennial summer phloxes (*P. paniculata*), which we have been growing in our gardens for years. And just think of all the varieties there are to choose from. Although these are native American plants, the many varieties available have been developed or selected in Britain and Europe for many decades. This is an example of a native American plant being valued more by the British and Europeans than by American gardeners.

All phloxes, including the taller species, are best cut back after they have flowered. This keeps them more vigorous, and—in the case of the taller, sun-loving varieties and species—will often induce them to rebloom. A good shearing back will keep the mossy phloxes bushier and prevent the typical browning of the central growth, which, if neglected, becomes sparse and unattractive.

Many of the large-leaved phloxes tend to suffer from mildew. Apart from adherence to good cultural practices—in particular, providing good air circulation and surface drainage—an occasional dousing with a fungicide will control this. New varieties with mildew resistance are being developed, but in the meantime, a few of the old favorites—paniculata types 'Reine du Jour', 'Bright Eyes' and 'Fairest One'—seem quite mildew-resistant. These varieties exhibited no problems with mildew when I grew them in the hot, humid climate of South Carolina.

A personal favorite is *P.* 'Miss Lingard', for its early displays of white flowers, medium size and general durability. Unfortunately, it does not show the same resistance to mildew in the South as it does in northern gardens.

🌹 *Polemonium reptans* Jacob's Ladder

What a sweep of rich, intense blue a planting of Jacob's ladder gives to the spring garden! At 8 to 10 inches in height, it is ideal for a foreground position in a shady place and the perfect companion for the early woodland primroses, especially the pale yellow English primrose (*Primula vulgaris*), which flower at the same time. Jacob's ladder makes an especially distinctive show when its flowers are displayed and contrasted with the white-flowered form of creeping phlox (*Phlox*

stolonifera 'Alba') and the showy trillium (*Trillium grandiflorum*).

This is an easy, undemanding plant, but it dislikes drought intensely, and should be watched during dry spells, especially in spring. By early summer it is beginning to go dormant, so companion plants will be needed to fill in the space it leaves. Choices for this would include maidenhair fern, which is only just beginning to show when Jacob's ladder is in full flower; the astilbes, which also have a later display; and the fall-flowering species of bugbane and toad lilies.

Look for the several relatives of Jacob's ladder, one of which, *P. carneum* (from the Pacific Northwest), is a charming plant that requires a humusy but well-drained soil. It makes a rainbow of color, from the salmon pink buds to the rich pink of the mature flowers that fade into purple with age.

The European species *P. caeruleum* is a taller plant, growing up to 24 inches in height. It is well suited for a border location, as it will tolerate sun, but for best results give it summer shade and deep watering in dry weather.

Polygonatum biflorum
Solomon's Seal

The tall (20 to 24 inches), gracefully arching stems of the Solomon's

seal bring a hard-to-find vertical dimension to the shady wildflower garden. A clump or two near the back of a planting or in front of a wall or fence, or a single clump beside a bench or statue, gives a dignity to the setting not provided by other plants. Solomon's seal also appears to accentuate and, at the same time, soften the fullness and patchwork appearance of the mixed plantings that happily grow beneath and around it.

Any of the ground covers are well suited as companions for Solomon's seal, providing an attractive stage for it. A particularly pleasing combination is the native vancouveria, Asian epimediums and variegated wild oats. Ferns and the baneberry are also good companions to mix with Solomon's seal, as are the native azaleas.

The giant Solomon's seal (*P. canaliculatum*), shown here, which can reach 5 feet in height, is a striking plant. It is perfect for the back of a planting, where it ties together the lower herbaceous plants with the shrubs and trees. Its dark foliage makes a sharp contrast, in particular, with the pale greens of the taller ferns.

Both Solomon's seal and giant Solomon's seal provide interest in the garden all through the growing season. In spring, creamy white bells, overlaid and scalloped in green, hang beneath

the strong arching stems. By late summer, the flowers are transformed into large black berries reminiscent of edi-

ble blueberries. Then in fall, the foliage becomes a straw yellow.

There is also the exquisite variegated Japanese Solomon's seal (*Polygonatum odoratum* 'Variegatum') with its pale green foliage brushed in cream along the margins, and pendulous flowers hung on pink stems. The charming dwarf Solomon's seal (*P. humile*)—only 4 inches high—is also well worth looking for. It has dark, heavily veined foliage and spreads to form a pretty little ground cover. The English species (*P. multiflorum*), rarely seen in this country, is quite distinctive with its wavy foliage.

Smilacina racemosa
False Solomon's Seal

One of my favorite places to walk takes me past a shady bank (60 feet or more in length) that is solid with false Solomon's seal, with occasional clumps of cinnamon fern mixed in. This walk is enjoyable all through the growing season because this plant is always interesting.

In spring, the tiny ivory flowers, held at the tips of bright pink stems, form large terminal clusters. These gradually develop into berries that are first mottled in translucent burgundy and green. Then by late summer, these berries have developed into full clusters of bright red. In fall, the foliage turns a soft yellow which creates highlights amongst the remaining greens and other colors of the season.

An easy plant to grow, attaining a height of 24 to 30 inches, false Solomon's seal is suitable for use as a background in large colonies or as small clumps in a foreground position, mixed with many other favorite wildflowers. These might include Jack-in-the-pulpit, golden seal and bloodroot. Over time, the large fleshy underground roots of false Solomon's seal form dense colonies, making them especially suitable for erosion control on banks.

While this woodlander does not like drought (few plants do), it is tolerant of it, although it may go dormant early to overcome this unfavorable condition.

✿ *Stylophorum diphyllum* Wood Poppy

In spring, wood poppy's many large flowers (up to 4 inches across) provide a bright, cheerful display of sunny yellow that brings the warmth of summer to a shady garden. It is a color infrequently seen at this time of year and is one of many good reasons

to have wood poppy as part of a spring display.

It blends well with all the other plants of this season, and a favorite group of mine shows it in a shady spot with blue wood phlox, pink bleeding heart and waldsteinia. The latter also has yellow flowers similar to the wood poppy—but in miniature—and the waldsteinia's dark green foliage provides a striking contrast to the flowers of the other plants.

Wood poppy grows to about 12 inches high with attractive glaucous-green foliage that is heavily scalloped, making a pretty display even after the flowers have passed. Its ornamental green seed capsules look like bristly miniature mayapple fruits.

It readily self-sows throughout the

shady garden but never becomes so prolific as to be a problem. It will, however, build up its number in a new planting with swiftness and ease, a distinct advantage for the gardener. Whether it is used in small groups or as a specimen, this little-seen wildflower is a delight and deserves to be used more.

Sometimes called celandine poppy, these beautiful native wildflowers should not be confused with the pernicious weed of Europe, the lesser celandine (*Ranunculus ficaria*).

✿ *Tiarella cordifolia* Foamflower

Foamflower is, without doubt, one of the easiest and most rewarding of woodland plants to grow. In spring, swaths of the bright green foliage will define a meandering path or the gentle curves of a shady border, or sweep around stone steps and the trunks of trees. It forms dense mats that make a handsome ground cover through which a multitude of other wildflowers can grow, including the European wood anemone (*Anemone nemorosa*), trout lily (*Erythronium americanum*) and wild columbine.

The foliage is handsome by itself, but it is absolutely beautiful when covered with the fluffy spires of flowers, which make a sea of foamy white 8 inches or so above the ground. *T. cordifolia* spreads by stolons, much as a strawberry does, and small rosettes of leaves form intermittently along the stems, beneath which develop a vigorous cluster of roots. This creates small plantlets that are easy to dig up and transplant to another location.

As delightful as this species is, its close relative, Wherry's foamflower (*T. wherryi*), shown here, surpasses it for sheer loveliness. The distinctive, sharply pointed foliage, overlaid in burgundy, forms a solid clump from which rise many stems 8 to 10 inches high. It does not have the stoloniferous growth habit of *T. cordifolia*. The stems are topped with elegant spears bearing pink buds. The creamy white flowers maintain a note of pink even when fully mature. Because the blossoms at the bottom of the cluster open first, the distinctive bright pink

buds above them only add to the charm of this plant.

Wherry's foamflower is a specimen plant to set in front of dark foliage—perhaps that of Christmas fern, fetterbush or cliff-green (*Paxistima canbyi*)—or with a background of false Solomon's seal, blue cohosh and marginal shield fern. A flat ground cover of dewdrop (*Dalibarda repens*) in front of Wherry's foamflower looks particularly attractive.

The foliage is evergreen in both species. In early spring it usually looks rather bedraggled for a week or two, but the bright new leaves are quick to cover up the old, and the plant once again regains its perfect appearance.

There are other foamflowers to seek out, such as the species *T. × collina*, and a fine new selection that appears to be a hybrid of *T. wherryi* and is currently called 'Oakleaf Form'. It is aptly named, with distinctive oaklike foliage and pink-hued flowers similar to Wherry's foamflower.

✿ *Uvularia sessilifolia* Wild Oats

Wild oats makes a loose, 12-inch-high carpet of soft green and, before the leaves are fully expanded in spring, it produces long, dainty, tubular flowers in pale yellow. This is a useful plant to grow on a bank where the resilient twining roots will help hold the soil.

It is prettiest with other wildflowers growing through it. For spring color, use the wake robin (*Trillium erectum*), Ozark phlox (*P. pilosa* ssp. *ozarkana*) or rosy twisted-stalk; for fall interest, plant the Asian toad lilies among wild oats. It also makes a good foreground planting for shrubs, especially those with somber, dark green foliage, as its delicacy

lightens them and softens their heaviness. For a planting in front of wild oats, the foliage of the Labrador violet (*Viola labradorica*), with its deep purple overlay, makes an attractive contrast.

For a truly striking display, plant the variegated form of wild oats (*U. sessilifolia* 'Variegata'); its prominent foliage brings pale, creamy ribbons of light to a shady location, and will always draw attention.

A close cousin of wild oats, merrybells (*U. grandiflora*), forms sturdy clumps 15 to 18 inches high. The foliage and flowers are similar to those of wild oats, but both are larger, and the pendulous flowers of merrybells bear deep yellow petals that have an unusual and attractive twist to them. This is an ideal specimen plant that works well either as a focal point or mixed with low-growing ferns and other wildflowers that bloom at the same time, such as trout lilies, wild bleeding heart, crested iris and a background of yellowroot. Merrybells looks especially striking when grown with the variegated wild oats and the deep maroon flowers of wake robin.

Vancouveria hexandra Vancouveria (Inside-out Flower)

Vancouveria closely resembles the

well-known Asian epimediums, but its pale green leaves are more ornate. To my mind, this easily offsets the fact that its flowers are smaller and less prolific than those of the epimediums.

A woodland vista with a sea of vancouveria as a ground cover is a refreshing sight. On sunny days in a garden setting, the leaves of vancouveria shimmer and gleam among companion plants such as crested iris, hepatica and wood poppy. The taller wildflowers, like baneberry and false Solomon's seal, and ferns with strong, heavily dissected foliage, such as Christmas and autumn fern (*Dryopteris erythrosora*), make ideal backdrops for vancouveria. Another attractive planting would include a foreground of waldsteinia, with its dark foliage providing contrast, and a sprinkling of spring bulbs in bright yellow adding a cheery beginning to the gardening year.

Given good woodsy soils and shade, vancouveria proves to be an easy, long-lived wildflower with a tenacious root system, much like that of twinleaf and the epimediums.

Viola species Violets

There are many violets to grow in the wildflower garden, but some of them, although pretty, are a frightful nuisance, as they self-sow far too readily and create endless hours of weeding. I have discussed three here that I feel are exceptionally fine garden plants — Canada violet (*V. canadensis*), Labrador violet (*V. labradorica*), and bird's-foot violet (*V. pedata*), shown here — although I realize there are others that are suitable for a shade garden, particularly if you have a spacious area.

The Canada violet has stems 6 to 8 inches tall that in spring carry many sparkling white flowers with a hint

of yellow at their throats. It is a pretty plant and, in my experience, quite well behaved, spreading gradually to form a drift.

For an unusual and striking display, use the Labrador violet, whose foliage forms a low carpet of dark green heavily overlaid in purple; it makes a stunning contrast with the lavender flowers that cover the plant in spring. The Labrador violet threads its way beautifully around trillium, merrybells, the taller baneberry and umbrella leaf. If grown with the variegated wild oats and variegated Japanese Solomon's seal, it will give a shady corner a dramatic look all through the growing season.

The lovely bird's-foot violet is quite different. Although it can be found in light shade (especially in hot summer climates), it prefers full sun and an acid, sandy soil. I first saw this plant growing in the wild along an old railroad track in the sandy soils of New Jersey. This gave me a good sense of what I would need to provide for it in my garden. In May, it covers itself with large, lavender flowers; in the striking bicolored form (*Viola pedata* var. *bicolor*), the top two petals are a dark velvety purple. There is a lovely and very rare white-flowered form (*Viola pedata alba*) that wildflower enthusiasts covet and pass on to their friends, but I have never seen it listed for sale in a nursery catalog.

Although the main flower display is in spring, bird's-foot violet will continue to produce some flowers on and off into fall, and the attractive foliage will expand to make its own display throughout the growing season.

🌹 *Waldsteinia fragarioides* Waldsteinia (Barren Strawberry)

Here is a dense and handsome ground cover that is far too infrequently used. In spring, it is covered with golden yellow flowers that look like miniature single roses. But it is the glossy dark foliage of waldsteinia that makes it the perfect companion for all the colorful, shade-loving plants of spring. When it is settled around trillium, with lady fern and wild bleeding heart, it accentuates the form and colors of these companions.

A bed of waldsteinia beneath blue cohosh, variegated Japanese Solomon's seal, or rodgersia provides not only a pleasing contrast but also a solid visual anchor for the airy effects of these tall plants.

Waldsteinia also provides a fine carpet beneath pastel azaleas and the lovely yellow-flowered Asian winterhazel (*Corylopsis pauciflora*), both of whose flowers become much more prominent above this dark ground cover. I also interplant waldsteinia

with early miniature bulbs, like narcissus 'April Tears' or squills (*Scilla sibirica*), and with spring ephemerals that include trout lily or squirrel corn for a striking early display. And if you like a strong splash of color, plant a few small clumps of the tulip 'Red Riding Hood' among it.

This is a plant that tolerates a wide range of growing conditions, is easy to grow, resilient and long-lived. To keep the growth dense and the foliage looking its best, it should be given a rich humusy soil in a shady spot.

Bulbs and Herbaceous Plants (Sun)

🌹 *Amsonia tabernaemontana* Blue Star

Blue star's crisp foliage and full clusters of sky blue flowers make this an easy choice for early color in a sunny spot. I don't know of another plant with such clear lines and simple, natural beauty.

It is one of the very first flowers to bloom in a meadow or a sunny border, where the blue blends perfectly with the rich pinks of early azaleas. Growing to approximately 3 feet in height, *A. tabernaemontana* is the tallest and the one most familiar to gardeners. After flowering, the foliage remains attractive and unblemished all through the summer and into the fall, when it turns a soft yellow that accents the lavender and purples of the fall asters and ironweed (*Vernonia noveboracensis*), and contrasts perfectly with the scarlet foliage of the staghorn sumac (*Rhus typhina*).

There are several other species, all of which are good garden plants. The dwarf form grows to only 15–18 inches and is usually listed as variety *montana* or sometimes as a separate species. This is my favorite of the blue stars, both for its low, compact growth and because it is a true miniature of the blue star that I have loved for many years. Two other less well known species, *A. hubrectii* and *A. salicifolia*, are both well worth looking for.

Blue star is ideal for the sunny border or meadow. It is also quite tolerant of moist soils, which is a distinct advantage in some gardens, as it looks perfect beside a pool or stream. I have yet to find any problem with this easily grown charmer that is high on my list of best garden plants.

🌹 *Aquilegia canadensis* Wild Columbine

Wild columbine, probably one of the best known and loved of our native wildflowers, gives a beautiful display to a sunny area barely awake in early spring with its brightly colored red and yellow flowers that nod on gentle spring breezes. It can be found in a variety of habitats. It might be scattered through a sunny glade in company with merrybells, wood phlox, and wild cranesbill, but

is equally at home in a sunny border with golden ragwort (*Senecio aureus*), bowman's root and dwarf coreopsis (*Coreopsis auriculata* 'Nana'). Wild columbine might also be found growing along the edge of a meadow path, where the competition from other plants is not so great.

Its airy grace and delicate appearance bring a softness to heavily textured ferns and shrubs, and the flowers are a beacon for hummingbirds. Like all columbines, it is an easy plant to grow, preferring an open, well-drained soil and—in hot climates—some shelter from the afternoon sun.

Wild columbine is also a good choice for a large rock garden. In the wild it can often be found growing out of tight crevices on rocky ledges where the seeds, which germinate easily, have fallen. In this situation, it will be much smaller, not attaining its usual 15 to 18 inches in height.

Another excellent native columbine is the blue-and-white Rocky Mountain columbine (*A. caerulea*), which also reaches 15 to 18 inches in height. This is also an undemanding plant, but it does need high shade and a cool, moist spot with good drainage.

The enchanting Japanese columbine (*A. flabellata* 'Nana') has glaucous-green leathery leaves that always look in perfect condition and provide just the right setting for its large blue-and-white flowers. (There is a pure white form (*A. flabellata* 'Nana Alba'), but the typical blue-and-white flower colors are much more showy.) Because of its compact growth habit and 8- to 10-inch height, this is an ideal plant for a rock garden.

🌸 *Aster* species

The best known of the asters are the New England (*A. novae-angliae*), shown here, and New York (*A. novi-belgii*) asters, which are so much a part of the fall wildflower display. These have been cultivated and superior color forms selected and named by the English, who greatly value them in their herbaceous borders.

No fall garden is complete without the imposing forms of the asters, which splash pink, lavender, purple, blue and white across the fall landscape. The taller ones can be kept at more reasonable heights by shearing them back in early summer. There are also a number of named varieties of both the New England and New York asters that are naturally low-growing—12 to 15 inches at most—and therefore suitable for the smaller garden or a foreground planting.

A number of excellent but lesser known and generally overlooked native asters are especially suitable

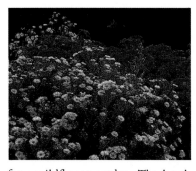

for a wildflower garden. The heath aster (*A. ericoides*), 18 to 20 inches tall, features a mound of small star-like flowers that cover the plant in late summer through fall. The heath aster is not at all fussy about soil and will do well in dry or lightly shaded places where some of the other kinds will not prosper.

Then there is the calico aster (*A. lateriflorus* 'Horizontalis'), whose dark, mahogany-red foliage is almost invisible beneath the myriad small white flowers that cover the plant in fall, each of which is enhanced by the central mass of tiny red stamens. This midsized aster, at 24 to 30 inches high, is very tolerant of a wide range of soils, but is at its best when grown in an average garden soil in full sun or light shade.

The smooth aster (*A. laevis*) adds a wonderful splash of light blue late in the growing season. Put it in a sunny, moist spot, where it will grow to a height of 18 to 24 inches. Look for the other asters to mix into your wildflower garden; they are relatively unknown and wonderful, garden-worthy plants.

A. × frikartii (of hybrid origin, and not a native) is a superb plant, growing to 24 to 30 inches in height, with glaucous gray-green foliage. Its large lavender flowers bloom for an unusually long time, beginning in summer and continuing through autumn. This is considered one of the most ornamental of asters, and is a truly pretty plant.

Most asters benefit from being divided every few years to keep them vigorous and floriferous. They do best in a deeply worked soil that is not too rich, with the exception of *A. × frikartii*, an excellent performer that prefers a rich soil.

🌸 *Baptisia australis* Wild Indigo

This is a bold, long-lived and tough plant with strong spires of intense blue flowers similar to those of lupine. Wild indigo is particularly eye-catching in a spring meadow, but it can also be effective as an early accent in a sunny border, where its 3- to 4-foot height is impressive but not overpowering. Later in the growing year, when the majority of sun-loving plants flower, wild indigo's lovely gray-green foliage provides a good foil for the bright colors associated with summer. The foliage remains as umblemished at the end of the year as it is in early spring, which is another reason to grow this plant.

Wild indigo's deep taproot resents disturbance, so plant it in a permanent location when it is young and leave it undisturbed to mature. In a lean soil and full sun, it will be a strong, upright grower that mixes well with other early-flowering sunlovers like wild senna (*Cassia hebecarpa*), leopard's-bane (*Doronicum caucasicum*) and bowman's root, to name a few.

Look also for the white-flowered species *B. pendula*, which grows to a height of about 3 feet. It is a stunning plant, with clear white flowers clasped by charcoal calyxes carried on stems of the same color. *B. pendula* makes a dramatic accent, especially when combined with the pink flowers of the fleabanes (*Erigeron* species),

the white flowers and dark green leaves of the hairy beard-tongues (*Penstemon hirsutus*) and the purple foliage of *Heuchera micrantha* 'Palace Purple'. I planted *B. pendula* in a border set against a brick wall, up which I grew *Clematis* 'Nellie Moser'. This made a wonderful background for the baptisia's white, gray and charcoal colors.

All the baptisias tolerate—and in fact, prefer—poor soils and a certain amount of benign neglect, if it's only occasional! They are therefore well suited to the informality of a meadow or a border that may be far away from a convenient water source and will not always receive enough supplementary water in dry weather.

🌿 *Cassia hebecarpa*
Wild Senna

Wild senna is a tall, imposing plant to spot through a meadow or to use as a bold accent. In summer, its bright yellow flowers mix well with purple coneflower (*Echinacea purpurea*), pink beebalm (*Monarda didy-*

ma 'Croftway Pink') and blazing star (*Liatris spicata*) in a sunny corner. It is also a good companion for tall ornamental grasses.

In the south I grew it with the dwarf pampas grass (*Cortaderia selloana* 'Pumila'), *Artemisia* 'Powis Castle' and the lavender-pink flowers

of wild bergamot (*Monardia fistulosa*) with a foreground sweep of *Aster* X *frikartii*. Another good companion is the queen-of-the-prairie (*Filipendula rubra*), whose fullness, dark foliage and feathery pink flowers provide a nice contrast to the yellow flowers of wild senna all through the growing season.

In a moist area, I like to grow it with the equally imposing native hibiscus—either the soft pink of the rose mallow (*Hibiscus palustris*) or the rich, fiery red of *Hibiscus coccineus*.

Wild senna provides a great textural accent in a large formal or informal garden and blends well with many plants that offer a less impressive countenance. The soil needs to be kept on the lean side for the growth to be strong, compact and in character.

🌿 *Chelone lyonii*
Pink Turtle-head

To me, a streamside or moist summer meadow is incomplete without a planting or two of this attractive, long-blooming and colorful plant. The strong stems are clothed in rich, dark foliage, creating the perfect foil for the plentiful, intense, pink summer flowers.

I have a favorite planting of turtle-heads in a damp meadow with a nearby stream and pond. In spring, the meadow is a carpet of pink and white from ragged robin (*Lychnis floscuculi*), with a sweep of blue from the blue flag iris (*Iris versicolor*) that grows at the pond's edge. Later in summer and into the fall the pink turtle-heads provide the dominant color among the full clusters of Joe-pye-weed (*Eupatorium purpureum*), goldenrod (*Solidago* species) and tall three-lobed coneflower (*Rudbeckia triloba*). Each spring I look forward to the unfolding of this cheerful display, and I miss it in fall after the first hard frost has browned all the foliage—even though on many early mornings everything is beautifully coated in hoarfrost.

The white-flowered species (*C. glabra*) of turtle-head is not as showy as the pink, but it is just as long-lived and easy to grow, and is as full of flow-

ers from summer to the end of fall. I first saw it in summer, growing in shallow water at the edge of a sunny brook with swamp milkweed (*Asclepias incarnata*), royal fern (*Osmunda regalis*) and cardinal flower. It was a pretty display in a pretty setting, simple but effective, and a welcome change from the exuberance so often associated with summer perennials.

Both species do well in a traditional summer border, but they must be

given a soil rich in organic matter and deeply watered during dry spells.

C. obliqua is a southern species of turtle-head, less frequently grown. It is even more ornamental than the other species, with striking deep pink flowers that last a very long time. This species seems better adapted to growing in a sunny border away from the constant moisture of a streamside or water garden.

🌿 *Chrysogonum virginianum*
Golden Star

What a marvelous, undemanding and versatile plant this is. It can be used to edge a path in light shade, swirl around a rock in sun, or form a dense ground cover beneath shrubs. It is especially useful on banks where the stoloniferous roots help to hold the soil. The dark green foliage and golden-yellow flowers are perfect together and create as cheerful a picture as can be found. Golden star is an ideal companion for interplanting with wild columbine and merrybells in light shade, or fleabane, Carolina phlox (*Phlox carolina*) and wild cranesbill in sun.

The primary flowering time is spring, but golden star has the

delightful habit of reblooming on and off even into fall.

There are several selections available, ranging in height from a completely prostrate form to one 8 inches tall. Each has its own charm, and selecting which one to grow is a matter of personal preference.

Few wildflowers are so easy to grow as golden star. It is undemanding but will do best and be most floriferous in good garden soil with some additional organic matter. It is also a good plant to practice your dividing skills on, as it is very forgiving and easily reestablishes itself.

✿ *Coreopsis auriculata* 'Nana' Dwarf Coreopsis

There are several native coreopsis, and all are easily grown garden plants for sun or light shade, which is preferable in areas with hot, dry summers.

The dwarf coreopsis is, to my mind, the best and most versatile member of this group. Its dark foliage forms low, 4-inch-high mounds that provide a fine base for its multitude of large, golden-orange flowers, shown here, resting atop the strong, supple stems, 10 to 12 inches high. The flowers are so numerous that there are ample to cut—not something often said of wildflowers.

The flowering period for dwarf coreopsis is a long one, extending from spring into summer with some reblooming often occurring in the fall. While it is best suited to a sunny spot, it will flower well in light or part shade, even though the growth habit is not as compact. As a ground cover it is a delight: edging and accentuating the lines of a pathway or border, or twining around rocks or statuary. Set as a foreground plant in a sunny border mixed with columbine or wild pink (*Silene caroliniana*), it looks especially lovely. It also makes a good display in light shade with cliff-green and the tall Asian bleeding heart.

I once saw a planting of dwarf coreopsis so pretty that it always comes to mind when I see this plant. It was growing in a small garden edged with a low boxwood border that was no more than 8 to 10 inches high. A mass of multicolored pansies swirled behind it in a thick cover, creating a marvelous, colorful herald to spring.

Another particularly good coreopsis for the sunny wildflower garden is the threadleaf coreopsis (*C. verticillata*), which usually grow 24 to 36 inches high. An especially outstanding variety is 'Moonbeam'. This plant is just 15 inches or so tall, with soft yellow flowers that bloom for weeks and form a dainty sea of color, interspersed with the narrow needle-like foliage. The recently introduced *C. rosea* is also 12 to 15 inches high, and literally covers itself with small pink flowers. It has the distinction of being the only coreopsis tolerant of moist soils.

The taller varieties are ideal for the meadow garden, where they provide broad splashes of color. They grow rapidly in the rich soil in borders, and should be watched so they do not take up too much space.

✿ *Echinacea purpurea* Purple Coneflower

This stately summer perennial, native to the prairies, is as durable a plant as I know. It produces large heads of rosy purple flowers and goes on blooming—seemingly without end—from summer through fall. This already spectacular display can be greatly enhanced by removing the old flowers, which will encourage the plant to produce flowers even more prolifically.

A meadow full of the yellows of sneezeweed (*Helenium autumnale*), goldenrod and three-lobed coneflower is greatly enhanced by clumps of purple coneflower scattered through it, especially as the flowers attract a multitude of insects, particularly butterflies. In a sunny border, I grow it with pink phloxes, the bright purple of false dragonhead (*Physostegia virginiana*), the gray foliage of the fall-flowering boltonia, the flowering spurge (*Euphorbia corollata*) and—to provide a backdrop—a clump or two of the ornamental grasses. A pretty display can be created in autumn with the purple coneflower blooming beside the buttery yellow fall foliage of blue star.

In the wild, coneflower is usually found in moist areas, but in a well-cared-for garden it seems to do well in any location, and for me it has actually proven to be quite drought-tolerant.

Keep an eye out for a new introduction called 'Crimson Star'. Its flowers are somewhat smaller than those of the familiar purple cone-flower or the variety 'Bright Star', but are produced even more prolifically. They seem totally unaffected by the searing heat of a southern summer that could, in very dry years, scorch the flowers of the other kinds.

Eupatorium purpureum
Joe-Pye-Weed

Joe-pye-weed is the best known and most frequently seen species in this genus of diverse, sun-loving wildflowers. The dusky, old-rose-colored flowers form a cloud atop the strong 5- to 6-foot-high stems. They

stand like sentinels above the tall lushness of a meadow or in the back of a sunny border. The large flower heads soften the strong vertical accent of meadow grasses, and they also provide a lovely display when grown in conjunction with the colorful rose mallow, billowy queen-of-the-prairie and tall Indian-cups (*Silphium perfoliatum*).

In the wild, Joe-pye-weed is generally found in moist areas, but it will thrive in a typical sunny border garden if it is given good soil and is deeply watered during dry spells.

The 3- to 4-foot-high boneset (*E. perfoliatum*) is another robust plant for a meadow; it is similar in looks to the Joe-pye-weed but with white flowers and distinctive foliage.

The lower-growing species called hardy ageratum (*E. coelestinum*) is a long-lived perennial that grows to a height of 12 to 15 inches. It has lovely clear-lavender flowers held in tight clusters, and is well suited to be grown in large colonies in rich, moisture-retentive soils.

Filipendula rubra
Queen-of-the-Prairie

A damp summer meadow can be a sea of feathery, bright-pink plumes when this lovely plant is in bloom. It is tall, 5 feet or more in height under optimum conditions, but has a delightful tendency to recline gently on surrounding vegetation, so it often appears to be much lower growing (perhaps 3 feet high). It is very effective when grown among ornamental grasses. I have grown it both in a wet meadow along with great blue lobelia (*Lobelia siphilitica*), boneset, three-lobed coneflower and sweet pepperbush, and in a sunny border where it makes a striking accent and good background for other plants such as blazing star, wild senna and beebalm.

Queen-of-the-prairie grows best in a lean soil; in rich soil, it will in a relatively short time form sizable clumps that may be too large for a typical border. Even so, for me it is too beautiful to be excluded for any reason, so I sometimes plant it in a bottomless container. (See page 108.)

It is a good idea to cut off the flower heads of this prairie plant after it has bloomed, before they become bowed over from the weight of ripening seed. Then the foliage can be better seen and admired.

Another species well worth including in a sunny wildflower garden is the European queen-of-the-meadow (*F. ulmaria*), especially the double form (*F. ulmaria* 'Flore Plena'). This is a lower-growing plant with strong stems 20 to 24 inches tall and similar, but smaller, feathery white plumes. It looks marvelous behind a planting of culinary sage (*Salvia officinalis*), whose blue flowers and gray-green foliage are a pleasing contrast. There is also a form with rich yellow variegated leaves (*F. ulmaria* 'Aurea-variegata') that grows in a low mound of foliage, making it an attractive foreground plant, useful for edging or as a colorful highlight.

The engaging dwarf Siberian meadowsweet (*F. palmata* 'Nana') grows to a height of approximately 12 inches. It is a plant of greatly refined charm that, in summer, is covered with misty clouds of pink flowers, making it a must for a very special location in a sunny border. In the South, I grew it in light shade and a humusy soil, where it did very well with extra summer water. In temperate climates, such as those of England and the Pacific Northwest, it can be grown in full sun. It is also tolerant of quite wet soils. Obviously, this is a plant that adapts well to a wide range of growing conditions, and it lends itself well to the diverse climates in North America.

Geranium maculatum
Wild Cranesbill

There are a number of excellent hardy geraniums in this greatly overlooked and underused genus that are suitable for the informality of the wildflower garden, and gardeners are missing an opportunity if they do not include them in their gardens to create attractive, long-lasting displays.

Our wild cranesbill is one of the prettiest and most appealing of native wildflowers, with its light pink flower cups that sway gracefully in the gentlest of breezes above its 10- to 12-inch-high foliage. It will do well in a sunny or lightly shaded spot. In dappled shade, it makes a beautiful companion for waldsteinia and wood phlox, while in sun it creates a cheerful early display with bowman's root, nodding onion and blue star.

Wild cranesbill is an excellent choice for use in the transition zone along a woods margin or at the edge of a meadow path. In a sunny border, it can easily be grown in amongst

ornamental sedges and smaller grasses or wild columbine and the European globe flower (*Trollius europaeus*). Use wild cranesbill to form airy colonies for a favorite spot, perhaps near a special bench in a quiet retreat.

There is a beautiful white-flowered form that I like very much (*G. maculatum* forma *albiflorum*). It is just as easy to grow as the pink species but harder to find. Another excellent member of the genus is the non-native *G. macrorrhizum*, which prefers shade and spreads to form dense colonies. The flowers are purple with a touch of pink; in the form 'Spessart' they are a delicate pale pink. The intensely fragrant foliage turns to a brilliant scarlet in fall.

Geranium × *cantabrigiense* 'Biokovo', a hybrid between the European *G. macrorrhizum* and *G. dalmaticum*, is an outstanding plant, incorporating the best features of both parents. The leaves, which form a compact mound of glossy dark green, resemble those of *G. dalmaticum*. These turn a rich red touched with purple with the approach of cold weather. In warmer climates, it remains evergreen through the winter months. In sum-

mer, this mound is covered with white flowers flushed with soft pink. The abundance of flowers and the great hardiness of this plant come from the other parent, *G. macrorrhizum*.

These are undemanding plants with a wide tolerance for different soils and garden situations. Their ease of culture and attractiveness make them very desirable choices for a wildflower garden.

Geum triflorum Prairie Smoke

The native prairie smoke is a very different plant from the bushy perennial geums seen in summer borders and rock gardens. A low ground cover, it is a delightful plant for a sunny spot, if the soil is well drained

and it is not overwhelmed by boisterous neighbors.

This plant comes from our western mountains, where I have seen it form extensive carpets on the windswept slopes. It grows most often in sparse, rocky soil, but once in a while it will be found in damp meadows mixed with the dwarf mountain delphiniums and potentillas.

Prairie smoke produces a vast number of summer flowers, held on stems 4 to 6 inches high. The flowers are a deep rosy pink, pretty but not spectacular. It is prairie smoke's fluffy seed heads that put on the real show, turning the ground into a haze

of dusky rose in their profusion.

In the rock garden—natural or manmade—it is a perfect plant, pleasantly easy to grow and undemanding. There are many other plants of equal charm to grow with prairie smoke. Miniature bulbs are pretty popping up through the foliage, while yellow star grass (*Hypoxis hirsuta*), bird's-foot violet and wild pink are other good choices. You may also want to consider for companions other western plants that are suitable only for a rock garden, including the lewisias (*Lewisia* species) and fameflower (*Talinum calycinum*).

Gillenia trifoliata Bowman's Root

This has long been a special favorite of mine. Bowman's root has one of the most delicate of flowers, with a gracefulness that brings an ethereal quality to the garden. When the plant is in bloom, it appears from a distance to be heavily speckled in pure white, but on closer examination, the individual flowers are seen to be clasped in pink calyxes and carried on pink stems.

It does well in full sun if the soil is enriched and moisture-retentive, but in areas that have harsh summers it will be happier in light shade. In the sun, bowman's root has many companions, from the tall bush pea (*Thermopsis caroliniana*) and wild indigo to the lower-growing evening primrose (*Oenothera fruticosa*), hairy

beard-tongue and wild petunia (*Ruellia humilis*).

In a lightly shaded area, it looks particularly attractive with lowbush blueberry (*Vaccinium angustifolium*), native azaleas—especially the later-flowering species such as the fiery red-flowered Cumberland azalea, (*Rhododendron bakeri*)—stately foxglove (*Digitalis purpurea*) and colorful astilbes. It is also a good choice for a container where the nuances of its attractive floral display can be seen and admired.

The strong stems grow 24 to 36 inches tall and are clothed in foliage that remains unblemished during the entire growing season. This is a trouble-free wildflower and a top choice for a sunny border, informal meadow or lightly shaded woodland garden.

✿ *Helenium autumnale*
Sneezeweed

Any summer or fall display is greatly enhanced by the bright, cheerful yellow flowers of the sneezeweed. Growing 24 to 30 inches tall, it mixes easily with other plants and makes a pretty combination with the pink and the white turtle-heads, Joe-pye-weed, monkeyflower (*Mimulus ringens*) and the intensely dark blue bottle gentian. For me, the simple yellow flowers of the wild species are far prettier and infinitely more pleasing than the gaudy oranges, reds and browns of the cultivated varieties that are currently in vogue.

Although in the wild sneezeweed is found in moist or wet areas, it adapts well to growing in a sunny border with good soil and occasional summer waterings. Sneezeweed, with its prolific flowers and strong, up-right stems, brings a soft quality to the rigid formality so often seen in traditional borders.

✿ *Hibiscus palustris*
Rose Mallow

Here is a wonderfully exuberant herbaceous perennial with an expansive nature. The summer flowers, shown here, are a good 6 inches across and are held on strong stems 4 or more feet tall. The foliage is bold and attractively balances the blossoms, which in this species are a soft pink (or sometimes white) with a red eye.

One plant is all that is needed for a small area, where, because of its size and growth habit, the rose mallow easily takes on the role of a shrub. In a large moist meadow or swampy place, several plants are needed to bring soft highlights of color to contrast with the greens and strong colors of other meadow plants.

There are other, closely related species to look for. The halberd-leaved mallow (*H. militaris*) also has pink flowers with a red eye, on plants that grow to about 6 feet in height. The wild swamp mallow (*H. moscheutos*) is a more southern species (hardy to north of Boston) with 8-inch white flowers and a red eye. A favorite of mine is *H. coccineus*, which is quite different from the others (and not as hardy). It has intense scarlet flowers whose petals taper at their base. These flowers, along with the finely cut leaves, give this species a more delicate appearance than that of its bold cousins.

I love to mix all of these extravagant-looking mallows with the bright yellows of the tall Indian-cup, the royal purple of ironweed and the bountiful pink of queen-of-the-prairie—together, they make a marvelous, bold summer display. The swamp mallow flowers appear especially bright and clear when grown with white flowers, such as those of Canadian burnet (*Sanguisorba canadensis*).

There are also several named varieties to look for. A favorite of mine which I grew in the south is called 'Cotton Candy'. It was the showstopper of my garden. Even young children would pause to admire the mul-

titude of gorgeous mid-pink flowers. These wild mallows, with 6- to 8-inch flowers, are far more attractive and better proportioned than the gigantic, ungainly hybrids currently offered for sale with flat platelike flowers 12 to 15 inches across.

Swamp mallows like moist soil, and are perhaps at their best when mixed with grasses, sedges and other flowering plants in large, informal, moist places where they provide a haven for birds. What better remembrance of summer is there than red-winged blackbirds amongst the exotic-appearing pink flowers? Mallows will, however, also do just fine in the drier soils of a sunny garden, if deeply watered in summer.

✿ *Liatris spicata*
Blazing Star

I remember the deep lavender flowers of blazing star, shown here, from my childhood in England, where I first saw it growing among a multitude of other summer flowers in a perennial border.

I liked it then, but I was even more delighted the first time I saw sizable clumps of it in a New England meadow. There, it was mixed with black-eyed Susans (*Rudbeckia hirta*) and white beard-tongue (*Penstemon digitalis*) in a seemingly random and informal display, where the color combination and setting were nearly perfect, in my view. With its strong vertical lines, tidy growth habit and trouble-free nature, blazing star is a very good choice for a sunny border. It grows 30 to 36 inches tall and can also be set as a specimen beside a walkway.

There are several other species well worth growing. Two of the more easily found are button gay-feathers (*L. squarrosa*), a 3-foot-high species with rounded flowers set loosely along the stems; and prairie blazing star (*L. pycnostachya*), a taller (up to 4 feet) and more slender species. I think one of the best is the dwarf form of *L. spicata* 'Kobold', just 15 to 20 inches high—an ideal size—and perfect for any setting. There are also white-flowered forms to look for.

All blazing stars will succumb to rot in wet soils, especially in winter, so drainage is important—although *L. spicata* and *L. pycnostachya* are more tolerant of moist soils, where they are often found in the wild.

All are easy to grow and are popular as cut flowers that sell for outrageous sums. No one who sees blazing star sitting rigidly in a vase, however, can associate it with the informal and soft appearance it has in a natural prairie or meadow garden.

🌿 *Monarda didyma* Beebalm

The bright scarlet beacons of beebalm are well known to gardeners both here and in Britain, where it is kept within the restraints of a herbaceous border. Although it provides a bright spot of color for the sunny border, beebalm really comes into its own in the freedom of a meadow—woven through the grasses and complementing the other denizens of this habitat, where it sends a signal to every butterfly and hummingbird for miles around.

There are several named cultivars of *M. didyma* well worth trying. 'Croftway Pink' is an old favorite, while 'Beauty of Cobham' has dark red flowers and good resistance to mildew. 'Marshall's Delight' is the newest selection and the one that promises, after many trials, to be mildew-free.

If beebalm is too well tended and given too rich a soil, the growth will tend to be too vigorous for most borders. In such a place, beebalm is best planted in some kind of bottomless container that is plunged into the ground. An old plastic or galvanized bucket with the bottom cut out, or a clay drain pipe (15 to 18 inches in diameter) set on end will work well. This will contain the stoloniferous roots and limit the plant's tendency to spread.

Another wonderful monarda is the delicate wild bergamot (*M. fistulosa*), which I first remember seeing scattered through old pastures. I like the soft lavender color of its flowers and the more open habit of growth; it also has less inclination to spread. *M. fistulosa* seems little, if ever, affected by mildew.

Mildew can be a problem with beebalm, especially in areas with humid summers. To combat this, I cut the stems back hard (down to a height of 4 to 6 inches) right after their flowering, and douse the remaining foliage and soil with a fungicide. (A second treatment may be needed, six to eight weeks after the first.) This has controlled the problem quite satisfactorily for me.

🌿 *Penstemon digitalis* White Beard-Tongue

The beard-tongues come in a variety of colors, sizes and forms that add much to the sunny wildflower garden. Several of the more refined species, such as *P. pinifolius*, have long been grown in Britain, where the best forms have been selected and named.

Americans have tended to ignore the beard-tongues, however, perhaps because those species that do well in

Britain are generally not as easy to grow over here in our more demanding climates. But the white beard-tongue and several close relatives are easily grown, resilient plants that have proved to be well suited to our sunny borders and meadow gardens. And while other people may not consider them as choice as those grown in Britain, they do have a favored status with me because they are tough and long-lived, and so don't have to be replaced every few years.

With a height of 24 to 30 inches, the white beard-tongue can be grown in a variety of places. They are especially useful where the white flowers can add a softness to the more intense colors of the early summer garden. When they are spotted through a meadow, they bring an unusual element of light to it. A recently developed selection of the white beard-tongue called 'Husker Red' is quite striking, with dark burgundy-red, almost deep purple, foliage that is dramatic against the white flowers.

A smaller species is the hairy beard-tongue (*P. hirsutus*) whose 12-inch stems carry a number of white flowers heavily overlaid in dark lavender, making a striking early summer display. It also has a beguiling dwarf form, 'Pygmaeus', a treasure no more than 8 to 10 inches high that is perfect for a rock garden or container garden.

These herbaceous beard-tongues should not be confused with the shrubby species from our western mountains, which are quite demanding and difficult to get established even in a carefully prepared rock garden.

Physostegia virginiana False Dragonhead

This plant's tall, strong stems grow up to 3 feet and are clothed in rich, dark foliage that makes a lovely contrast to its abundant, deep lavender-pink summer flowers.

False dragonhead mixes well with the soft colors of musk mallow, summer phloxes and meadow-rues (*Thalictrum* species). Its dark foliage is particularly striking among the gray leaves and white flowers of boltonia, and I like to add a plant or two of Joe-pye-weed and artemisia to provide the finishing touch for this attractive group.

In a moist location, a clump of variegated Japanese iris (*Iris kaempferi* 'Alba Marginata') set near false dragonhead (perhaps at a waterside) will create a dramatic picture.

My favorite of the false dragonheads is the form 'Vivid', with its intense, lavender-pink flowers. It is only 20 to 24 inches high, and therefore particularly suitable for a small garden or a terrace planting. In such a place, it will make a lovely display with northern sea oats (*Chasmanthium latifolium*), a grass that has very ornamental seed heads and turns a soft straw color in fall.

There is also a good clear white form of false dragonhead (*P. virginiana* 'Alba') that is perfect for either the border or meadow.

False dragonhead is another robust grower that is well suited to a meadow garden. But, like a number of our native flowers, it will spread rapidly if planted in too rich a soil. This can be a problem in a sunny border, where it will need to be restrained (perhaps by growing it in a container), but in a meadow this trait produces lovely effects as false dragonhead can be allowed to form graceful drifts weaving through the other meadow vegetation.

Stokesia laevis Stokes' Aster

A more delightful and amenable plant than Stokes' aster is hard to think of. The large, lavender, disk-shaped flowers, similar to those of the China aster (*Callistephus chinensis*), fill the early summer garden with a cheerful elegance not always found in the more robust growers of summer. (There is a white form available also.) Its glaucous-green foliage makes neat mounds that can be used as an edging and, over time, can become a ground cover.

So many of the familar flowers of summer, especially the yellows, are ideal companions for Stokes' aster. The soft yellow flowers of *Coreopsis* X 'Moonbeam' or the intense yellow blossoms of *Coreopsis* 'Zagreb' are both excellent choices. Or, for a very different color combination, consider combining Stokes' aster with the pale pink flowers of the dwarf baby's breath (*Gypsophila paniculata* 'Compacta Plena') and the white flowers of the phlox 'Miss Lingard'.

This is a long-lived, undemanding plant. Its only requirement is good drainage and protection from winter wetness, which would soon rot the crowns. A good soil mix with some extra-coarse sand added, or a gently sloping bed, will correct this problem.

Thalictrum dioicum Early Meadow-Rue

Although delicate in appearance, the early meadow-rue has resilient stems 12 to 24 inches high that carry the airy clusters of small flowers. These have the appearance of drifting slivers of snow above other woodland wildflowers.

It prefers light shade and blends in well with ferns, baneberries and tall bugbane, with its blue-tinted foliage creating a particularly good foil for these plants. Easy and undemanding, this plant brings to the early spring

garden the same qualities the bowman's root does to a later display.

In moist, sunny places, the tall meadow-rue (*T. polygamum*) is a graceful spectacle, dancing above the ferns and other vegetation of summer. While their cousins from abroad (such as *T. minus* 'Adiantifolium' and *T. delavayi*) are much more showy—and also wonderful for mixing into the wildflower garden—they lack the wildness of these natives. The lavender-flowered meadow-rue, *T. rochebrunianum*, with its eye-catching flowers and 4- to 5-foot purple stems, makes a beautiful, delicate accent for any location.

Seek out all of the thalictrums, as they are all fine garden plants of easy culture and offer not only engaging flowers but wonderfully attractive foliage. They do well whether they are planted in a sunny border or set at the edges of a meadow, where they appreciate the greater movement of air and the relatively uncrowded location.

🌼 *Thermopsis caroliniana*
Bush Pea

The bright yellow flowers of the bush pea are carried on tall, strong spires that grow 4 to 5 feet high and add a cheerful splash of color to the early summer garden. It looks especially attractive growing among the soft pinks and lavenders of fleabane, the white of bowman's root and the blue of wild indigo.

It is also an ideal companion for the billowy goatsbeard in a partially shaded corner, or in a sunny spot, where the goatsbeard will grow well if summers are not too hot or long.

The bold flowers of bush pea resemble those of lupines (*Lupinus polyphyllus*), but it is far easier to grow. It may be too large for the average or small garden, but a single specimen can be used in many gardens to give height and fullness, much as a shrub does. In a meadow garden or large border, bush pea's bold appeal is very pleasing.

The mountain bush pea (*T. montana*) is a rarely seen dwarf species that grows 18 to 24 inches tall. This is also a fine garden plant and is well worth acquiring if it is offered by a nursery or at a plant sale.

Bush pea, like most legumes, resents root disturbances, so it is advisable to set out young seedlings into their permanent homes. Once it is established, it is a long-lived and resilient wildflower.

🌼 *Vernonia noveboracensis*
Ironweed

Nothing quite matches the richness and clarity of ironweed's deep, velvety purple flowers. Held high above all surrounding vegetation, they are bold sentinels standing out against the other colors of a meadow. Strong, sinewy stems easily carry the terminal clusters of flowers. In a spacious meadow, they can be grown with the giant cow parsnip (*Heracleum mantegazzianum*), which resembles a tree in miniature and is a good companion plant because of its size and contrasting foliage. And in the back of a sunny border ironweed serves as a magnificent specimen plant, surrounded with less imposing ones. Its height does preclude its use in all but a large border, island bed, or meadow, but when a clump of ironweed can be used, it creates a marvelous sense of height that no other plant can quite match.

Ironweed offers a nice contrast of color when combined with the tall ornamental grass *Miscanthus sinensis* 'Morning Light', with its graceful silvery foliage. In warmer climates, dwarf pampas grass makes an elegant neighbor, as its flurry of white plumes provides the perfect match for ironweed's purple flowers.

Ironweed is found growing natu-

rally in damp, even wet meadows, so it is a good choice for planting in a swampy area—but it will also do well in a typical meadow or garden setting if given extra moisture in the summer.

12
The Intermediates

Shade

🌸 *Anemonella thalictroides*
Rue Anemone

This is perhaps one of the most captivating and dainty of all the spring wildflowers. Its intricately shaped foliage forms delicate whorls beneath an airy cluster of purest white flowers—and the plant is all of 6 inches high.

Rue anemone is delightful sprinkled in small groups along a path, or perhaps nestled against an old, moss-covered tree stump, where it can be shown off and not lost amongst the luxuriance of other spring wildflowers. Hepatica (*Hepatica* species), partridgeberry (*Mitchella repens*) and dewdrop (*Dalibarda repens*), with

their dark foliage, will highlight the pale green leaves and pristine flowers of the rue anemone, while the rosy twisted-stalk (*Streptopus roseus*) will add a little height to such a group. Any of the woodlanders with a similar mild nature and grace are suitable

companions. In time, a single plant will develop into a fair-sized clump from self-sown seedlings and the expansion of the roots. These clumps can be carefully and gently divided to begin new plantings.

The real showstopper in this genus is *Anemonella thalictroides* 'Schoaf's Double Pink'. Despite its small size, its sheer beauty is so exceptional that it always draws attention. The fully double flowers are a deep pink, and they bloom for weeks on end. This plant is not hard to find, but it is essential to locate just the right spot for it to take full advantage of its special qualities. There is also a rare, double white-flowered form (*Anemonella thalictroides* 'Flora Plena') of great charm.

Despite the delicate appearance of the rue anemone, it is a long-lived plant and will bring many years of delight to a shade garden, making this always a place to have as a destination.

🌸 *Caltha palustris*
Marsh Marigold

Not long after the spring peepers signal the beginning of a new season, splashes of sunshine appear in wet places and streamsides as bold clumps of marsh marigold come into bloom. Frequently, they will be growing in or near the icy waters of a brook, or in swampy places that are often still encrusted with frost early in the morning. In such a wet, shaded habitat, marsh marigold's natural companions are skunk cabbage (*Symplocarpus foetidus*), false hellebore (*Veratrum viride*) and, on the low hummocks, ferns whose tightly curled croziers are just beginning to unfold. This is the time of year, also, when the flowers of vernal witchhazel (*Hamamelis vernalis*) scent the air.

The leaves on deciduous trees are still in tight buds when the marsh marigold flowers, so it is essentially in full sun at this time and receives the warmth of the sun it needs to be coaxed into growth and flower. But as the season progresses, this area will gradually receive more shade, and will ultimately be in full shade. However, because marsh marigold goes dormant by summer, it can be planted in a place that stays sunny, as long as the soil does not become hot or dry out. In a shaded area, the moisture-loving ferns, like the interrupted (*Osmunda claytoniana*) or royal fern (*Osmunda regalis*), will fill in the

spots left by its dormancy.

This plant will be long-lived and easy to maintain if it is given the same conditions in a contrived garden as those found in its wild habitat. A lightly shaded waterside where the vegetation does not grow too thickly is good. Marsh marigold will also be happy beside an artificial pool in an area where water is allowed to overflow in order to keep the surrounding soil wet, though not necessarily saturated. A short distance away, but still where the soil is moist, the wood anemone (*Anemone quinquefolia*), dwarf ginseng (*Panax trifolium*) and early meadow-rue (*Thalictrum dioicum*) can be grown. All of these plants favor moist soil and will thrive on hummocks that rise slightly above standing water, but they will have to be kept away from the really wet spots that the marsh marigold needs.

🌸 *Claytonia virginica*
Spring Beauty

Spring beauty is an early spring-flowering ephemeral with a cheery countenance. Over time, it will form extensive colonies both in the wild and in the garden. In early spring, it creates a 2-inch-high sheet of delicate flowers of white with a hint of pale pink and deeper pink veining.

Its natural companions are the other spring ephemerals, along with rue anemone, wake robin (*Trillium erectum*) and a light ground cover such as oak fern (*Gymnocarpium dryopteris*) and creeping phlox (*Phlox stolonifera*).

Spring beauty grows abundantly in shade, and also in sun if the soil remains moist and cool. I have seen it in great swaths along the Blue Ridge Parkway, growing easily among the sparse grasses, which protect and shade its dormant roots in summer. The Carolina spring beauty (*C. caroliniana*) is a more southern species with broader leaves, but it is no less hardy or beautiful.

This delicate-looking wildling spreads mostly from self-sown seed and, like the Dutchman's-breeches (*Dicentra cucullaria*) and squirrel corn

(*Dicentra canadensis*), must be handled carefully during transplanting. The small tubers should be set shallowly, only 1/2 to 1 inch into the ground. New plants are easiest to handle if they arrive established in pots. If the plants are acquired bare-root with their tubers wrapped in moist sphagnum or similar material, it can be mystifying to someone who has never seen them before to identify the top. Remember the old adage: "When in doubt, plant them on their sides."

This is another of the many plants that in the wild are most often found in neutral to alkaline soils, but will, in the garden, adapt well to most soils, providing the pH is not extremely acid.

Cypripedium calceolus var. *pubescens* Large Yellow Lady's-Slipper

The roots of all terrestrial orchids have a symbiotic relationship with a soil mycorrhiza (fungus), and if this organism is not present in sufficient quantity in the soil, the plants cannot survive, even in the wild.

The large yellow lady's-slipper is less exacting in its need for this mycorrhiza than any other terrestrial orchid, which is why it is the only lady's-slipper that should be considered for cultivation in the wildflower garden. The large yellow lady's-slipper, which can reach a height of 12 to 15 inches, can be adapted to a garden situation under favorable conditions. It needs shade and a deep, rich soil on the alkaline side, with ample humus to keep it buoyant and hold extra moisture during the warmer summer months.

Because the large yellow lady's-slipper is so special and so rarely seen, it should be the focal point of a planting. For instance, it can be very effective grown as a single specimen, with just a ground cover around it and some ferns for a background. Another beautiful picture is created when yellow lady's-slippers are grown with crested iris (*Iris cristata*), showy trillium (*Trillium grandiflorum*) and the maidenhair fern (*Adiantum pedatum*).

Because this lady's-slipper likes an alkaline soil and my woods are acidic, I always bury some limestone material near the plants to offset the soil acidity. Every spring, I sprinkle the area around them with dolomitic lime to maintain the pH balance they prefer. Even a specially prepared lime bed should have a yearly top dressing of lime, worked lightly into the soil. Under such conditions, this species proves to be a long-lived plant in cultivation and will increase in size every year.

The small yellow lady's-slipper (*C. calceolus* var. *parviflorum*) grows 8 to 12 inches high. It does not adapt quite as readily to cultivation and tends to require more moisture than the larger one, and in the wild is

most frequently found in places that are always moist such as bogs and swamps. Like the larger-flowered variety, it has a broad global distribution including Europe and Asia; in North America, it is found in its favored habitat from coast to coast.

Large yellow lady's-slipper can be successfully divided in late summer as the plants approach dormancy. This stage can be recognized when the foliage is withering to a yellow brown. To divide them at this time, carefully dig up the clump, cutting into the soil with a spade well away from the central crown so as to do as little damage to the root as possible. The goal is to separate the secondary crown(s) from the parent by gently pulling them apart. A gentle twist will aid in this procedure, although it may break a few of the smaller roots which often become snagged together.

Trim any torn roots with a sharp knife, as they will be susceptible to disease. A clean knife-cut will usually heal well and quickly, but as a precaution, I dust any cut surfaces with a fungicide. Sometimes I make up a solution of fungicide and dip the whole root system into it, then cover the plants with newspaper to be sure they don't dry out while the solution dries (which it does quickly).

Although *C. calceolus* is the only species of lady's-slipper that I would recommend be grown in a garden, there are a couple of others that can be introduced into cultivation if they are given the specific growing conditions that are essential for them. The overwhelmingly beautiful showy lady's-slipper (*C. reginae*), with large pink-and-white flowers, can grow to 24 inches or more in the wild, where it is found in cool bogs overlaying a limestone bedrock. It can also be grown in a bog garden, but requires great skill. The white lady's-slipper (*C. candidum*) and mountain lady's-slipper (*C. montanum*) may both be found in the gardens of specialty wildflower enthusiasts, but neither is suitable for an average wildflower garden.

I feel bound to say something about the pink lady's-slipper (*C. acaule*), if only to discourage its continued collection from the wild, however enticing the plant and well-meaning the collector. Although this plant does grow in great abundance in the wild, and is without question one of our loveliest wildflowers, it is nearly impossible to transplant successfully.

Of all the lady's-slipper orchids, *C. acaule* has the greatest need for the soil mycorrhiza associated with terrestrial orchids. Only very rarely can a gardener provide a place suitable for it, and only then where this mycorrhiza has been added to an area and is in sufficient quantity to satisfy the pink lady's-slipper's needs.

Occasionally, it will survive transplanting, if it has been moved with a very large rootball and into an area where it is already growing naturally. Most often, it will struggle for a year or two—rarely more—before disappearing. And no one has ever been successful in propagating it; any seeds that germinate in cultivation quickly die.

So instead of trying to move it from the wild into our gardens, we should concentrate on providing protection for its natural habitat, and educating others about this and other wildflowers to prevent their certain demise.

☙ *Dalibarda repens* Dewdrop

I was enthralled by everthing about this engaging plant the first time I saw it growing along a woodland path, where it formed lovely ground-hugging mats of dark green. The small, symmetrical leaves with scalloped edges were dusted with snow-white flowers that looked like

tiny single roses, and the whole plant spread out beneath the other woodland plants in a rich carpet.

The next time I came across dewdrop, I saw it growing wild in the Adirondacks in a heavily shaded area; later the same day, I found it in a moist location, tucked into a bed of sphagnum moss in light shade. This gives some indication of its wide tolerance for different growing conditions. I have successfully grown dewdrop with ease ever since in a typical deciduous woodland, using a deep, humusy, slightly acid soil.

This small treasure never becomes invasive, and it appears always to be in harmony with its surroundings. It also sets off the other plants it grows among to great advantage: the flowers of showy trillium look whiter, the pink of Henderson's trout lily (*Erythronium hendersonii*) is more intense and the blue of Virginia bluebells (*Mertensia virginica*) is clearer when set in contrast with dewdrop.

Like most trailing plants, dewdrop takes some extra attention initially to get it established. It requires careful planting to be sure the sparse roots are securely tucked into the soil, and at no time should the plant be allowed to dry out.

It's hard to understand how a plant that is so beautiful and undemanding can be so little seen in gardens, especially as it roots easily from cuttings.

☙ *Dentaria diphylla* Toothwort

Sadly, this charming little (4 to 6 inches tall) spring ephemeral is rarely seen in cultivation, even though it is easy to grow once established. The clear white flowers and dark, finely cut foliage provide a very pretty display. I like to see it scattered among clumps of Solomon's seal (*Polygonatum biflorum*), trillium, primroses (*Primula* species) and Jack-in-the-pulpit (*Arisaema triphyllum*). It will also form small colonies from the self-sown seeds and the expansion of the brittle roots.

All signs of toothwort disappear after it has flowered and its seeds have been scattered. It is therefore a good idea to grow it among a light ground cover of oak fern, dewdrop, or creeping phlox.

There is another striking species, the cut-leaved toothwort (*D. laciniata*), that is even more infre-

quently seen. This plant has heavily dissected foliage and is especially pretty grown with the wild bleeding heart (*Dicentra eximia*) and Labrador violet (*Viola labradorica*).

☙ *Diphylleia cymosa* Umbrella Leaf

In late spring, a cool, shady, moist spot can be impressive with just one bold clump of this imposing native.

Its height will vary somewhat according to how moist and rich the soil is, but it can easily reach 18 to 24 inches or more. The large, parasol-like leaves provide just the right setting for the loose cluster of white flowers that appear in spring. In late summer, these are followed by dark blue berries on eye-catching red stems.

Mixed with the moisture-loving ferns and a swath of Japanese primroses (*Primula japonica*), umbrella leaf makes a lovely picture, especially with the tall columns of the false hellebore's foliage placed behind it. Such a planting is not hard to accomplish in the setting of a wildflower garden.

Dodecatheon meadia Shooting-Star

When they first see the flowers of the shooting-star, many people cannot decide if it is an orchid or a special kind of miniature cyclamen. In spring the soft pink flowers, brushed with yellow at their throats, dance in the air on pliable stems that grow 8 to 15 inches high.

Shooting-star prefers a lightly shaded place and a cool, damp soil rich in humus, so it is a natural choice to mix with the various primroses, dwarf ginseng, and little wood anemone. Bloodroot (*Sanguinaria canadensis*) is another good companion, because its broad leaves unfurl after the shooting-star has gone dor-

mant and disappeared in early summer, thus protecting the latter's crowns resting in the soil beneath.

Although in the wild this dainty, elegant wildflower is found in alkaline soils, I have grown it successfully in an acid soil with oconee bells (*Shortia galacifolia*), partridgeberry and even golden star (*Chrysogonum virginianum*). It will do well as long as its companions are not those that grow too enthusiastically and would smother it.

I remember seeing the eastern shooting-star's close cousins (such as *D. jeffreyi, D. alpinum*, and *D. pulchellum*) growing in the wet meadows of our western mountains. Most are taller and a little stouter than the eastern species, but all have that gentle grace that endears them to everyone. Their colorful flowers are reminiscent of exotic little pink birds hovering above the ground, and they always make me homesick for the cool clear air and multitude of flow-

ers that share the mountains with them.

The western species do not always take as kindly to our gardens as the woodlanders from the east do, but if the habitat is cool and moist enough for them, they will put on a fine display. They may even grow in full sun in a favorable situation and temperate summer climate.

All are also a good choice for a brief sojourn in a container so their beauty can be savored often.

Galax aphylla Galax

To see the dark green, highly polished foliage of galax is enough to make any gardener covet it. Here is a plant that is in top condition year-round. The evergreen foliage is never blemished and, with the onset of cold weather, takes on a rich plum color that remains into early spring. In early summer, elegant spikes 12 to 15 inches high rise up through the leaves, each encrusted with small snow-white flowers of such beauty as

always to stop me on a walk and entice me to take a few minutes to savor them and ponder how anything could be so lovely.

Galax needs a deep, organic, acid soil that is always cool and moist. In such a location, it will form a sizable clump. It is wonderful when planted close to a path, beside stone steps or a rustic bench. Or, it can be grown as an integral part of a larger display, where it will always capture center stage. For an enviable show, grow galax beside a group of showy trillium—to my eye, this makes one of the finest sights to be seen in a garden.

This is one of the few plants that will flower well in quite dense shade. I have seen galax in the wild, growing in what appeared to be unending colonies beneath tall, gnarled mountain laurels (*Kalmia latifolia*) and rhododendrons so ancient their lower branches had long since died. Beside narrow trails, where there was a little more light, it grew even more densely.

The plants form a mass of fibrous roots and take quite a long time to settle into a new location after transplanting. Be patient and watchful to see the soil never dries out, and in eighteen to twenty months they will have become well enough established to begin expanding into what will eventually be a sizable plant. Mature clumps can be divided with care, but success requires some previous experience in dividing plants. Once it is well established, galax is a tough, long-lived plant that will bring years of delight.

⚘ *Gaultheria procumbens*
Wintergreen

This is primarily a plant of acid woodlands, where it can be found as an extensive ground cover. The texture and color of its evergreen foliage are quite similar to those of galax: a rich, glossy dark green.

Unlike galax, however, wintergreen will thrive in a dry, impoverished soil. Spring sees this 1- to 2-inch-high plant speckled in small white flowers similar to those of the bearberry (*Arctostaphylos uva-ursi*). Later in summer and early fall, the flowers are replaced with bright scarlet berries that make a striking contrast to the dark foliage. Any berries not eaten by wildlife during the winter can be found still on the plant when it blooms in the spring, making an unusual display.

Wintergreen takes time to get its roots firmly settled into the soil. It needs to be planted carefully and watered well until new roots have begun to move out into the surrounding earth. Plants that have been grown in containers are the most easily transplanted. If it is dug out of the ground (I transplanted them from my own woods into a shady wildflower area near the house), a large, deeply dug clump should be taken so the majority of

the root system remains undisturbed. Plant this firmly into the new location and soak it in well but gently to settle the soil down around the roots and underground stems.

Ideally, it should be grown in shade. In areas with cool summers, wintergreen will tolerate full sun, although I do not recommend this as a regular practice. Under these conditions, the foliage will develop a prominent plum color usually seen only in winter.

Plant it under shrubs that have an upright branching habit, such as the pinkshell azalea (*Rhododendron vaseyi*) and pinxter bloom, (*R. periclymenoides*), and among other plants that enjoy the same acid conditions, such as shinleaf (*Pyrola elliptica*), trailing arbutus (*Epigaea repens*), and bird's-foot violet (*Viola pedata*).

⚘ *Mertensia virginica*
Virginia Bluebells

Come early spring, I start searching for the first signs of this endearing plant—the tiny shoots that push up through the cold soil. The flowers, which quickly follow the early gray foliage, produce the sweeps of blue typically created by Virginia bluebells. And then when I discover it, I always linger to enjoy the design and different color phases of the

flowers, from pink buds that turn to the familiar blue, accented by the pale green leaves. I cannot imagine a woodland garden without the delightful presence of this lovely wildflower.

A drift of Virginia bluebells, beneath the spicebush's (*Lindera benzoin*) pale yellow flowers that look like tiny sparklers, makes an unmatched spring picture. As this is an ephemeral that goes dormant soon after dispersing its seeds, it is best mixed with later-flowering astilbes and ferns such as lady (*Athyrium filix-femina*) and marginal shield ferns (*Dryopteris marginalis*), whose fronds are not fully expanded when Virginia bluebells is at its peak of bloom. A ground cover, too, is a good companion to protect the resting roots of Virginia bluebells later in the season. I often use the Allegheny spurge (*Pachysandra procumbens*) or golden Alexanders (*Zizia aurea*) for this purpose.

There are areas along the Brandywine River in Pennsylvania that are solid carpets of blue when this plant is in bloom. These are mostly wettish places that, at times, have been inundated by spring floods. But the floods do not last long, and the soil drains quickly.

The strong, fleshy rootstocks of Virginia bluebells dislike any disturbance, so they are best left alone. Colonies develop not only by these spreading roots but by the abundantly produced seeds. If they require dividing or transplanting, it should be done in late spring to early summer when the plant is going dormant and the leaves have turned a papery brown but can still be traced to the roots.

There is a seldom-seen white-flowered form (*Mertensia virginica* 'Alba'), which is pretty but not nearly so robust or tall as the blue-flowered one. When the whites are spotted in with the blue, they make an attractive color combination.

⚘ *Mitchella repens*
Partridgeberry

The ground-hugging mats of partridgeberry's dark green foliage stand out in a shady garden all year round. What a pleasure it is to find it revealed beneath snow that has been brushed aside by a wild animal looking for the small scarlet berries, which remain for many months, even through the winter and into spring.

In early summer, the pristine white flowers appear. They are exquisitely beautiful, with such fine detailing that they need to be examined through a magnifying glass for their intricacy to be fully appreciated.

An easy plant to grow once estab-

lished, partridgeberry will unhurriedly spread over the woodland floor, forming a rich dark carpet around plants such as the yellow lady's-slipper, wood poppy (*Stylophorum diphyllum*), or double bloodroot (*Sanguinaria canadensis* 'Multiplex'). It is also the perfect companion for the delicate spring ephemerals, which can grow easily and unhampered through its trailing stems and are then well protected by them once they have gone dormant.

As with most trailing plants, when transplanting partridgeberry care needs to be taken so that the sparse, fine roots are undamaged and are securely tucked back into the soil to encourage the plant to successfully reestablish.

❦ *Mitella diphylla*
Bishop's Cap

Another infrequently seen woodland treasure, this plant forms trim clumps with delicate, small leaves and many diminutive white flowers held closely along the stems. These flowers, reminiscent of a bishop's mitre (hence the name), are jewels, and well worth taking the time to savor their beauty.

Bishop's cap is lovely in my woodland garden, where it is set against an old mossy log with spring beauty and squirrel corn around it and the small bulblet fern (*Cystopteris bulbifera*) growing nearby. I like to see it

with a backdrop of dark foliage—perhaps Christmas fern (*Polystichum acrostichoides*) or the waldsteinia (*Waldsteinia fragarioides*)—and a foreground of two or three hepatica set close together. It is also lovely when tucked into a niche in a shady rock garden.

This is such an unassuming plant that it is often overlooked in a garden, so make a special place for it and surround it with a framework of plants to give it center stage—even if only when it is in flower. Or, to better enjoy the flowers, grow bishop's cap in a planter, where its size and growth habit are well suited to the confinement and scale of a container.

It prefers a neutral soil, so when I plant it in my acid woodlands, I give

it the same treatment as I do with my large yellow lady's-slippers: I bury a couple of pieces of old mortar or limestone nearby and give it an annual top dressing of lime to reduce the effect of the acidity. This treatment has kept it happy year after year.

❦ *Polygala paucifolia*
Fringed Polygala

The exotic and unusual flowers of the fringed polygala cause most people to mistake this ground-hugging plant for an orchid. The trailing stems and leaves are joined in midspring by flowers of the clearest, most intense purple, each with a tiny firecracker whorl of yellow stamens

at its tip. These are carried on stems no more than an inch high. Despite the plant's small size, the flowers stand out like tiny beacons in the greens of the woodland floor.

Whether grown beneath taller plants like baneberry (*Actaea* species), blue cohosh (*Caulophyllum thalictroides*) and marginal shield fern, intertwined with starflowers (*Trientalis americana*) and rue anemones, or placed around oconee bells and trillium, the fringed polygala is a delight. It is also perfect for growing in a shady rock garden. Each spring, I eagerly await the time when these flowers open.

There is an equally exquisite white form (*Polygala paucifolia alba*), with the same velvety texture to the miniature, birdlike flowers. Both require constant shade and an acid soil that does not dry out.

Like many of the trailing plants, fringed polygala needs special care when moved or transplanted. I have found that plants grown in pots will reestablish best. New plants can be grown from stem cuttings that—for an experienced propagator—root easily.

❦ *Sanguinaria canadensis*
Bloodroot

The simple beauty of this woodlander has often caused the start of a love affair with wildflowers. What gardeners could resist imagining their own woodland oases, with this elegant, easily grown plant sweeping through them? And each spring, I impatiently await the day when the bloodroot's tight buds, furled by the leaves, push through the earth and then quickly open to large, glistening flowers.

A group of bloodroot grown anywhere in a shade garden is a treat.

Long after the flowers have passed, the gray-green foliage will continue to hold interest, even well into late summer, if the soil is not allowed to dry out.

The bloodroot's white saucerlike flowers, mixed among the tiny blue flowers of squills (*Scilla sibirica*) and grape hyacinths (*Muscari armeniacum*), are a warming sight on a spring day. Consider a ground cover of dewdrop for contrast, and then something taller such as wake robin, merrybells (*Uvularia grandiflora*) and ferns set behind as a background. Place bloodroot against a weathered rock and, in the foreground, add the native Allegheny spurge, whose dark evergreen leaves provide just the right setting.

In the wild, bloodroot is quite often found in alkaline soils, but in the garden the quality of soil and care the plant receives matter more than the pH. When its needs are met, the thick, fleshy root will gradually form a large mat. Over the years, the plants will continue to spread until large drifts cover the ground.

When the rootstock is cut, it exudes a red juice—hence the common name. This tends to run rather freely (except when the plant is dormant), and its loss can greatly weaken the plant, so any transplanting or division of bloodroot should be done as it approaches dormancy, when the foliage is withering away but can still be easily traced down to the roots.

If the soil becomes dried out for any length of time, bloodroot will respond by going prematurely dormant. As a result, the plant may be smaller and less vigorous during the following year, as it will not have had enough time to manufacture sufficient food reserves.

There is an outstandingly beautiful double form called 'Multiplex', that fortunately is not hard to come by and is no more difficult to grow or divide than the single form. Its flowers resemble those of a camellia but have more delicacy and brightness.

Shortia galacifolia
Oconee Bells

This is, without a doubt, one of the very loveliest of all plants and a special favorite of mine. To see a clump of oconee bells planted against a weathered, lichen-covered rock is always a highlight of my garden walks.

The dark, glossy evergreen foliage forms a striking mound which, with the onset of cool weather, turns a rich plum color that is especially beautiful against the snow. This color persists into spring and can still be in evidence when the flowers open.

The single-frilled white bells of absolute perfection are held in pink calyxes and carried on 4- to 6-inch stems, making a picture so lovely it needs no staging.

Several plants make particularly good companions for oconee bells. Variegated Japanese Solomon's seal (*Polygonatum odoratum* 'Variegatum'), with its creamy variegated leaves, presents a striking contrast to the dark green foliage of the oconee bells. Another good choice is rodgersia (*Rodgersia* species), with its tall architectural foliage and feathery plumes of flowers, perhaps set nearby in a background position. The light green foliage of vancouveria (*Vancouveria hexandra*) and golden seal (*Hydrastis canadensis*) also make good backdrops. The delicate rue anemone, wild bleeding heart and Jacob's ladder (*Polemonium reptans*) provide beautiful finishing touches to this lovely spring picture.

I have only once had the good for-

tune to see oconee bells in the wild, where they were growing in dense colonies along the rock-strewn banks of a river. In places they were so close to the water that ripples often flowed over the foliage. The air was damp and cool, and plenty of spray drifted over the plants. The shade was heavy and the soil an acid black humus.

Sadly, this plant has been almost entirely eradicated in the wild, both because of collecting and the destruction of its habitat. Fortunately, it is well established in gardens where an experienced gardener can propagate it by division and grow it readily once the right spot has been found. Oconee bells requires cool, moisture-retentive soils that are rich in acid humus and never permitted to dry out. It consistently does well on gentle slopes, but this is certainly not a requirement. When it is happy, it will slowly form handsome colonies that are a wonderful sight all year round.

Streptopus roseus
Rosy Twisted-Stalk

I first saw this spring woodland wildflower growing beside the moss-covered remains of a small tree stump. The soft green foliage and 12-inch height were perfect in this setting. Near the rosy twisted-stalk were the sparkling white flowers of false rue anemone (*Isopyrum biternatum*), to the side was a large clump of oconee bells, and the dark fronds of marginal shield fern formed the background. But it was not until I got quite close to this group that I saw the rosy twisted-stalk's small but very beautiful dusky pink flower. The whole plant reminded me of a refined Solomon's seal, especially the pendulous flowers.

Other good companions for this plant are Christmas fern, crested iris, partridgeberry, dewdrop and spring ephemerals such as the trout lily

(*Erythronium americanum*) and toothwort. Rosy twisted-stalk brings a hard-to-find vertical dimension to lower-growing woodland plantings, and it is a perfect choice for any situation that calls for some extra height and a frame for foreground plants.

Perhaps because its flowers are not large or showy, it is not frequently seen in gardens, but its ease of culture in a rich woods soil, its longevity and its overall charm should be enough to recommend it. Unfortunately, very few nurseries or catalogs carry it.

🌹 *Trientalis americana*
Starflower

The dainty foliage of starflower gives a light but pretty and highly appealing cover to the woodland floor. It looks attractive scattered among Christmas and marginal shield fern, beneath wake robin, around oconee bells and among mats of creeping phlox and crested iris. Once plants are established in a location, they will easily seed themselves about the woodland.

This plant is not often seen in gar-

dens, which is unfortunate, as it is a charming wildflower with a distinctive whorl of leaves set beneath the terminal white flower. The 4- to 8-inch-high stems are brittle and easily broken. While this does not necessarily kill the plant, it can weaken it, as

only one stem per plant is usually produced. Great care should be taken, therefore, when handling or working around starflower.

Once settled in, it becomes a long-lived and reliable woodlander, and is well worth the extra effort that may be necessary to locate it for your own garden.

🌹 *Trillium* species

No wildflower garden is complete without a planting or two of these favorite woodlanders. Whether it is a group of just three to five flowering stems in a mixed planting or a drift of twenty or more, trilliums will always cast a special air of beauty in any shade garden.

Few of us will be able to plant trilliums as they are frequently seen in the wild, in extensive colonies that seem to go endlessly on into the woods. In the garden, a small group with a few companion plants is more effective to draw attention to its simple elegance.

The showy trillium (*T. grandiflorum*) is probably the best known, perhaps because of the unmatched loveliness of its snow-white flowers. But I enjoy the wake robin (*T. erectum*), shown here, too, with its velvety

maroon blossoms, maybe because it grows wild in my woods where it forms sizable groups at the base of large hickories among wild oats (*Uvularia sessilifolia*), Christmas and cinnamon ferns (*Osmunda cinnamomea*). Close by is a beautiful meandering brook with dwarf ginseng, royal fern and the fall-flowering witchhazel (*Hamamelis virginiana*) growing along the banks.

All too frequently overlooked are the sessile trilliums, *T. sessile* with its deep maroon flowers, and *T. luteum* with soft yellow blossoms. They are probably neglected because their upright flowers remain closed and are not spectacular. Nonetheless, the blossoms make an attractive display above the beautifully mottled leaves, which adds to the pleasure of growing these species.

I have a favorite planting that consists of just three stems of the sweetly fragrant yellow trillium mixed with wood phlox (*Phlox divaricata*) and maidenhair fern. Nearby is a colony of spring beauty that swirls around primroses. But it is the planting with the trillium that always catches my eye, and I often make it my destination on a quiet evening stroll.

Look for the other species as well.

Give all of them deep rich soils, and ample water in dry spells. Most trilliums seem unconcerned about soil pH—provided it is not too extreme —but the tiny, 2-inch-high snow trillium (*T. nivale*) must always have a limy (alkaline) soil. And the rare painted trillium (*T. undulatum*), the most strikingly beautiful of all these lovely plants (and the hardest to grow), needs a moist acid soil if it is to prosper.

Trilliums can be propagated by seed or by division of the tubers. They take a long time to flower when grown from seed (five to seven years), and are slow to propagate by division. Old colonies will have self-sown seedlings scattered through them, and when the seedlings are 4 to 6 inches high, they can be transplanted elsewhere to begin another planting. In time, the tubers increase in size until they have several stems and are large enough to be divided if this is desirable. Skilled gardeners and nurserymen have good success with these methods, even though it is a slow process.

If trilliums become dry, they will go prematurely dormant, which is not harmful if it occurs only occasionally. The plants may be smaller the following year, however, as they will not have had enough time to manufacture the food reserves necessary for vigorous growth.

The trilliums' only leaves are carried at the top of the stems, just beneath the flowers. If the stems are broken, the plant will be unable to manufacture sufficient food, and it will do poorly the following year. A new transplant may not recover from such an incident, so it is important to handle them carefully. Transplanting is best done very early, before they have started into growth, or very late in the year as they are approaching dormancy.

If these basic precautions are heeded, most trilliums are easy wildflowers to grow and will be very long-lived.

Sun

🌿 *Asclepias tuberosa*
Butterfly Weed

Whether it is just a couple of clumps growing in a sunny border or many plants scattered through a meadow, butterfly weed is always a pleasure to see. Its brilliant orange flowers stand out strongly among other plants and play off the yellows, greens and pinks that are the pre-

dominant colors of a summer garden. A recently introduced seed mix called Gay Butterflies has a whole range of lovely colors in shades from yellow to deep orangy-red to scarlet. These wonderful flower displays are followed by the fluffy seed heads that create one of the prettiest late summer displays.

Butterfly weed naturally grows in lean, impoverished soil, often with a high sand or gravel content. The plant soon develops a deep fleshy taproot that greatly resents any disturbance. Young plants or seedlings should therefore be set into their permanent places early and left to mature into the bold clumps we so admire.

It grows easily from seed, and root cuttings can also be used to maintain a particularly good color form, but these require some experience with propagation to yield success.

A close and equally delightful relative is the swamp milkweed (*A. incarnata*), which has deep pink flowers with a hint of white. This plant likes damp meadows or wet soils beside water, where it mingles with sedges (*Carex* species), turtle-head (*Chelone* species) and Canadian burnet (*Sanguisorba canadensis*). Both butterfly weed and swamp milkweed are favored by all manner of butterflies, and this makes an already beautiful display even more attractive and appealing.

🌿 *Camassia cusickii*
Camas Lily

This striking native plant from Oregon should have much more of a presence in our gardens. In the wild, its 2- to 3-foot spires of intense blue can be seen rising through the tapes-

try of the wet meadows of our western mountains, where it is one of a rainbow of flowers that bloom at high altitudes in summer. (In gardens at lower elevations, the flowering time will be earlier—late spring to early summer.)

The wild companions of camas lily are often shooting-star, cotton grass (*Eriophorum* species), the various mountain species of potentilla (*Potentilla* species), Indian paintbrush (*Castilleja* species) and wild geraniums (*Geranium* species), to name just a few.

Despite its natural proclivity for moist or even wet soils in the wild, this bulb grows well in cultivation if it is given a rich, moisture-retentive soil that is not allowed to dry out. Given the right conditions, camas lily is quite hardy and long-lived. It is important to ensure good drainage around the bulb itself, just as with the other liliaceous bulbs. After flow-

ering, the plant goes dormant, so the soil does not have to be kept as moist after this time.

Camas lily grows well in full sun or in light shade. In lightly shaded areas, it can be mixed with the deep pink of the Asian bleeding heart (*Dicentra spectabilis*), foxglove (*Digitalis purpurea*), false Solomon's seal (*Smilacina racemosa*) and taller ground covers such as golden seal, yellowroot (*Xanthorhiza simplicissima*) and epimedium (*Epimedium* species). A simple and very lovely combination mixes camas lily with the graceful ostrich fern (*Matteuccia struthiopteris*).

In sunny spots, an attractive picture can be created by using it with white-flowered wild indigo (*Baptisia pendula*), hairy beard-tongue (*Penstemon hirsutus*) and bowman's root

(*Gillenia trifoliata*). In a sunny location, add extra humus to the soil to hold additional moisture.

Several other equally good species are also available. *C. leichtlinii* grows 24 to 30 inches high, with very dark blue flowers. *C. quamash* is a lighter blue and grows to 12 to 18 inches high. *C. scilloides*, the eastern representative, also produces flowers of pale blue—although all camas lilies tend to be quite variable in color, and white-flowered forms can be found.

These easily grown, free-flowering natives are generally to be found in bulb catalogs listed under "miscellaneous" or "minor bulbs." Once you have seen this plant you will quickly elevate it from this rather nondescript status to a favored one in your garden.

✤ *Campanula rotundifolia*
Harebell

This engaging little plant is native to many temperate regions around the world. I have seen it growing on the edges of the geyser basins in Yellowstone National Park, in rocky outcroppings on the wild moors of Scotland, and on talus slopes in Iceland. Its natural preference is for places with cool summers, low ground temperatures and lean, gravelly soils with excellent drainage.

Starting in summer, slender stems 8 to 12 inches tall carry captivating

bells in deep sky blue. The shade of blue can vary considerably, and some good color forms have been selected. There is also a rare, white-flowered form (*Campanula rotundifolia* 'Alba') to keep an eye out for.

Harebell is ideal for the uncrowded environs of a rock garden, where it can be planted with wild pink (*Silene caroliniana*, bird's-foot violet and the three-toothed cinquefoil (*Potentilla tridentata*). It is a tough, long-lived plant in a northern climate. When I grew it in South Carolina, it seemed, at least in appearance, undaunted by the heat of the South, but it did not live long in the hot soils and humid air. I could not get it to last longer than two years at most.

✤ *Houstonia caerulea*
Bluets

Bluets grow in a wide variety of places, providing the soil is not too rich; a lean one is more to their liking. In late spring, masses of their small flowers can be seen as sheets of pale blue in sunny glades, or in rocky areas where self-sown seedlings will become established and thrive in crevices and other places where it is too hard for the gardener to get plants started.

Bluets can also be found in grassy expanses where the vegetation does not grow so tall or thick as to overwhelm these beguiling treasures, and I have seen them growing equally as well in dry areas as in moist ones. Bluets are challenging to get established initially because of their lilliputian size and sparse roots, and it may take several tries. But once they are growing, the plants will self-sow and, in time, form the colonies that make such appealing pictures.

If you are fortunate enough to have them popping up in a lawn, don't mow them until the seeds have had time to ripen and disperse.

If you are getting bluets from a friend, be sure to dig deeply and broadly around the clump so the central part of it will have plenty of undisturbed roots. Or purchase plants well established in a pot. Because of their shallow roots and delicate nature, these transplants

need to have a close eye kept on them until they have attained a good foothold, after which time they are trouble-free.

Bluets are usually found growing with few other plants close by, but they can be mixed with restrained companions such as yellow star grass (*Hypoxis hirsuta*), blue-eyed grass (*Sisyrinchium angustifolium*) and harebells in sunny places; in light shade, they find squirrel corn, Dutchman's-breeches, and rue anemones to be perfect neighbors.

Look for both the mountain bluet (*H. purpurea*), with large pink flowers

on 8- to 10-inch-high stems, and the low, mat-forming thyme-leaved bluets (*H. serpyllifolia*), with clusters of pale lavender-purple flowers on stems 2 inches in height. The latter is a treasure to be set in a rock garden or tucked between paving stones, where it will form a low carpet. In too rich a soil, however, the flowering stems can grow to be 4 to 6 inches in height, which will cause the plant to grow out of character and lose its compact, prostrate growth habit.

✤ *Hypoxis hirsuta*
Yellow Star Grass

A much-overlooked wildflower of great charm, with its upright, grass-like foliage, this plant grows just 6 to 8 inches high. The bright yellow flowers make pinpoints of sunshine in early summer and, sporadically, into fall. Its preference is for a moist, well-drained soil. A sunny spot set back from a pool or stream is ideal, with extra sand or other drainage material mixed into the soil; it will also grow well in a rock garden, where it can be placed beside a rock

so its roots can grow down into the cool dampness beneath.

Because of its small size, the yellow star grass should be grown with other plants of similar stature so as not to be overshadowed by its neighbors. Blue-eyed grass, monkeyflower (*Mimulas ringens*) and wild petunia (*Ruellia humilis*) are good choices, as are some of the smaller sedges like the blue sedge (*Carex flacca*) or miniature variegated sedge (*Carex conica* 'Variegata'). The dwarf white-striped Japanese sweet flag (*Acorus gramineus* 'Albo-variegatus') is also an amiable companion.

✿ *Lilium canadense* Canada Lily ✿ *Lilium superbum* Turk's-Cap Lily

In early summer, while the grasses and other general summer vegetation are still quite low, the Canada, shown here, and Turk's-cap lilies are in their full glory. Under optimum growing conditions, their supple, strong stems will grow as high as 5 feet (occasionally higher) and carry a multitude of flowers in stately opulence.

They are both generally found in wet meadows in the wild, especially the Turk's-cap. They favor slightly elevated ground so the bulbs are away from the wetness. Under cultivation, they do very well in rich, organic soil that has extra drainage material added and is kept well watered. In fact, they will consistently produce many more flowers in cultivation than they do in the wild.

If you are not going to keep the seeds, cut the top third of the stem back after flowering. This leaves ample foliage for food production and removes the quite unattractive (and highly visible) top portion. All lilies begin to look rather disheveled as the season progresses, and setting tall companion plants around them is important to hide the foliage as it dies back. In a meadow, ironweed (*Vernonia noveboracensis*), blazing star (*Liatris spicata*), Joe-pye-weed (*Eupatorium purpureum*) and goldenrod (*Solidago* species) are good plants for this task, as they have plenty of foliage and are tall enough to mask the stems and foliage of the lilies.

Because so much of the natural habitat of both these lilies has been destroyed, and they are still being extensively collected from the wild, they need to be grown more frequently in cultivation to protect and preserve them. They are not difficult

to raise from seed, but they take from five to seven years to reach flowering size.

Many years ago, I was fortunate to see a wet meadow, several acres in size, that was full of Turk's-cap lily —it was spectacular. But on my return to that spot several years later, I found an industrial park paved with concrete and macadam. Sadly, no one knew about this development in time to rescue the lilies, so hundreds of plants perished.

There are also other native lilies to find and grow. The rarest is the wood lily (*L. philadelphicum*), with upright flowers on 20- to 24-inch stems, which—as the name implies— grows in light shade.

✿ *Lobelia cardinalis* Cardinal Flower

What lovelier sight is there in summer than the elegant spires of the cardinal flower, with its brilliant, almost electric, red flowers? It is beautiful anywhere, but especially so when seen beside water (which is its preferred habitat) and mixed with grasses, sedges and sun-loving ferns with some added color from turtleheads, meadow-rue (*Thalictrum polygamum*) and queen-of-the-prairie (*Filipendula rubra*).

There are a number of different color forms of cardinal flower, including a rare, elegant white-flowered one (*Lobelia cardinalis* 'Alba') and an unnamed white one with pink stripes down the petals. There are also several hybrids between the classic cardinal flower and its close relative, the great blue lobelia (*L. siphilitica*), that yield flowers in shades of rich dark purple.

Hybrids from a cross with *L. fulgens*, a more tender species from Mexico, are readily available, too, under names such as 'Bees' Flame' and 'Queen Victoria'. These hybrids have dark red flowers and, as an additional attraction, have purple foliage so dark that it is almost black, which is quite eye-catching against the flowers and provides a good color accent after the flowers have passed. Favorites of the British, who developed them, these hybrids can be seen planted in large swaths in damp places in their gardens—areas that, earlier in the year, were ablaze with moisture-loving primroses. This scene can be duplicated in places that have the cool climates in which moisture-loving primroses do well. I have found, however, that hybrids of *L. fulgens* do not do well in areas with extremely cold winters, where they are not hardy.

While the great blue lobelia lacks the elegance and brilliance of its red cousin, it brings a rare color to the damp meadow or flower border and is valued for its ease of culture and durability. This also has a white-flowered form of great charm.

Neither species seems very long-lived—usually three to five years—but as they both produce ample seedlings, there is alway a good display. In a formal garden, a determined effort must be made to remove the many seedlings produced by the great blue lobelia, leaving only those that are in the right place and in reasonable numbers. In a meadow or wild place, this isn't necessary, because there are never too many of these bright blue spires. (Although the cardinal flower also produces an abundance of seed, not as many will germinate or reach maturity as with the great blue lobelia.)

When grown in wet soils—which is their preference—these native lobelias will tend to heave out of the ground if subjected to winter freezing and thawing. To help counteract this, they should be well mulched and checked often so the crowns can be gently pressed back into the soil when they have been heaved out, before the roots become desiccated and the plant dies.

Orontium aquaticum
Golden Club

The golden club grows in shallow, still water where its gray-green leaves

float on the surface. In spring, the plant develops ornate structures of white tipped in gold that carry the insignificant flowers. Golden club is an engaging, showy plant that creates a bright highlight of color against the dark greens of water.

In such a place it is quite easy to grow and, once established, produces large numbers of seeds. These quickly germinate along the water line around a pond; the seedlings can easily be transported in a bucket of water to a new location.

The major obstacle to getting golden club established and keeping it is the fact that muskrats seem to love it above all else. I have gone to great lengths to protect my plants: I have surrounded the roots and crowns in wire cages, and I've taken the dogs for frequent walks around the pond just to convince the muskrats it is hazardous for them to stay around. In the main, this approach has been successful. Because of the muskrat problem, golden club makes a good specimen plant in an artificial pond, well away from the natural habitat of the pond dwellers who so enjoy its taste.

Pontederia cordata
Pickerel Weed

Although the summer-blooming pickerel weed enjoys much the same environment as does the golden club, it is also frequently seen in handsome bands around the edges of a sunny pond, in open water in a swamp or even along a slow-moving waterway.

This plant's mound of lush foliage forms a marvelous platform for its numerous flowering stems, which grow to a height of 12 to 36 inches above the water and carry a multitude of bright blue flowers. These

appear in midsummer and look particularly beautiful reflected in the shallow (12 to 18 inches deep), still water of its preferred habitat.

Although I usually take great trouble to plant the tubers carefully, I have also, on occasion, tied the dormant rootstock to a brick and unceremoniously tossed it out into a more distant spot in my pond. After a while, the foliage appears, confirming the plant's survival in defiance of my harsh treatment.

Pickerel weed makes a lovely display along with waterlilies (*Nymphaea* species) when they are grown close to a bank with a background of sweet pepperbush (*Clethra alnifolia*), Joe-pye-weed and turtle-head.

Ruellia humilis
Wild Petunia

The supple, upright stems of wild petunia are clothed in summer—and often well into fall—with 2-inch lavender flowers, similar to those borne by the monkeyflower. The soft but striking color and velvety texture bring a particularly attractive note to the summer garden. The wild petunia is approximately 20 inches high and is especially lovely when grown among golden aster (*Chrysopsis mariana*), hardy ageratum (*Eupatorium coelestinum*) and Barbara's buttons (*Marshallia grandiflora*).

Here is a plant that will tolerate quite alkaline soils, and, as it prefers those on the sandy side, I have grown

it in a rock garden with harebell, prairie smoke (*Geum triflorum*) and the annual California poppy (*Eschscholzia californica*), set against the dark evergreen foliage of candytuft (*Iberis sempervirens*).

In the North, wild petunia seems to do well in sun, but in southern areas it prefers light shade.

There are several other species well worth looking for, but they are not as hardy as this one and are therefore suitable for more southern gardens, where they put on a long display.

Sagittaria latifolia
Arrowhead

The dramatic, highly stylized foliage that gives this plant its

name is a great addition to a waterside planting, where its distinctive form and 18- to 20-inch height make it an excellent specimen plant. In summer, the arrowhead produces many crisp, sparkling white flowers.

This plant is greatly overlooked, but it should not be, because it is quite easy to grow in the right habitat. Arrowhead is found in the wild in still or slow-moving shallow water, or in the wet muck at water's edge where it forms fine clumps.

I have potted a single plant up into a container (12 to 15 inches in diameter) to use in a small pool. This method not only stops it from spreading but also accentuates the natural proportions of the plant by restricting it to a tight clump, making it an impressive accent.

Silene caroliniana
Wild Pink

In a sunny rock garden in spring, bright spots of rich pink are created by the small parasol-like flowers of this showy plant, which grows in dense little clumps.

The strong pink harmonizes well with the whites, pale pinks and lavenders of the mossy phloxes (*Phlox subulata*); they also make an attractive display with the bird's-foot violet, especially the bicolored form (*Viola pedata* var. *bicolor*). The pasque flower (*Anemone patens*) is also a good companion: although its bloom time is over by the time wild pink blooms, its attractive foliage and feathery seed heads make a delightful background for the wild pink.

This is an easy plant to grow if it is given a well-drained soil. Perfect drainage is vital, particularly around the crown, which will quickly rot if subjected to any lingering soil moisture, especially in winter.

Wildflower enthusiasts have selected several exceptionally good color forms; unfortunately, no special names have been given to these to distinguish them from others. One of the best is only 8 to 10 inches high, bearing deep pink flowers and producing an even more compact, sturdy growth

habit than the straight species. I hope that one day it will be named and offered for sale.

The wild pink has a beautiful relative, the fire pink (*S. virginica*), which grows taller (12 to 18 inches high) and has brilliant red flowers. It will grow in light shade or full sun if the summers are not excessively hot. In New England, I have found it to be somewhat short-lived, lasting for only two to four years. This, I think,

is mostly a problem of winter hardiness and wetness, as it is even more fussy about excellent drainage than the wild pink, and wet springs will take their toll in all but the best-drained locations. In the wild, I have often seen it surrounded by a ground cover of bluets, growing in sandy, dry soil in light shade where it forms large, open colonies of great beauty.

13 Specialty Plants

Shade

Clintonia borealis Blue Beadlily

Just seeing a bold clump of blue beadlily in the dappled shade of a garden brings back fond memories of visits to Maine, where I have seen this engaging plant growing in sizable groups. There, they colonized the woods floor beneath spruce trees, where the soils were black, moist, humusy and acid. They grew even more densely in areas where additional sunlight filtered through the shade canopy.

In the mountains of the South, the speckled beadlily (*C. umbellulata*) can be found growing in the same kind of cool habitat and acid soil.

When they are in flower, beadlilies are very appealing. The blue beadlily, shown here, has stems 8 to 10 inches tall with loose terminal clusters of greenish-yellow flowers that resemble miniature Canada lilies (*Lilium canadense*) in shape. The speckled beadlily features clusters of sparkling white flowers. The fruit that gives this plant its name is reminiscent of the edible blueberry, and replaces the flowers in late summer.

Both species require the same conditions in a garden, though they need not grow under spruce. They will also do fine beneath oaks and hickories, but the air must be cool and the soils intensely acid and always moist. The beadlilies, therefore, are obviously not plants for the warmer parts of the country or those areas that have long, hot summers.

If they are happy, their stoloniferous roots will gradually spread and, in time, form sizable clumps reminiscent of those found in wild stands. Their succulent, pale green foliage overlaid with fine white hairs gives them a glaucous-gray appearance that is always a welcome and cooling sight.

Natural companions include plants that require strongly acid soil and a cool environment, like the painted trillium (*Trillium undulatum*), bunchberry (*Cornus canadensis*), twinflower (*Linnaea borealis*) and goldthread (*Coptis groenlandica*). Other plants that do not require these conditions but will tolerate them can be added to the display, including other species of trilliums, devil's bit (*Chamaelirium luteum*), oconee bells (*Shortia galacifolia*), box huckleberry (*Gaylussacia brachycera*) and cliff-green (*Paxistima canbyi*).

Coptis groenlandica Goldthread

One of the loveliest sights I've ever seen was a sunny, wet glade with an edging of cinnamon fern (*Osmunda cinnamomea*) and moisture-loving coast azalea (*Rhododendron atlanticum*). The setting became even more appealing when, on closer inspection, I saw a carpet of goldthread running over the ground. In the background along the wood margin were wayfaring trees (*Viburnum alnifolium*) and other native azaleas, and in the sunny foreground at the edge of standing water were cardinal flowers (*Lobelia cardinalis*) and sphagnum moss (*Sphagnum* species), through which goldthread was intertwined.

Goldthread will form beautiful colonies in cool, damp, shaded spots where the soil is humusy and acid. The small, intricate foliage is extremely pretty and is topped in early summer with tiny sparkling-white flowers. Under good cultivation, the inch-high mats, which follow the contours of the woodland floor, will grow thickly. In heavy shade, however, goldthread will be somewhat sparse and will not flower as well.

This is a perfect plant for the acid, moist environs of a bog. It is particularly attractive trailing over hummocks and growing beneath the bog orchids that favor such spots. In the cool air of this environment, goldthread is happy growing in full sun. If plenty of well-decomposed leaf mold is added to the soil in a cool, moist woodland corner, goldthread will prosper, even if the area is not as wet as a bog would be.

🌸 *Cornus canadensis*
Bunchberry

When it is happy, bunchberry will cover the ground in dense mats of evergreen foliage. And, as it is a stoloniferous plant, it has the potential to form sizable colonies in the garden or in the wild. In spring these mats support myriad white flower-like structures. These flowers' white "petals" are really bracts; the true flowers are the insignificant small clusters of stamens in the centers. (This is also true with the ornamental tree-forming dogwoods—relatives of bunchberry—that are so highly praised for their outstanding "floral" displays.) By late summer, the flowers have developed into clusters of spectacular bright red berries.

Bunchberry is a plant for cool acid soils that never dry out—even in summer, the soil must be damp. Although it does not have to be grown in a bog garden, a hummock in a bog is an ideal location for it. Planting it beside a rotting log or tree stump will also make it happy, because it will easily be able to get its roots down into the soft, crumbly wetness of the moisture-retentive wood. This is also a good way to display this delightful plant, especially if the remnants of wood happen to be covered in moss. In a garden, bunchberry is most usually seen in association with beadlilies, twinflower, dwarf ginseng (*Panax trifolium*) and the other plants that must have similar growing conditions.

If possible, try to acquire bunchberry plants that are well established in containers, as they transplant more easily. These will have originated from seed or from cuttings; the latter are quite difficult to produce. If you are rescuing this plant, be sure to dig large, deep clumps, just as you would for other trailing plants. This ensures that the majority of the finely rooted stolons are essentially undisturbed.

🌸 *Linnaea borealis*
Twinflower

Here is a plant for cool, moist shade where the soil is acid. In such a place, twinflower will thrive, and its prostrate stems clothed in tiny leaves will gradually weave themselves over the ground, eventually forming dense mats. In late spring 1-inch-high stems rise from the bed of dark green, each carrying a pair of white trumpets flushed with deep pink. If you get close to them, their delicate fragrance is an added pleasure.

Twinflower is one of the most delicate and enchanting of flowers, and it is a perfect companion for other plants that also need northern conditions, such as grass of Parnassus (*Parnassia glauca*), goldthread, bunchberry and the bog orchids. It is also beautiful grown beneath painted trillium, showy lady's-slipper (*Cypripedium reginae*) and grass pink (*Calopogon pulchellus*).

In the northern parts of New England, I have seen cold sphagnum-covered bogs hidden beneath solid mats of twinflower many feet square growing among an equally dense cover of bunchberry. Both were so thick and luxuriant that one would

never have believed how difficult both species are to get established in cultivation. Both will grow in shade or in full sun in cool northern climates or at high altitudes.

As with so many plants, however, once the right place has been found for it and the climate is to its liking, twinflower will be a long-lived and easily maintained wildflower. If this plant is not grown in a bog, the soil must be kept moist and enriched with well-decayed acid leaf mold.

🌸 *Panax trifolium*
Dwarf Ginseng

A diminutive treasure just 1 or 2 inches high, dwarf ginseng is often found in heavily shaded areas alongside a stream or in wet places where the soils are acid and dark from the high humus content. I have often seen them beside a brook on slightly elevated ground that escapes most spring floods. (An occasional inundation does it no harm.)

The intricately cut, deep green foliage is in perfect harmony with the tiny globes formed by the white flowers. It is a companionable plant and grows well with trout lily (*Erythronium americanum*), dewdrop (*Dalibarda repens*) and oak fern (*Gymnocarpium dryopteris*). The dwarf ginseng may be crowded out, however, by larger or more vigorous neighbors.

Great care is needed in transplanting, especially with tiny seedlings.

The stems are brittle and can easily be damaged if they are not handled with care. Planting dwarf ginseng in a sheltered niche will give it protection and provide a setting to show off its special charm.

Sun

✿ *Calla palustris*
Wild Calla

Wild calla is found only in the specialized habitat of acid bogs in the cool climates of North America, Europe and Asia, where it forms extensive colonies. There, calla grows luxuriantly, along with cotton grass (*Eriophorum* species) and bog orchids, among the sphagnum moss that lies over the water of these bogs. In such settings the large white spathes—reminiscent of huge petals—appear in spring and seem to hold the very essence of wild, isolated places.

Early in the year, calla can be found growing in shallow standing water. As the seasons advance, this surface water may disappear, but the black, oozy-muck soils are always

saturated. In a garden setting, it will grow in the wet edges of a pond or swampy place so long as the soil is very acid and has a high humus content, and so long as there is no competition from other plants.

Once it is given the conditions it must have, it is not difficult to grow and often reblooms in summer. Later in the year, thick clusters of scarlet berries, reminiscent of Jack-in-the-pulpit (*Arisaema triphyllum*), develop from the insignificant flowers that were produced inside the decorative spathes.

✿ *Drosera filiformis*
Threadleaved Sundew

Sundews are small, inconspicuous plants that can be found nestled down in cushiony mats of sphagnum moss along with the wren's-egg cranberry (*Vaccinium oxycoccos*), rose pogonia (*Pogonia ophioglossoides*) and creeping snowberry (*Chiogenes hispidula*), all of which thrive in the highly specialized environment of a bog.

Most people, especially children, are familiar with this insectivorous plant that is covered with sticky hairs that entrap unsuspecting

insects which the plant then digests. The drops of sticky fluid on the plant's hairs sparkle like tiny crystals in the sun, rewarding with their great charm anyone who lingers to examine them, while the dark red color of the stems provides an additional handsome accent.

Sundews are easy to miss, but when they flower (especially the threadleaved species) they become quite noticeable. The delicate stems carry several beautiful small flowers in a soft pink that is attractive against a bog's carpet of pale green sphagnum.

In a carefully built contrived bog, the sundews will grow easily wherever their fine, filamentlike roots can thread themselves through beds of sphagnum. It is vital that this covering mat never dry out, for if it does, these delicate structures will quickly die.

In time and with attention to the plant's needs, tiny seedlings will be found scattered near the parent; these will be the foundation of the colonies that are typically seen when sundews are growing under favorable conditions.

✿ *Habenaria psycodes*
Purple Fringed Orchid

Although creating an artificial bog garden is a great deal of work, the labor is amply rewarded when the flowers of this beautiful plant bloom. The sturdy stems grow 15 to 18 inches high and in summer carry numerous rich light purple flowers. These are so unusual and beautiful that I enjoy any excuse and opportunity to savor them and the overall pleasant environs of a bog garden, however small it is. It is here that the soft green of sphagnum moss, laced with creeping snowberry, casts a refreshing mantle and provides just the right setting for cotton grass, purple pitcher plant (*Sarracenia purpurea*), and the other species of this lovely orchid.

Other members of this particular group of orchids include the delicate yellow fringed orchid (*H. ciliaris*), with its many soft orange-yellow flowers, and the ragged fringed orchid (*H. lacera*), which has very deeply dissected white flowers with a distinctive green overlay. The white fringed orchid (*H. blephariglottis*) has clear, sparkling white flowers and less fringing than others of the species.

Though all of the fringed orchids vary somewhat in the size and color

of their flowers and in the depth of the flowers' fringe, all of them can be grown in an artificial bog and will produce a magnificent display.

These are very specialized plants, suitable only for the environs of a bog garden, where they are best planted on low hummocks. Their crowns should be above any standing water, but their thick fleshy roots must be set into the soil of the hummock so they can grow down into the permanently wet ground. The crown should have its tip just at or slightly above soil level, and a protective layer of live sphagnum needs to be tucked around the crown as a moist cover.

In time, a single crown will grow large enough to produce small secondary crowns that can be separated by experienced hands.

Plants should be purchased only from a reputable nursery that produces plants by division and does not collect them from the wild. Or plants should come from friends willing to part with extras.

Sarracenia purpurea
Purple Pitcher Plant

The unusual—almost prehistoric —appearance of the insectivorous pitcher plant creates dramatic, eye-catching splashes of maroon among what, from a distance, appears to be the predominantly green palette of a summer bog. The pitchers grow to a height of 4 to 6 inches. In summer, rich maroon flowers bloom on 12-inch-high stems.

Its cousin, the much taller trumpet pitcher plant (*S. flava*), is even more ornamental, with its yellow-chartreuse flowers and leaves. It can be expected to reach 15 to 18 inches in a garden, though it will attain a height of 2 to 3 feet in the wild.

Both are truly spectacular plants, and both have the well-known pitcher-shaped leaves that form highly stylized tubes and hold a pool of water at the base. The lips of these pitchers have a dense covering of downward-pointing hairs which prevent insects that have ventured into them from escaping. After the plant has trapped its prey inside the pitcher, enzymes in the pool digest the insects.

Both of these pitcher plants are

relatively easy to cultivate in the environs of a bog garden, where they can be planted either on level ground that in spring may have considerable standing water, or on the elevated hummocks where their roots can grow down into the dark, wet, acid humus.

Pitcher plants germinate easily from seed and thus can be readily grown by a nursery for sale. There should be no need to collect them from the wild.

There are other species of pitcher plants that are quite rare and even more ornate. Some have especially strange-looking pitchers, and, in the white trumpet pitcher plant (*S. leucophylla*), they can reach 36 inches or more in height. It is a thrilling sight to see a large wild stand of white trumpet pitcher plant, but unfortunately, it is a rare sight today because of the destruction of their habitat and overzealous collecting by unscrupulous individuals. I am always saddened to see these wildlings of cool, spacious bogs stuffed into cramped, stale terrariums—where many people put them—and I remember vast, wild and uninhabited areas I have been fortunate to see covered with these plants.

PART III
Creating
Your Garden

*A garden is a grand teacher.
It teaches patience and careful
watchfulness; it teaches industry
and thrift; above all it teaches
entire trust.*

GERTRUDE JEKYLL

TO CREATE A WILDFLOWER GARDEN, a gardener must first learn as much as possible about each plant's natural environment, as explained in Part II, "The Wildflowers." When you understand the needs of the plants you want to grow, you can decide whether they will fit into your garden, and, if so, where. The following chapters will help you determine the kind of adjustments necessary to grow them successfully.

Site selection and soil preparation are key elements of a flourishing garden. For example, think of the differences between the soil of a cultivated rose garden and that of a woodland. In a woodland, the soil has developed relatively undisturbed for years. There is far more decomposed organic matter (humus) and far less loam in the woodland than in the rose garden. Of course, woodland soils in different parts of North America will vary, depending upon quantity and type of vegetation, underlying soil, climate and so on—but there is no cultivated rose garden anywhere that is similar in soil composition to an undisturbed woodland floor.

As your knowledge of specific plants, soils and other factors in plant growth expands, a cohesive garden design can evolve through your understanding of the plants, the nature of the site and your own love of color and form.

Plant selection must take all these elements into consideration. During this process, you may discover that some of the plants you had hoped to grow are just not suitable for your particular location. The plants you do choose to grow, however, should prosper, because you will have acquired an awareness of their needs and of your ability to create a suitable environment for them.

Once the plants are established and thriving, good regular maintenance is crucial. In the wild, these plants maintain their ecological position through complex relationships with other plants, animals, insects and climate. In your garden, you will need to substitute your own careful maintenance schedule to approximate the balance of the natural cycles, and you will need to orchestrate all the interrelated factors that influence the success of a garden.

*The stately flowering spires of tall
bugbane (*Cimicifuga racemosa*) make
it suitable not only for the woodland
garden but also for the formal border.*

14

What Kind of Wildflower Garden Is Right for You?

PATIENCE AND PLANNING. How dull that sounds to a gardener who is eagerly awaiting the time when the digging, planting and nurturing can begin! But plan you must, and patience you must have, to achieve a successful garden and provide the best conditions for the plants you have been longing to grow.

Garden plans of some kind are necessary, but these do not have to be flat, sterile-looking blueprints, which are never able to convey all the colorful images you have created for your garden. For most people, something simpler will do: a list, perhaps some notes, and a few basic sketches gathered together during the time you have been thinking of having a wildflower garden.

The planning of a garden should not be a hasty process; ideally, it should take no less than one full growing season so that all the necessary information can be compiled. A good garden plan stems from a full understanding of the site, plus as much knowledge as you can gather about the plants you hope to grow. (See Appendix B for a list of recommended books on gardening.)

Because this planning phase is the most critical stage of creating a successful garden, you should expect to put at least as much time, effort and thought into planning your garden as you would into redecorating your house. If the garden is well planned and well cared for, it will certainly last longer than wallpaper and paint!

In the first section of this book, we looked at different types of gardens that feature wildflowers and also examined how these plants can be incorporated into an existing garden. This chapter will help you determine what sort of garden you'd like to have, what will be involved in its creation and whether this undertaking is possible for you.

To help you begin the planning process and decide what kind of garden will work for you, I have listed below a number of questions. If you jot down the answers and make notes of other ideas that may occur to you while you go through this list, you will begin to develop a clearer understanding of what it is that you really want and what's involved in achieving it. Then you can decide if it's feasible.

Restraint used here will prevent frustration and disappointment later and will bring ample rewards in the end, in the form of the enjoyment you will get from having a garden you are proud of and plants that grow well for you. If you have tried to grow wildflowers before and have been unsuccessful, these questions may also reveal why you were disappointed and how things might be done differently in the future.

This evaluation process should not be very time-consuming, and it can be an enjoyable pastime, especially in winter or summer when gardening demands are not great. If you have planned well, then when the time comes to make the design, lay out the beds, prepare the soils and finally put in the plants, you will have solved most problems ahead of time. Things should progress smoothly because you have a clear objective in mind. It's still important to be flexible, of course; even with all this preparation, I still find I make some on-the-spot changes and refinements when I am preparing and planting the garden, and this is all to the good.

The first objective in the initial planning stage is to have a good understanding of the cultural requirements of the wildflowers themselves. Then you will know what plants will be most suitable for you to try and where they will be most likely to grow best. So much can be learned from observing plants in their natural habitats, where conditions are best suited for their optimum growth. A great deal of information can be gleaned from books, and all this information can make good sense, but it does not offer the same immediacy or clarity as seeing plants in the complexities of real life. Plants growing in the wild also sharpen one's powers of observation, challenging our ability to reason why some plants are adapted to particular conditions.

The second objective is to fully understand *your* garden environment, so you will be able to take advantage of all the special places and microclimates within it. This knowledge will enable you to grow a broader range of wildflowers, because you will be able to find that special spot where a certain plant will grow—perhaps even after it has defied cultivation elsewhere on your property.

This information will also give you a good idea of how to use and integrate the wildflowers most effectively in the garden. At this point, the natural features of the property should be considered to determine how they can become part of the design. What will the overall design be, where can any new beds or areas be planted, how large will they be, what changes must be made to existing beds, and what effects are desired?

To help the garden begin to take shape in your mind and on paper, consider the following questions.

1. Why do you want a wildflower garden?

This is a question so basic that few of us ever consider asking it. Instead, our gardens usually evolve rather randomly in response to any number of things: a desire to grow certain plants, the need to find a place to plant the wildflowers a friend has given us, or perhaps a sudden impulse that results from reading an exciting article about growing wildflowers.

There is a better (and certainly more successful) way to find the answers to this question, but it does require a little forethought and—as I mentioned earlier—some patience. Give some thought to these questions:

Is this wildflower garden going to be a place to work in for the sheer pleasure of pottering about with the plants? Will you be working actively with them a great deal of the time? Or do you primarily want to have a display garden that, once created, will be easily maintained with a minimum of personal involvement?

Do you want to grow rare and difficult plants, or do you want a garden with a grand and spectacular display?

Are you looking for a special kind of garden? Perhaps you want a garden to attract butterflies or provide food for birds. Or you might want to introduce young children to the concept of preservation and develop in them an appreciation for wild things in general.

Do you want to incorporate wildflowers into an existing garden? Or will this be an entirely new area, previously uncultivated?

What are the effects you're looking for? Do you want to enhance an existing woodland area by adding plants and a path or two? Perhaps the path is in place, and your goal is to make the area near it more beautiful.

What sort of look do you want to achieve? In a woodland setting, you might want intense plantings near paths that fan out into the woods; or perhaps the idea is to create a lighter planting spread through the whole area to give a feeling of a natural wood rather than a garden environment. In a meadow garden, do you prefer a natural-appearing display of random colors, or a more ordered design?

2. When and where do you want the primary displays to occur?

You may, as I do, hope to be out enjoying your garden every month of the year, or you may want the primary display to occur during a particular month or season. If, for instance, you are away at certain times of each year, there is little point in having the garden look spectacular and full of color during those times.

List all the months in which you would like to have something of interest in the garden, and note those months when you'd like to have the most impressive displays. (And remember to consider not only the flower, but *all* the different attributes of a plant that may contribute to its display, from the first shoots in the spring to the seed heads and dried stems in the winter.)

Ask yourself if it is important to have something of specific interest in your wildflower garden during the winter months. If winters in your area are severe, you may not be too concerned with this, although anything that reminds us of spring—a hint of color from some berries, clusters of fluffy seed heads, or better still the expanding buds of witchhazel (*Hamamelis* species) and Christmas rose (*Helleborus niger*)—will provide a welcome uplift in those long dormant months. If you live where the winters are mild and short, you can plan to have a fine display throughout this season, which is far from a dormant time in many parts of the country.

From where will the wildflowers be seen most often? Is there a particular window, patio or doorway from which you like to view your garden? Perhaps you will most often see it from a deck or terrace. It is not hard to plan displays around the time of year these areas are most often used. Or your decision might be as simple as planting a few favorite wildflowers in the immediate area near a log you like to sit on for a few quiet minutes at the end of the day.

Christmas rose (Helleborus niger) *is an early harbinger of spring.*

3. How big do you want the garden to be?

What size do you envision the final garden to be? If it is a large area, can its creation be broken down into manageable stages that can be developed over a period of time? This is an important consideration for a large garden area.

How much of the property do you want to ultimately develop or convert to wildflowers? Will it be a small shady corner, a border running along a fence, an island border curving through a lawn or along a driveway? Perhaps your goal is to turn an abandoned wild place into a beautiful meadow, or you might secretly want to have wildflowers growing over your whole property. (This isn't such a far-fetched idea with a small area.)

And most importantly, can you reasonably maintain—and enjoy—the size of garden you hope to have?

4. Who will use your garden, and how?

Will your garden be a private place for your own enjoyment, or do you anticipate having family and friends visit it with you? Sharing your garden with others can bring great enjoyment, but if your wildflower garden is to be frequented by many people and pets (especially exuberant children and dogs) you will want to be sure you have allowed enough room for walking and browsing. You may want to place some sturdy plants near the edges of the planting beds to protect other, more fragile ones. And if you have very young children, remember to keep all toxic plants out of their easy reach.

If your garden is going to be where your children and pets take a short cut to their friends' house next door, will it be easier to relocate the planned border or retrain them to take another route? Or should you simply put in a path? All of us have unplanned paths in our gardens, worn from constant use by people and animals who have found the most convenient way to go from point A to point B. This may seem like a minor problem, but it can become a major and unattractive annoyance.

5. Where do you want the garden to be?

If you have a location already in mind, consider its advantages and disadvantages and think of how these will affect what you can grow and maintain. Will the garden be at the bottom of an incline or in a water-catchment area? Is it a frost pocket or on the north side of a house, with little sunlight? Do you have a windy, exposed hillside or a protected bank?

Remember that with wildflowers we need to select the plants that we think are most suitable for the environment we have, rather than acquire the plants and then find a place for them. (Although this inevitably happens, from time to time, with all gardeners.)

6. What does the "site analysis" show?

An informal but detailed site analysis will give you some very specific information about your property and your garden site. (See pages 134–141 for more information about evaluating your site.) If you are starting with a wild area, there will already be some plants growing there naturally, and you should identify and list them. These are "indicator plants" and, once you find out what they are and what kind of habitat they prefer, you will have a good idea of what your present conditions on this site are: whether the soils are infertile or rich, dry or wet, and so forth. (You may even want to keep some of these plants and incorporate them into the new planting.)

What is the soil like? Is it acid or alkaline? Is it a heavy clay soil or a light one with plenty of sand or gravel mixed in? Is it high in organic matter, or relatively infertile and lean? This information will affect the amount of preparatory work you'll need to do, and it will also—to some extent—dictate your selection of plants.

How much moisture is in the ground? Is there a high water table that keeps the ground damp or wet all year round? Are there seasonal wet spots? What happens during the summer months? If there are areas that become severely dry during the summer, can you easily get water to them? When it rains, are there low spots that always accumulate rain and might be prone to flooding or damage from runoff?

How much shade is there, and how much shade do you need to have for the plants you want to grow? If the area consists of sparse grass under some shade trees because there isn't enough light under them to establish a really good lawn, it might make sense to turn this area into a garden for shade-loving plants instead.

How does the shade change throughout the day and the seasons of the year? Where is it heaviest and lightest? Do you need to remove a tree or two, or some of the lower limbs from the trees, to improve the quality of light for certain plants?

What is the lay of the land? Is it flat or undulating? Are there rocky outcroppings or a stream? How could these be worked into a garden?

If your property is flat and there are no special features, don't be discouraged. You can create a delightful garden, full of interest and surprises, in such a place. Because we are stimulated by natural features, we often think it is necessary to have some particular attraction to work with—a few shade trees, a woodland stream, or some sort of beautiful setting—before we can have a beautiful garden. These are definitely assets, but they aren't prerequisites to having a fine garden.

7. *What plants do you want to have growing in your wildflower garden?*

This question comes toward the last, not at first, because the wildflowers you can grow successfully will be influenced by all the other factors listed above.

As you begin to make a list of plants that might do well in the site you have chosen for your garden, you'll be thinking of additional factors as well:

How tall does a particular plant get? How much room does it need?

What are its displays? When does it bloom and for how long? What colors will it add to the display?

These last issues are covered more fully in Chapter 15, "Using Wildflowers in Your Garden," but you'll need to keep them in mind even in the earliest stages of planning.

As you draw up your list of plants, I strongly suggest that you follow these recommendations:

Begin with just a few varieties or species of plants, no more than six or seven at most, and choose ones that are easy to grow. Any of the Stalwarts would be excellent choices. By starting with a simple design and a manageable number of plants, you will be better able to keep track of what works and what doesn't—and you'll also be more certain of success in your first attempts.

Expand gradually. As your knowledge of the plants and of your property increases, you'll be able to experiment with different plants and broaden the scope of your garden. During this time, your original planting will be growing, filling out and becoming the body of the design you have been working to achieve. You will be, in fact, getting the look of a garden while learning how the wildlings will grow for you.

Be flexible. In a wildflower garden—as in any garden—you will probably want to move some plants, change some groupings, and

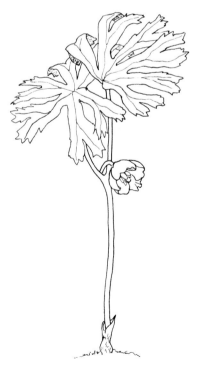

Mayapple (Podophyllum peltatum)

improve or alter the original design. Think of these changes as refinements, not radical revisions, to your overall ideas.

8. What sort of an effort will be required to create and maintain your garden? (And how much will it cost?)

It is vital to have a realistic understanding of everything that may be necessary to create your garden before you take out the chain saw, garden fork and wheelbarrow.

Tree work will be required for any woodland garden and may entail hiring professionals. (See Chapter 16, "Building a Wildflower Garden.") Building the beds—even small ones—entails some rather strenuous work, especially in a wooded area. Beds near trees will probably have to be dug by hand because the tree roots make it very difficult to use machinery.

Putting a new bed into a lawn area requires removing all the existing grass and deeply working and improving the soil. If you are planning to renovate a bed, the plants that are already growing there will have to be dug up and moved to temporary homes while the bed is reworked if they are to be part of the new garden, or relocated to another garden. Any old, straggly shrubs should be taken out and hauled away.

Once the clearing work is done, you must acquire and incorporate the necessary materials to improve the soil, and you must obtain the wildflowers, plant and mulch them, and keep them watered and cared for as they establish themselves.

Then, of course, there is the general maintenance—the weeding, watering, fertilizing and (where necessary) winterizing. This is just as much a part of wildflower gardening as it is of any other gardening endeavor. For most of us, this work is a true pleasure—if it is kept within sensible bounds so we don't feel overwhelmed by it.

The financial outlay can vary considerably. If you plan to do all of the labor yourself, if you have a ready supply of manure, leaf mold, sand or whatever you might need for improving the soil, if you can trade plants and seeds with friends—you will be able to create your wildflower garden with relatively little expenditure. For most people, however, a realistic budget will have to include initial expenditures for most if not all of these items, certainly in the early stages.

For each person and for each garden, the necessary tasks will be different and will depend on any number of factors—from the type of soil, the availability of organic matter (compost or manure), and how far you will have to haul everything, to how much time you have available to spend in the garden.

So the question of "What commitment can you comfortably make in terms of time, effort and money?" is a valid one. The goal is not only to have a beautiful garden, but also to enjoy planning, installing and taking care of it.

Considerations for Site Evaluation

To answer some of the questions raised above, it will be helpful to take a closer look at the various elements that are essential to any successful garden.

Water

Water plays a vital role in the cultivation of wildflowers, beyond the basic need for water shared by all plants. How much is enough, and what is excessive? This is an area where close observation and a sound understanding of a plant's requirements will mean the difference between success and failure.

Not all wildflowers need equal amounts of water, nor do they need it in the same quantity throughout the growing season. In this way, wildflowers differ greatly from more traditional garden plants, almost all of which have similar needs and are tolerant of a broader range of watering practices (or the lack of them!).

For instance, some wildflowers need a summer baking, while others do best if the soil is moist all year round, even if they go dormant in the summer like shooting-star (*Dodecatheon meadia*) and spring beauty (*Claytonia virginica*). In the wild, these plants are generally found in soils that have additional moisture in spring and never dry out completely during the summer. In a garden, they will do best if they are placed in similar conditions and planted in a moisture-retentive soil that is kept well watered.

It is crucial to understand the difference between "moist" soils and "wet" soils. Wet soils have a high water content: when they are squeezed, water runs or oozes out of them. Moist soils have a nice damp feel, but there is no excess water; this degree of soil moisture closely resembles what you have in your garden or in your houseplant soil the day after you have given it a deep, thorough watering.

If your property encompasses several different habitats, it will be important for you to learn of any differences in the groundwater and to find which areas, if any, have a high water table, before you select the site for your gardens or choose the plants.

How do you learn about this? Indicator plants (those that are currently growing on the land) will tell you quite a bit about the soil moisture.

Skunk cabbage (*Symplocarpus foetidus*) and false hellebore (*Veratrum viride*), for example, mark a wet, swampy area with a high water table. There may not be any water visible during a dry August, but these plants flourish because the high water table keeps the ground itself wet year-round. You can further determine soil moisture by digging into the soil with a trowel to see just how wet it is. Sometimes when I have done this in an area that I suspected was rather wet, the hole has slowly filled with water seeping in from the surrounding saturated earth, even though there was no indication of this degree of moisture on the surface, a situation that can be especially deceiving to an inexperienced eye. On the other hand, if a pool visible in April is still there in August, this definitely indicates the presence of a high water table and abundant soil moisture.

By contrast, a vernal pool is a depression that is fed by water from the winter and spring runoff, and it will dry out in the summer. Here the effect is temporary and is not due to the level of the water table. Because of this, plants grown near a vernal pool will have an abundance of natural moisture in the spring but no more than those on the rest of the property in summer. Therefore you are going to have to water during the dry months if you decide to plant this area, especially if you have chosen to grow plants that are suited to the wet soils found in spring.

I have often seen people misled by these seasonal pools and wet areas. A gardener will set plants that need plenty of year-round mois-

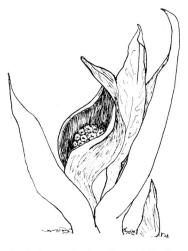

The dark green leathery leaves of skunk cabbage (Symplocarpus foetidus) *are good companions for ferns and other plants with more delicate foliage.*

ture near a vernal pool or stream, and then as the season advances the water dries up. This means that either the plants languish and perhaps die or the gardener spends hours of toil dragging hose lines around to water the garden.

The presence or absence of water (natural or artificial) greatly affects the range of plants that can be successfully grown in any garden. This is because the soil temperature of a permanently wet or a moist area will be several degrees cooler than that of a dry one in the same general location. In hot weather, both a moist soil and a wet soil have a cooling effect on the roots and above-ground parts of plants. This is created by the simple presence of moisture and by the process of its evaporation. Depending on where the plants are located in relation to the source of water, the amount of soil moisture will vary considerably, enabling you to grow many plants with different soil-moisture requirements in a relatively small space.

It is also important to know how long moisture remains in the upper soil levels, as this is the "root zone"—the area where the vast majority of perennials (and many trees also) have their roots. The depth of this will vary according to where you live, but 12 to 15 inches is a good guideline to keep in mind when you examine your property and prepare your soil.

Once you understand the importance of soil moisture, you will have a much clearer idea of what plants you can grow well. Some want a high degree of moisture, while others will rot if they are planted in soils with a high moisture content (especially around their crowns), or if water does not drain away quickly after a rain or snowmelt. (One way to deal with a plant known to be sensitive to excessive soil moisture is to set it on a gentle slope or raised area, thus facilitating drainage.)

For most plants, there must be a balance between moisture retention and good drainage. This is frequently referred to in gardening literature as: "Needs a moisture-retentive soil that is well drained." At first, this sounds like a contradiction; what it is saying, however, is that the plant needs a soil that has enough organic matter (humus, compost, manure and the like) mixed into it to absorb and retain water, and at the same time has enough drainage material (sand, small stones, or gravel) in it to allow excess moisture to drain off after the organic matter has soaked up all the water it can.

There is always competition in the soil for water. Think of the amount of soil moisture needed to support all the plants in a woodland area, from 80-foot trees and young saplings to the daintiest of wildflowers. In nature, these plants and their environment will be in a balance that has evolved over eons; in our gardens, we have to create that balance in a relatively short period of time, by using a well-prepared soil, selecting and placing the plants properly and providing sufficient water during dry spells.

In general, the sun-loving wildflowers grow well in a rather infertile, lean soil that is low in organic matter, nutrients and moisture. Their requirements are very different from the soil and moisture needs of shade-loving plants. As a result, the wildflowers that prefer sun have a deeper and more tenacious root system to enable them to find available moisture and compete with other, often aggressive plants found in their habitats.

At the other extreme are the plants that grow beside or in perpetually wet places—bogs, swamps, streams and ponds. Some water-loving plants are found growing on slightly elevated ground or hummocks, with their crowns above the water or the saturated earth but their roots down in the wet soils. This is the case with many of the bog plants—in particular the orchids. I have also seen highbush blueberry (*Vaccinium corymbosum*) and the osmunda ferns thriving in the wild in what initially appeared to be a pool. On looking closer, however, I found that they were set up on hummocks covered with sphagnum moss. These plants, like many other wetland residents, also grow well under more usual garden conditions, provided they are given a moisture-retentive soil and ample water year-round (which may mean no more than a good soaking once or twice a week during hot, dry summer months).

The same is true of two of our loveliest meadow plants, Turk's-cap (*Lilium superbum*) and Canada lily (*Lilium canadense*). In nature, these are found in damp meadows, but a lily's worst enemy is too much soil moisture around the bulb, because this will quickly cause it to rot. If the bulbs of these somewhat specialized plants are elevated above the wet so there is good drainage around the bulb itself but the roots can get down in the cool, damp—even wet—soil, they are perfectly content. Knowing these things makes it possible for you to select plants that will do well in a wet area, even though your first thought might have been that few plants with attractive flowers or any ornamental value could be grown there.

With some plants, it is a combination of factors that causes them to thrive or languish. Many of the plants from northern locations or high elevations need a cool, moist root zone and cool air temperatures (especially during the summer months); they also dislike high humidity. Simply giving them a well-prepared, moist soil isn't enough. This is the case with bunchberry (*Cornus canadensis*) and goldthread (*Coptis groenlandica*), both of which soon succumb to dry, warm soils, high air temperatures and high humidity. In nature, these two (along with many companion plants) are found mostly in cool bogs in the North, or in high mountain wetlands in the South where the elevation creates conditions similar to those of the North.

What are the seasonal needs of a plant for water? Some tolerate very cold weather but dislike cold, wet soils in winter and spring, and will tend to rot if drainage is not good at that time. Stokes' aster (*Stokesia laevis*) and mossy phlox (*Phlox subulata*) are examples of this. Both are easy, tough plants, but both have one prime requirement: good drainage. So often when a plant is lost over the winter, someone will say, "Oh, it's not winter-hardy," when in fact the plant died because of sodden soil in February or March. This is a cultural problem, not a climatic one. If you can find out what caused a plant's demise (and this is not always possible), then you will have an opportunity to succeed with it next time by changing the unsuitable conditions or relocating it.

Both the distribution and circulation of water in a soil are important to maintain the proper level of moisture and disseminate nutrients through the soil. When we consider good water circulation, we should also realize that good air circulation in the soil is just as important and also affects how well plants perform. If a soil is properly prepared, both air and water will move through it well. (See Chapter 16, "Building a Wildflower Garden.")

The Turk's-cap lily (Lilium superbum) *is a stately plant for a sunny place where its large, bright flowers will always attract attention.*

Light

Sunlight, like water, plays a vital role in determining the degree of success you will have in your wildflower garden. It is light that enables plants to produce the food they need to grow, and each one requires a certain quality and quantity of light to prosper. A surprising number of plants seem to do well in sun or shade—as long as neither condition is really extreme—while many others simply will not grow in what is, for them, the wrong light conditions. Consider, especially, the area of transition from sun to shade that is typically found at the edge of a wood. In such a location, plants must be able to tolerate variations in both the quantity and quality of light, from shade to full sun. A number of lovely wildflowers find this transition zone much to their liking. Bowman's root (*Gillenia trifoliata*), wild cranesbill (*Geranium maculatum*) and golden star (*Chrysogonum virginianum*) all do well here.

The quality of light is one of the more complex and misunderstood of horticultural elements. To understand fully its importance, we must clearly define the terms we use: shade, part shade, partial shade, filtered light, and so on. Interpretations will vary from gardener to gardener, so it is often useful to refer to light conditions in terms of what will grow in them.

For instance, English ivy (*Hedera helix*) is one of the few plants that grows well in dense shade—and even it will grow only if that shade is primarily from deciduous trees, not from the almost-impenetrable cover created by conifers (especially hemlocks). I am always surprised by the number of gardeners who try to grow things in such dark, gloomy places and wonder why everything is doing poorly. Then they want to know what sort of plants can be grown there, instead of asking what they can do to improve the site so that plants will grow well and bloom.

Woodland plants actually require good light conditions in which to grow vigorously and bloom well. Although we think of these primarily as shade-lovers, remember that most woodland wildflowers bloom early in the spring, before the leaves of deciduous trees are fully expanded, so these plants are, in fact, flowering in full sunlight (or close to it). In most places, the sunlight in early spring is neither intense nor hot—but it is warm, and this warmth on soil and plants is important, because it induces the plants to grow and flower. Once the deciduous trees have fully leafed out, the plants then grow happily in the shade, which is essential because it protects them from the searing summer sun. (When soil is exposed to sun and wind, it dries out far more quickly and also warms up faster than shaded soil, and this can have a detrimental effect on many plants.)

What we call woodland "shade," then, is actually a seasonal shade. It is never the deep, dark shade of a hemlock or pine grove. A shade cover should be high enough and light enough so that diffused or dappled light filters down onto the plants. The shade canopy breaks up the direct rays of sunlight, so that light is present without the full intensity of the sun. In a woodland, plants will receive filtered light all day—perhaps with occasional periods when the sunlight may stream through an opening in the canopy—but they will never have full sun beating relentlessly down on them.

If a shady area receives direct sunlight at any time of the day other than in the early morning or late afternoon, you will have to select

Wild cranesbill (Geranium maculatum) *is an easily grown wildflower for sun or light shade.*

plants for that location that will tolerate this amount of sun. If you have studied the area, you will know where these spots are, when they are in sun, and for how long.

The shade doesn't always have to come from tall trees. Many times, light can be deflected in simple ways: smaller plants can be shielded by taller ones or nestled behind a rock or tree stump. This will give them extra protection especially at ground level where the shade will help reduce the evaporation of moisture from the soil and keep it cool. The north side of a building can create a perfect spot of shade for those wildflowers that do not want any exposure to sun. This shade will be denser and more uniform, and it will not have the dappled effect produced by tree leaves. This may cause some plants, however, to exhibit less compact growth habits and somewhat lighter flowering.

"Part shade" is such a nebulous term that it's next to impossible to know what people actually mean by it. Even among gardeners, there are widely differing interpretations for it. For my purposes, part shade simply means shade of some kind during part of the day and sun during part of the day. The more important questions are at which time of day and during what part of the year the shade occurs. These factors are critical, as they will have a marked impact on how well a plant grows and performs. So, unless you actually know when a site receives shade or sun, "part shade" is a relatively unhelpful term of reference, and needs to be explained.

Remember that the afternoon sun is always the hottest and most intense, no matter where you live, and any wildflowers with sensitivity to the effects of the sun must be shaded from it during those hours. This may all sound very basic, but I often see shade-loving plants being subjected to strong, scorching afternoon sun in a "part shade" location, with shade occurring only in the morning, or I find such plants being placed in a garden setting that receives a lot of reflected light and heat from buildings or hardtop surfaces like driveways or paths. In many areas where summer temperatures and the intensity of the sun are not too strong, shade-loving plants will tolerate almost full sun if their environment is a benign one. They will need vegetation (rather than hard surfaces) around them and a spot where any breeze can move the air to cool them (they should not be set against a brick building or in an airless courtyard). And there are many shade-loving wildflowers (such as those recommended in the wildflower portraits for use in transition zones) that do enjoy several hours of sunlight each day— so long as it is during the early morning or early evening, not in midmorning to midafternoon.

The quality of sunlight is also affected by where you live. In southern areas the sunlight at all times of the year is much more intense than that received by the North. For instance, we cannot talk of California as having a certain amount or intensity of sunlight, because the intensity of the sun in southern California is far greater than in the northern part or the mountainous regions of that state. And the sun's heat in any area is more intense at sea level than at 5,000 feet. This is why the definition of "hardiness zones" can be so misleading; a Zone 7 in Oregon is a very different climate from a Zone 7 in North Carolina.

The best way to learn about the patterns of sun and shade in your area is simply to observe them closely. Walk around your property and through the woods at different times of the day, and notice how the shade patterns change. Observe the seasonal changes, also, and make notes of these observations in your journal. Ideally, you should do this *before* you make final plans for siting your wildflower garden and selecting the plants. Check a new garden frequently after you've set the plants out, to see if you have placed them correctly. Don't hesitate to move any that are not doing well, and give them another chance.

Frosts and Cold

It is important to learn as much as you can about the frosts in your area. Find out from the local weather bureau or county extension service whether there are frequent late spring or early autumn frosts and when they are likely to occur. Determine whether there are some parts of your property that receive a frost when the rest of it doesn't. Even in a small area, temperature ranges can vary quite considerably. Low temperatures and the effects of a frost can be deflected by the cover provided by another plant or the branches of a tree. The proximity of a building can also temper the effects of cold. These factors can make quite a difference in which plants you can grow and where.

Many other factors are also important, such as the presence or absence of a snow cover (and its depth), how much winter temperatures fluctuate, and the general health of the plants. Extreme temperature fluctuations can be harmful, but a good snow cover can insulate plants and maintain an even temperature through the winter. Plants that are in poor health are less able to cope with severe winter conditions, and plants that go into winter suffering from water stress after a particularly dry fall will be susceptible to winter damage.

Where a plant is sited on a property can greatly affect its winter hardiness. Plants that may be considered marginally hardy may also do surprisingly well if they are grown in a cold, sheltered spot—perhaps on a north-facing slope—that is slow to warm up in spring and becomes cold early in the fall. This puts the plants into dormancy early and keeps them dormant later into the spring, which helps them avoid the freeze-and-thaw cycles that can occur during the transitions into and out of winter and that are often the cause of a plant's demise. Frequent freezing and thawing, along with frosts, can be far more damaging to most plants than simple cold temperatures.

If you would like to try some wildflowers that are questionably hardy in your area, you might want to experiment by planting them when they are very young, even as vigorous seedlings (especially the woody ones). Often, these will develop more hardiness as they grow and mature. I found this to be the case with redbud (*Cercis canadensis*) when I tried it in southern New Hampshire. The young seedlings survived and gradually adapted to the climate, but I lost the five- and six-year-old plants I set out at the same time. (The young, smaller plants are also easier to give winter protection to for the first year or so.)

Soil

After many years of growing wildflowers in a variety of places, I feel that without a doubt the most important aspect of their successful cultivation is the soil. The closer the attention you pay to the soil, the more vigorous these wildlings will be, the more readily they will adapt to cultivation, and the greater your gardening success will be. It isn't so much a question of how acid or alkaline the soil is—this is only critical in a very few instances—but, more important, what the soil is made of and the resulting texture and structure it exhibits. The color, feel and even the smell of the soil are all vital. (Have you ever noticed the sour, stagnant smell of a poorly drained soil? This odor lets you know immediately that something must be done before plants will grow in that type of soil.)

Examine various soils in the wild, if possible, to learn what a particular plant's needs are. This can be quite an enlightening experience, because the "natural" soil often turns out to be quite different from what one might expect. For example, if you see the showy lady's-slipper (*Cypripedium reginae*) growing in a bog, you might assume that plant therefore needs an intensely acid soil—when in fact the bedrock under that bog is limestone and tempers the effect of the normally acidic bog, providing the more neutral pH level needed by this plant. I have also found fringed polygala (*Polygala paucifolia*)—a plant that is considered an acid-lover—growing among limestone ledges. Closer inspection revealed, however, that it was growing in crevices filled with acid pine duff which offset the effect of the alkaline limestone; the plant was actually growing in soil with a pH of 5.0 to 5.5. (For a full discussion of pH factors in soil, see Chapter 16, "Building a Wildflower Garden.")

If you don't have the opportunity to investigate soils in the wild, ask questions of all the gardeners you know who are growing the plants that interest you. Examine the soil closely, rub it through your fingers, ask what has been added, and be sure to discuss the problems as well as the successes. To get a clear picture of your local soils, consult your county extension agent.

Deep and thorough soil preparation is necessary for successful cultivation of wildflowers. If this work is done well the first time, it will not have to be redone for many years (if ever again); periodic additions of organic matter may well suffice, in most cases, to maintain a good soil. I know it is tiresome to haul and mix loads of soil and soil amendments, dig out impoverished soil and fill in the chasm with a well-prepared mix—but it is part of good gardening, and particularly important when you want to grow wildflowers. You can take encouragement from the knowledge that these beds, in all likelihood, will not have to be redug, and you will not have to add vast quantities of compost every year to rehabilitate the soil (as is the case with vegetable gardens).

Once you have your basic soil mix (a humus mix for the woodlanders and shade-lovers, and a rather lean one for meadow plants, or a typically loamy one for the sunny border, as described in Chapter 16), it can be adjusted by adding whatever other components are needed to meet the more specific needs of a particular plant or group of plants within these categories. It is a little like being a chef: at first, you follow the recipe and instructions quite carefully, but as you come to understand your plants and develop confidence in your skills, you will find it easier to blend the "right" ingredients by feel as well as by formula. For your first wildflower gardens, begin with a standard formula, keep a close eye on your plants' welfare, and work from there. When you move on to blend soil mixes for the more difficult plants, finding the right combination will become much more of a challenge.

Once established, fringed polygala (Polygala paucifolia), *with its exceptionally beautiful flowers, will put on an unmatched spring display.*

15

Using Wildflowers in Your Garden

OVER TWENTY YEARS AGO, I SPENT the long, bleak months of a winter anticipating the approaching growing season in my first "very own garden." What a satisfaction it was to know that, at long last, I had a permanent home for the treasured wildflowers that I'd kept in various containers during the years I had no other place for them. Soon their roots would be able to spread out into my well-prepared beds, and the plants could reach their full proportions under these optimum growing conditions.

That first year in "my garden" was spent in a flurry of activity. I had a beautiful, spacious corner of a New England woodland where I prepared bed after bed of rich, humusy woodland soil in which to tuck my wildflowers. As the huge manure pile dwindled, my satisfaction grew, because I was confident my wildlings would flourish in this location. I also had plenty of room for expansion, so I knew I could continually add to my collection of wildflowers.

And there, unrealized by me at the time, lay the crux of the problem that I soon became aware of. What I had was a *collection* of plants, or what I have often heard referred to since as a "horticultural zoo." It was not a garden, despite the idyllic setting, because it lacked the crucial element of design.

When I stood back and examined with a critical eye all the beds and plantings I had taken so much time and care with, and really looked at the overall picture, I saw a discordant, scattered array of lovely, often rare plants. These were most often one of a kind; seldom did I have more than a solitary specimen of my treasured plants. These single plants were growing here and there, with occasional small groups spotted along a path—and none of them had any relationship to each other, nor had they been tied into their surroundings. There was no continuity from plant to plant or from bed to bed. The garden did not flow together—there was no design.

What had happened to my vision of a woodland splashed with color, the drifts of plants woven together into subtle tapestries? Where was my recreation of images from remembered field trips? I had taken great care with each wildflower's horticultural needs, but I had never even thought of planning this garden beforehand from a design point of view. I took it for granted that the design would happen naturally, as an automatic consequence of good cultural care; but the natural harmony of a wild place, a thing so subtle as to be taken for granted, had been overlooked and pushed aside in my eagerness to plant.

It became painfully obvious that until I developed a design where the plants were arranged together in a visually pleasing way, my garden would not be the satisfying, pleasurable place I had anticipated, a place where I could realize the dreams I had nurtured for so long. Instead, it would be a thorn in my green thumb!

Gathering Design Information

There are several approaches to designing a garden. It may take some trial and error to find the method that works best for you.

I recommend that you keep a garden notebook or journal in which you include rough sketches of plantings or garden layouts that particularly appeal to you. Combine this information with ideas gathered from books, magazine articles and photographs—and don't forget the designs of Nature herself. All of this information will help you decide how the plants you select can be used to best effect in a garden.

As part of your "homework," try to read some of the works of the "old masters," such as Vita Sackville-West, Gertrude Jekyll and Louise Beebe Wilder, whose writings about garden design and plants contain wonderful ideas and useful tips that are easy to adapt to one's own garden. Their in-depth, hands-on experience is coupled with a superb sense of color, form and style to provide delightful reading and solid gems of information. (See Appendix B for a suggested reading list.)

Designing even the simplest of gardens is a constant process of refining your ideas and plans. Having a well-thought-out design enables you not only to use plants most effectively, but also to attain your goal in a logical way that helps you avoid making frequent and unnecessary changes once the plants are in the ground. You should, however, expect to make some revisions. You may find, as your design evolves, that you will need to change your selection of plants or your goals, so the live garden works best for you both visually and horticulturally.

All gardens take time to create, including the famous ones we admire and often try to emulate in some way when making our own gardens. Designs are drafted, revised and fine-tuned over several seasons or even years. Plants are moved, color combinations changed, heights and relationships revised until the gardener is satisfied. It is important both during this process and after the garden has been created to recognize when the elements of a design are not in harmony. It is even more difficult to figure out what adjustments need to be made to bring that harmony and cohesion to the design. The gardener also has to be willing to make the changes that are necessary. Sometimes it seems easier just to leave things the way they are, even if we are not satisfied with them.

Even when a new garden is well balanced and harmonious, its gradual realization unfolds over time. A young, seemingly sparse garden is a growing entity that will take a few years to acquire a look of permanence and maturity. During this period, you can observe how the various plants do in the locations chosen for them, see how the garden gradually fills in, and decide if the design elements (especially the color combinations) look as good in reality as they did in your mind or on paper.

Some gardeners prefer to have a detailed plan on paper to help them organize the garden before they begin laying out paths and beds, while others work best right at the garden site, marking out beds and paths and then writing notes to record their decisions. And some gardeners work from written notes only—without actually making a garden plan on paper.

However you decide to proceed, it is best to begin modestly. In the early stages of designing a wildflower garden, it is important to remember that nature cannot be captured in one or two seasons of enthusiasm and effort. Choose plants of simple form and culture at first, and then gradually expand into more complex designs and plant combinations, just as you progress from easy plants to more difficult

Twinleaf (Jeffersonia diphylla)

ones when you are learning how to grow them. As your confidence and familiarity with the plants increase, you can create more sophisticated designs or make further refinements to an existing garden. If you have a particular theme or special look that was created earlier in another garden on your property, you may want to embellish or expand this theme in the design for a new wildflower garden. To accomplish this, you may need to do no more than change the plants, use different colors or perhaps revise the seasonal focus.

When I create a garden in a wooded area or meadow, whether it is a quarter of an acre or three acres, I develop a plan that has one or more paths meandering among numerous beds throughout the whole area.

A path, no matter how long or short, creates interest, surprise and the illusion of greater space in the garden. The plants or vistas that are only glimpsed from the perimeter of the garden become easily accessible, and each aspect of the garden has more appeal as the path draws people into the garden, inviting them to investigate it further and savor it fully. A path also allows you to maintain the garden adequately.

Along the path, planting beds are developed. These are areas of various shapes and sizes (see the illustrations in Chapter 1, "A Woodland Garden," Chapter 2, "A Suburban Woodland Garden," and Chapter 3, "A Meadow Garden") that have been carefully planned and planted with a variety of wildflowers to form the body of the garden. My personal preference is to plant the beds along a path quite intensively and then tie them together with shrubs, large perennials or ground covers.

I also include some less dense plantings well back from the paths for added interest. (See Chapter 1, "A Woodland Garden.") This enables me to enjoy the unplanted areas, where my eye can wander into the woods, across a meadow or lawn into other areas and plantings. Even though some spots are only lightly planted, the whole area is not in complete view from a single vantage point, and this entices one to go into the garden to explore and discover all the nuances.

My eye might also be drawn by a distant spot of color, a simple clump of white birch (*Betula papyrifera*), or the rough, peeling bark of shagbark hickories (*Carya ovata*)—the small, subtle things as well as the large, dramatic features. I can notice the muted brown cover of fallen leaves from past years, a spider's web spangled in dew, a clump of goldenrod (*Solidago* species) by the remains of an old fence, or a mossy decaying stump with clubmoss (*Lycopodium* species) tucked around it. Scenes such as these are beautiful even when they are unadorned by a planting of wildflowers. They provide a few reflective moments away from the more intense vitality of growth and color in a garden. They also allow the busy gardener to suspend the gentle, nagging feelings that remind us of the many things we still want to accomplish.

A rotting moss-covered stump becomes part of a picture when surrounded by wildflowers and ferns.

What Look Do You Want?

Think of the look you would like your garden to have. This will, to some extent, be affected by where you live (whether in an urban, suburban or rural area) and by the local landscape and style of architecture, as your garden should not appear severely out of place

It is possible to create a small woodland within the confines of a town or city, but it should tie in with its surroundings. On the other hand, a southwestern garden and the plants that belong in it will not look appropriate in a traditional country setting in Virginia or New England. If you do choose to have a specialty garden of this sort, it is best to separate it from the rest of the property by a wall or fence, or to make it part of a terrace. It should not be set into a lawn or near a woodland.

Different looks can be grouped generally into formal and informal types, which depend, in large part, on the individual plants and how they are used in the bed. Formal plantings are set out in rows and distinctive, discernible patterns, while informal gardens appear to be randomly planted and have a flow to them. There is also much less definition between the groups of different plants in an informal garden.

A wood or meadow, for instance, is usually an informal garden, but if the plants selected for it are formal in appearance and planted in a conventional style, then the garden will acquire a less-natural look and become more contrived in appearance. The traditional border, on the other hand, is considered a formal garden, but if the plants in it have billowy, loose growth habits and are set in an unstructured pattern, the border will have more the look of an unconstrained cottage or country garden.

Consider the shape of different plants. Some are round and dense, others are cloudlike and open, and still others are narrow and upright. The other features of a plant—the flowers, seed heads, berries, foliage and the bark and shape of the branches of a woody plant—also play a role in this determination and create the "feel" of a garden.

The shapes of individual plants are equally important design elements as the flower colors, whether low, mounding plants like the golden star (Chrysogonum virginianum), *or upright and narrow like the blue flag iris* (Iris versicolor).

🌺 🌺 🌺

Whether your design is for a single border, a small area, or a large expanse, you should consider how to integrate into the plans (or remove, if necessary) any existing features. Plants, building, fences, paths, lawns and the topography of the land itself—all become part of the design.

In each garden described in the first part of this book, there are examples of preexisting elements. Each was carefully considered throughout the planning stages of the various gardens. These features may affect, perhaps to a great extent, where a garden will go and how it will relate to the rest of the property and to other plantings.

To tie a border in with other plantings in the general vicinity, repeat similar colors (but not necessarily the same plant) in these separate borders. To add continuity and the sense of a well-thought-out design, repeat a color within the border itself.

Think also of smaller, simpler elements that can be worked into a garden. In a woodland, decaying tree stumps and moss-covered logs can provide beautiful settings for shade-loving plants. Rocks, of course, are design elements in many gardens, not only rock gardens.

The careful, well-thought-out placement of rocks is very important. Dropping any old rock down on the ground won't produce anything of beauty, and the loveliness and aesthetic balance of a fine garden can be undercut by a pile of rocks or a few stark, solitary monoliths of amazing ugliness that are used without any real consideration of how they fit into a design—if indeed they belong in it at all.

Think of how unattractive a new building site can look, especially if the raw-colored rocks and boulders dragged out of the ground have been set in some form of haphazard plan at the end of a driveway or in conjunction with a parking lot. Sometimes they are painstakingly

arranged into a circle, often with a shrub planted inside it, but they always look crude and totally out of place. Yet in places where rocks and ledges are a natural part of the landscape, they are beautifully weathered and always attractive. (If you have to use newly exposed rocks that have been buried in the soil for eons, you can soften their harsh, unweathered color by trickling manure tea over them from time to time. Manure tea is simply made by steeping a shovelful of manure in a bucket of water for a few days. This method of "weathering" can also be used when the rocks have been scarred during the process of moving them and setting them in place.)

Rocks, like decaying logs or tree stumps, are not just design elements but also provide protected niches into which small, treasured plants can be tucked so they are not lost in the vastness of their surroundings. These niches also create small microclimates that are good places for the difficult plants that need something extra in their culture or require some moderation of the climate to enable them to do well.

Plant Selection

The development of any garden design should begin with a consideration of the plants you'd like to grow, even though the actual planting is the last step in the process. The design should be created before anything else happens and, as the plants are the primary elements of the design, they are the most vital part of all the early planning.

Shrubs play an important role in all wildflower gardens—not only for their contributions to the display of flowers, interesting berries and diverse foliage but also because they have wonderful shapes, and their height adds an often-needed dimension, especially to borders. They can also provide us with garden interest during the winter and early spring months.

If you have made notes about the growth habits and other characteristics of different wildflowers, you already have some of the information you need to create an effective design. Along with the cultural notes describing where and how each plant grows best, your list of favorite plants should tell you when they bloom, how tall and broad each plant grows, what colors the flowers and foliage are, what other special features they might have, and which other plants look good with them. Be sure to consider the plant's mature height and breadth, not just its youthful dimensions, and try to get some idea of how fast that plant can be expected to grow in your area.

Don't overlook traditional garden plants and non-native wildflowers in your selection. Despite many gardeners' intentions to feature only certain types of plants in a garden, I've found that it is difficult for plant-lovers to remain totally faithful to only one group of plants: perennials, woody plants, rock garden plants, native American wildflowers, whatever. Inevitably, companion plants from the other groups creep into our design, where they invariably blend perfectly with their wild cousins from this country and abroad. Think of the bulbs, so eager to herald the newness of another spring, or the Japanese primroses (*Primula japonica*) ablaze amidst the native royal fern (*Osmunda regalis*) in a moist area. By a wood's edge English primroses (*Primula vulgaris*) and bluebells (*Endymion non-scriptus*), so reminiscent of an English hedgerow, can be mixed with native merrybells (*Uvularia grandiflora*) and hepaticas (*Hepatica* species). And in a meadow, the pastoral charm of Shirley poppies (*Papaver rhoeas*) and Queen-

The early saxifrage (Saxifraga virginiensis) *is ideal to tuck into a crevice in a shady rock garden.*

Anne's-lace (*Daucus carota*) blends beautifully with the native black-eyed Susans (*Rudbeckia hirta*) and blazing star (*Liatris spicata*).

It is important to consider whether a favorite plant has a dramatic appearance that will automatically draw attention to it, or produces a more subtle effect. The quieter, less dramatic plants need to be supported and have attention drawn to them by other plants or landscape elements.

How permanent is the display of each plant? An evergreen tree or a woody plant with handsome bark will provide ongoing, year-round interest, while the spring ephemerals will disappear after they have flowered.

I always consider fragrance as well when I am working on my garden design, because the element of scent is important to me. I like to have fragrant plants near the house, terrace or a path, so I am always aware of their perfume. Sometimes, however, I intentionally set these plants well away from the house, so I have a destination to draw me out into the garden. Not all fragrant plants are beautiful in their growth habits or flowers—the winter honeysuckle (*Lonicera fragrantissima*) is one of these—so they have to be carefully worked into a design to capitalize on the scent and not let their looks detract from the rest of the display. Of course, many fragrant plants are also very beautiful, and some—like the fringe tree (*Chionanthus virginicus*)—make especially lovely specimens.

Much of the information you need in order to plan can be found in the wealth of garden literature, from books to nursery catalogs. You can easily become confused, however, because this information varies according to its source. It varies too because plants behave quite differently depending on where and how they are grown. Ultimate heights, bloom time and so forth will not only differ according to geographic location, but also due to the different microclimates within a garden.

There can also be a certain amount of variation from year to year within a single location, depending on changes in the climate (early frosts, unusually hot summers, drought and so forth). Some fall-blooming plants of great beauty flower so late in a northern garden that they do not have time to put on a display before they are killed by frost. Even if these plants are perfectly hardy, they can't be relied upon to provide a flower display each season, and they should be used instead in areas with longer growing seasons and mild winters, no matter how glowing the catalog descriptions of them are.

To help me organize all this information and have it easily available for reference, I began keeping a garden notebook when I started planning my garden many years ago, and I have continued to add information to it. (See the illustration.) I found it to be especially valuable in my early years of planning and designing gardens, and I still refer to it.

As I select plants for a wildflower garden, I look not only at their individual features, but also at the roles they will play in the garden. Some plants are used for structure and framework, some become the "body" of the garden, and others provide background, highlights, dramatic impact or carpets.

Framework Plants

The framework plants create the structure of the garden and define the garden space. Most often, these will be the woody plants—the

NAME	TYPE	DISPLAY	DISPLAY TIME	COLOR	HEIGHT	WIDTH	SOIL	SITE	SOURCE	COMMENTS
Hepatica americana	Herbaceous perennial	Flowers; evergreen foliage	Spring	Multi	2" - 5"	3" - 5"	Rich humus	Woodland	J.D. '82	Propagate by division after flowering. Plant singly or in small groups.
Osmunda regalis	Herbaceous perennial fern	Foliage	All seasons *Fall color	Spring: Copper Summer: Pale green Fall: yellow	24" - 30"	18" - 24"	organic, silty muck	Wet place in & beside water; sun or shade	Second Brook	Outstanding continuation of seasonal display. Optimum proportions=year-round wet soils.
Hydrangea quercifolia	Shrub	Year-round; flowers, foliage and growth habit.	Spring: Buds, flowers; Summer: foliage and growth habit; Fall: foliage; Winter: exfoliating bark & shape	Spring: White Fall: Deep purple	5' - 6'	4' - 5'	Woodsy, moisture-retentive	Shade; some sun if summer cool.	Gift from M.N. '86	Outstanding year-round interest; heavy flower display. Mix with *Anemone japonica, Cimicifuga simplex;* plants with cream variegations to foliage.

A Sample Page From My Wildflower Notebook

trees and shrubs (both deciduous and evergreen).

There are two kinds of frame for a garden. The first is a general visual one for the property itself; this is usually made up of trees and some shrubs. The second kind is more focused, is usually created by shrubs and large herbaceous perennials and relates to a specific garden area, which may be something as expansive as a woodland or as intimate as a terrace.

The plants used in this latter group are either used individually, with several spotted throughout an area, or grouped together. When they are planted in groups, they can also serve as noise barriers or make good background plantings and screens to block buildings, neighbors or another garden area. They also can themselves provide appealing color themes, as seen with the roseshell (*Rhododendron prinophyllum*) or the pinxter bloom azalea (*Rhododendron periclymenoides*).

Try to keep in mind how fast and how large the background plants will grow. The rose bay rhododendron (*Rhododendron maximum*), for instance, will become very large and need to be pruned regularly to keep it within the bounds of a garden. Plants of this type are best used in spacious areas that can accommodate their size and scale. Even in a large area, they will need pruning from time to time to keep them from getting too open and leggy.

If your garden needs a framework planting that is not as large and solid in appearance as the rose bay, consider the Carolina rhododendron (*Rhododendron carolinianum*), which is a lovely plant and very tough. Its only shortcoming is that at any sign of water shortage in summer the leaves curl. (On the other hand, this is a good reminder that the soil has dried out and needs to be watered.)

There are many shrubs, both deciduous and evergreen, that are suitable for the framework or background, and appealing effects can be achieved with either kind or a mixture of both. The choice depends on what look and feel you want to have and on the size of the overall area. The choice of plants can range from the oak-leaf hydrangea (*Hydrangea quercifolia*) to the redvein enkianthus (*Enkianthus campanulatus*) to tall bugbane (*Cimicifuga racemosa*) to boltonia (*Boltonia asteroides*).

Background Plants

The background of a garden has two primary uses: first, to provide a backdrop that will direct and focus interest onto the foreground planting and accentuate the subtleties and nuances of the primary display, and second, to define the space of a specific area within the overall frame.

Although I strongly recommend including a few evergreens such as the Carolina rhododendron, Oregon grape holly (*Mahonia aquifolium*), inkberry (*Ilex glabra*) or conifers in your design to give some substance, especially in winter and early spring, these can sometimes create a dense, almost oppressive feeling if they are used too often or in too large a number. Also, too much of any single plant is monotonous. It is a good idea to break up groups of these heavy-appearing shrubs with occasional plants that have lighter-textured foliage, a looser habit of growth or a bright flower display to soften the somber effect from too much dark green and sameness of form.

A smooth, settled effect is needed in the background to balance the gaiety and diversity found in the lower-growing plants that make up the body of a garden. In some cases, a single plant can achieve this if it is large and spreading like a viburnum or Cornelian cherry (*Cornus mas*). To achieve the same effect with smaller plants like winterberry (*Ilex verticillata*), sweet pepperbush (*Clethra alnifolia*) or the herbaceous goatsbeard (*Aruncus dioicus*), several plants would be required.

Plants with foliage that is dark or heavy in texture will appear brighter and more interesting if mixed with plants that have an airy countenance and lighter-textured foliage.

Whenever possible, I like to select background material that provides interesting effects at a time when foreground plants have not yet begun their display or when they have finished flowering, as this extends the period of interest for that area.

Many shrubs provide an abundance of color in their fall mantle, like the berries found on viburnum, the intense, rich purple-red foliage of oak-leaf hydrangea, and the bright scarlet leaves of winterberry. Clematis can be twined through the shrubs to add its fluffy seed heads (and sometimes late flowers) to the quietly receding picture.

Highbush blueberry (*Vaccinium corymbosum*) is an attractive shrub in a winter garden, and also offers a multitude of spring flowers, summer fruit and rich burgundy leaves in fall. The native beach plum (*Prunus maritima*) is another shrub that has winter interest, because of its shape and cinnamon-brown bark, and it covers itself with flowers in spring. If you plant beach plum, for best results place it in full sun, add extra sand to the soil and don't overfertilize it. In areas that do not have harsh, hot summers, witchhazels (*Hamemelis* species) and bottlebrush shrub (*Fothergilla major*) will both grow well in full sun or shade and are ideal selections: both have an interesting winter aspect followed by early spring flowers. The fall-flowering witchhazel (*Hamamelis virginiana*) has soft yellow fall foliage; the variety 'Sandra' and the bottlebrush shrub have fiery red leaves in autumn.

In summer, the native viburnums bring beautiful flowers followed by colorful fruit and fall foliage. And the native bottlebrush buckeye (*Aesculus parviflora*) has long been a favorite of mine. Its bushy growth habit and multitude of 8- to 12-inch spires that bear dozens of delicate, sweetly fragrant white flowers, make an impressive summer display.

A background planting can also serve as a screen. For an open screen along a wood margin, I have used shrubs such as barberries (*Berberis* species), witchhazel, fetterbush (*Leucothoe fontanesiana*) and wayfaring tree (*Viburnum alnifolium*), for their habit of growth, interesting foliage, flowers, bright fruit or fall color. Other plants commonly used in this situation would be mountain laurel (*Kalmia latifolia*) and azaleas. The native azaleas are particularly good choices because they prefer full shade to part shade (certainly afternoon shade). With careful selection of the various species and varieties of native azaleas, the flower display can be carried for a long period of time, from early spring to summer. For a sunny meadow the groundsel bush (*Baccharis halimifolia*) and meadowsweet (*Spiraea latifolia*) provide an excellent background for the garden itself, while in a wet area sweet pepperbush and the exotic-looking rose mallow (*Hibiscus palustris*) are good choices.

Other suitable plants for backgrounds are the tall herbaceous perennials. These can be arranged in groups of three or five and offer a pleasing contrast to the look of the shrubs and trees. They are also useful to bridge the changes in height between tall trees, shrubs and low-growing plants.

The design will be more interesting if background plants also have attractive foliage or growth habits throughout the whole growing season. In the shade, this would include herbaceous wildflowers like blue cohosh (*Caulophyllum thalictroides*), umbrella leaf (*Diphylleia cymosa*), goatsbeard and the Asian rodgersia. In a sunny place, Joe-pye-weed (*Eupatorium purpureum*), bush pea (*Thermopsis caroliniana*) and wild senna (*Cassia hebecarpa*) are good choices, as are some of the non-native ornamental grasses.

Only one such plant is needed to give emphasis to a small area, while in a large space a group set back into the woods, on the far side of a meadow, or behind a border will create an intimate feeling, bringing the perimeters of the garden into closer proximity.

Foamflower (Tiarella cordifolia) *interplanted with wood anemones* (Anemone quinquefolia). *The anemones flower first; as they begin to fade, the foamflower starts to blossom.*

Plants for the Body of the Garden

After the background material come the plants that form the body of a garden, those which create the main display and picture. The majority of these plants are herbaceous perennials which, unlike annuals, do not flower continuously. The perennial wildflowers are more likely to have one bloom time (which can be extended, in some cases, by the removal of the spent flowers). To have your wildflowers give you many months of flower displays, the garden will need to be planned with this in mind, just as you would plan any planting of herbaceous perennials. To extend the display time, plan your flowering groups so that one plant or group of plants is ending its bloom time as another is coming into flower and yet another is in peak bloom.

"Interplanting" is another tool that creates more and longer interest in an area. This can be as simple as underplanting a ground cover of foamflower (*Tiarella cordifolia*) with European wood anemone

(*Anemone nemorosa*). The wood anemones flower first amongst the old evergreen foliage of the foamflower, and then, as the anemones begin to fade, the flowers of the foamflower gradually open and the new foliage peeks through the old. After it flowers, the anemone totally disappears and its dormant roots are protected beneath the foamflower. (Blue cohosh, with its attractive glaucous foliage and midsummer blue berries, could be set behind this group to add another dimension to the planting.) In a sunny border, camas lily (*Camassia cusickii*) can be grown amongst the lower-growing form of false dragonhead *Physostegia virginiana* 'Vivid' in front of a stand of queen-of-the-meadow (*Filipendula ulmaria*).

The midsized wildflowers (24 to 36 inches tall) suitable for use in the body of the garden are many, and they come in a broad array of forms and colors. This group includes the baneberries (*Actaea* species), nodding mandarin (*Disporum maculatum*), Solomon's seal (*Polygonatum biflorum*) and ferns such as the ostrich (*Matteuccia struthiopteris*) and interrupted fern (*Osmunda claytoniana*).

Next in this group are those wildflowers that range in height from 12 to 24 inches. In a shade garden, we have—to name just a few—Jack-in-the-pulpit (*Arisaema triphyllum*), shooting-star (*Dodecatheon meadia*), the familiar beauty of the trilliums (*Trillium* species), the sparkling white of twinleaf (*Jeffersonia diphylla*) and the drifts of color from the woodland phloxes (*Phlox divaricata* and *P. stolonifera*), along with maidenhair (*Adiantum pedatum*), bulblet (*Cystopteris bulbifera*), northern beech (*Thelypteris phegopteris*) and lady fern (*Athyrium filix-femina*). In the sunny garden, we find the lower-growing asters (*Aster* species), the golden aster (*Chrysopsis mariana*), dwarf blue star (*Amsonia montana*), wild petunia (*Ruellia humilis*) and bottle gentian (*Gentiana andrewsii*).

Plants in this 12- to 24-inch range also offer us lovely ground covers, such as the wild oats (*Uvularia sessilifolia*), vancouveria, hardy ageratum (*Eupatorium coelestinum*) and *Coreopsis* X 'Moonbeam'. Highlights of color come from wood poppy (*Stylophorum diphyllum*), bleeding heart (*Dicentra eximia*), shooting-star, wild cranesbill (*Geranium maculatum*), dwarf blazing star (*Liatris spicata* 'Kobold') and ragged robin (*Lychnis flos-cuculi*). It is here that we see the full impact of the woodland garden in the spring pageant of color, so fresh and vital, as it blends with the bright greens of foliage, ferns and mosses, creating a sense of luxuriance and extravagance, while in summer, the sunny border is filled with a multitude of plants in all their vibrancy.

The plants that form the body of a garden offer so many lovely combinations and effects, from drifts of color provided by the ground covers and the delicate shows of the smaller treasures to those wildflowers that we can use as the highlights of our gardens, the "feature plants." These are plants of such outstanding beauty and form that we need to use only an individual clump to create a stunning effect. They include the large yellow lady's-slipper (*Cypripedium calceolus* var. *pubescens*), oconee bells (*Shortia galacifolia*), double hepatica (*Hepatica acutiloba* 'Flora Plena'), double pink-flowered rue anemone (*Anemonella thalictroides* 'Schoaf's Double Pink'), the double bloodroot (*Sanguinaria canadensis* 'Multiplex'), white-flowered bleeding heart (*Dicentra eximia* 'Alba'), galax (*Galax aphylla*), butterfly weed (*Asclepias tuberosa*), fire pink (*Silene virginica*) and pasque flower (*Anemone patens*).

These garden highlights should not stand entirely alone; just as the

Camas lily (Camassia cusickii) *interplanted with false dragonhead* (Physostegia virginiana) *and queen-of-the-meadow* (Filipendula ulmaria). *Camas lily dominates the planting in spring, but by midsummer it has died down; the false dragonhead and queen-of-the-meadow are now the stars of the show.*

entire garden needs a frame, these special plants need one as well, to focus attention on them. This frame should be an intimate, subtle setting. It could be ferns, a mossy old tree stump, a background plant with contrasting foliage color or a simple ground cover. Sometimes a plant's full potential is not realized until it is displayed in combination with other plants that highlight its true beauty.

Finally, we come to the low-growing wildflowers. Sometimes these are prostrate ground covers that trail over the ground, like partridge-berry (*Mitchella repens*) and fringed polygala (*Polygala paucifolia*) in a shady garden, or the three-toothed cinquefoil (*Potentilla tridentata*) and thyme-leaved bluets (*Houstonia serpyllifolia*) in sun. Others have foliage and flowers rising only a few inches off the ground. The dwarf crested iris (*Iris cristata*) is one of the prettiest of these and, because of its restrained habit, is very useful where space is limited. Others for a shady garden include Labrador violet (*Viola labradorica*), waldsteinia (*Waldsteinia fragarioides*) and dewdrop (*Dalibarda repens*). These plants also make a wonderful, safe haven for the resting roots of the spring ephemerals such as toothwort (*Dentaria diphylla*) and shooting-star. A sunny garden might feature golden star (*Chrysogonum virginianum*) and mossy phlox (*Phlox subulata*).

Trailing plants such as partridgeberry (Mitchella repens) *grown along the edge of a path will blend it into the garden and give a softer, more natural effect.*

The trailing and mat-forming wildflowers provide the continuity that ties all the other elements together. They can also edge path-ways, tumble down banks, nestle beside steps, appear as a cape care-lessly cast around the bottom of a tree or be focal displays on their own. The ground covers are often foreground plantings that spread out through the other wildflowers, creating unity in a planting or throughout the entire garden.

Combining all these various types and heights of wildflowers in a balanced design creates an image of harmony, variety and depth—and it is this that I wanted so much, but failed to achieve, in my first attempt at a wildflower garden.

Seasonal Interest

My overall goal is to have nearly year-round interest in my garden from late winter and early spring through the summer and fall and into early winter. Although the displays certainly include flowers, I always consider all the nonfloral features of the plants such as colorful or ornamental foliage, distinctive growth habit or a striking fruiting display.

In most sections of North America—even in the northern regions, which can have close to five or six months of winter—it is possible to have at least a few plants that provide visual interest during the off-season. These displays will certainly not match the vibrancy of the peak flower times, but they will still bring substance and structure to an otherwise bland landscape, and they are also a good reason to go into the garden on a cold winter day.

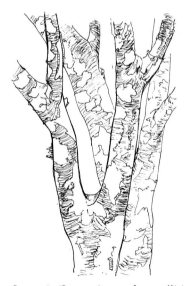

Stewartia (Stewartia pseudocamellia), *with its distinctive green and gray mottled bark and multitude of flowers in early summer, is a beautiful specimen tree.*

In addition to those shrubs described in the section on background plantings, there are many other deciduous trees and shrubs with beautiful bark and interesting branching habits which can be espe-cially lovely in winter. One of my favorites is the Asian paperbark maple (*Acer griseum*), with its peeling bark of rich cinnamon that shimmers as it catches the sunlight. In winter, this makes a dramatic contrast to the monotones of a snowy landscape. Or consider the beautiful, cream-striated green bark of the native goosefoot maple

(*Acer pensylvanicum*).

Woody plants with lovely architectural lines and beautiful forms are often fully appreciated and admired only when the cloak of leaves is gone and their structure is exposed. The river (*Betula nigra*) and white birch (*Betula papyrifera*), for example, become highlights at this time of year. In winter, the woods seem full of them, and we wonder why we had not noticed them in summer when nature's opulence overshadowed their quiet beauty.

Evergreens are at their most prominent in the winter garden. Their greens, grays, blues and yellows soften and warm the starkness of the season. Many have a graceful appearance with distinctive foliage textures that can be better enjoyed without the multitude of distractions found at other times of the year.

Some plants that are quite ordinary in shape can also be pruned into an interesting form that can dominate a winter scene, and others can be judiciously pruned to highlight an interesting growth habit. The weeping form of Canadian hemlock (*Tsuga canadensis* 'Pendula'), for instance, can have its cascading tiers of green emphasized in this fashion.

When there is little or no snow, ground covers that are unnoticed in the lusher seasons show themselves in winter. The clubmosses (*Lycopodium* species) appear as a miniature forest that spreads across the ground, while wintergreen's (*Gaultheria procumbens*) glossy mantle of dark green drapes itself around the bases of trees.

Think of the many plants that have interesting and colorful fruit. These often begin to appear in late summer, and many of those that adorn our gardens in late summer and fall will remain through the winter if they are not eaten by wildlife. Everything from rose hips to the berries of viburnum, hollies and barberry becomes precious jewels when they are encrusted with frost crystals glistening in winter sunlight.

*Evergreens are important to give emphasis to a garden, particularly in winter. Those with especially distinctive growth habits can have these further accentuated with careful pruning, as shown here with the weeping Canadian hemlock (*Tsuga canadensis* 'Pendula').*

Planning the Beds

Your earlier planning will now come into play as you select locations for the plants and the beds that comprise a large wildflower area or a single border. Beds can be of any attractive free-form shape that is in scale with the overall size of the property. If the beds are borders running in front of a background such as a building or fence, they will have straight back lines and, usually, front lines with interesting curves.

Start with the framework, and then add the plants that will form the body of the planting. Here, let your love of color and form guide you in selecting plants for your design. Those winter months spent with catalogs, reference books and your notebook will pay off now, enabling you to develop pleasing combinations of colors and shapes to create variety, harmony and the seasonal interest of an area.

Planting Density

Certain gardens—and certain beds within a garden area—are planted more heavily than others. A meadow or border garden, for instance, is usually more intensively planted than a woodland or rock garden.

In a large wooded area, it is unlikely that all of the space will be massed with plants—nor would this necessarily be desirable. Here, it will be the skillful location of woody plants—the smaller trees and shrubs—and the large herbaceous perennials that will define the intimate garden area and form the framework within which the main group of herbaceous plants and bulbs will go. (See details of the planting beds illustrated in Chapter 1, "A Woodland Garden.")

Small understory trees—ideally, flowering ones—can be spotted throughout a woods or small shade garden, just far enough back from the path to give the illusion of expansiveness, but not so far back as to be lost. If the area is small, one or two will be sufficient and still give the same effect as that of several in a large area. Shadbush (*Amelanchier* species), franklinia (*Franklinia alatamaha*), dogwoods (*Cornus* species), and sweet bay magnolia (*Magnolia virginiana*) are all excellent choices for sunny glades and marginal areas that also receive some sun. Suitable shrubs include the various rhododendrons, mountain laurel, viburnums and witchhazel. Lower background plants would be the fetterbush, chokeberry (*Aronia arbutifolia*), inkberry and dwarf bottlebrush shrub (*Fothergilla gardenii*).

When you set out the plants that form the body of the garden, remember that if they gradually fade out in density toward the edges of a group of plantings, however small this is, they will give the illusion of greater space and a more extensive planting. This is especially useful in a large area and when beds of wildflowers are spotted along a path. A more densely planted area emphasizes the immediate space and display.

Be careful of plants that are so strong and aggressive by nature that they will tend to take over the garden if not restrained. They can have a place in a garden design, but it is important to locate them carefully and perhaps curb their growth. In situations where they can be let go, they will provide a fine display and fill in large areas with pleasing forms and textures to balance the colors. For example, the mayapple (*Podophyllum peltatum*) can be quite aggressive, so it is not a plant for a small garden or one with delicate plants in it. It comes into its own in a large area, where its ground cover effect will fill in spaces or serve as an underplanting to tall herbaceous perennials or shrubs. Canadian mayflower (*Maianthemum canadense*), Canada anemone (*Anemone canadensis*), beebalm (*Monarda didyma*) and queen-of-the-prairie (*Filipendula rubra*) are all beautiful wildflowers that can be enjoyed and admired in a large space but will become a nuisance when placed in a small garden with small, unaggressive plants. It is the gardener's responsibility to be sure these plants are used appropriately.

Quantity and Placement

Generally, using just one plant—unless it is very special or a large, full specimen that has a definite presence in the landscape—is never satisfactory or effective. The principles of good garden design depend on the use of groups of one kind of plant grown in combination with other complementary plants. The essence of a wildflower garden can never be achieved by having just one trillium, a solitary Jack-in-the-pulpit, one bottle gentian or a single sneezeweed (*Helenium autumnale*). There should be clusters of these plants to suggest the groups they form in the wild.

The time to use a single plant is when you want to put it on stage. It should be something outstanding, a special plant of great beauty or charm, a wildflower that makes the viewers catch their breath. Such a display might be provided by the double trillium (*Trillium grandiflo-*

rum 'Flora Plena'), which is so beautiful that having more than a single plant with three to five flowering stems lessens the uniqueness of it. Oconee bells can be used in this way, also (although it also provides a different, though equally effective, look when used as a ground cover). The sun-loving pasque flower is another ideal specimen plant that also seems to lose its specialness when it is planted in a group.

You may want to use a group of a mat-forming ground covers to create a drift. This could be a patch of creeping phlox (*Phlox stolonifera*) no more than 18 to 30 inches across, and it doesn't have to be in a solid block. Rivulets can spread outward, intertwining with other plants and flowing around rocks or an old stump. Small groups of flowers can grow up through a drift for contrast in color and texture.

Consider repetition as a means of bringing a theme and flow to your garden. By repeating plants or colors within a group and groups within the garden, you will unify the whole planting, creating continuity and emphasizing the overall impact.

Height

Most often, the height change in a garden is gradual, with the different levels moving easily down from the tall trees to the lowest ground covers. The idea is to create different levels of visual interest, as the plants move from the tallest in the back to the lowest in front.

Once in a while, however, it is a good idea to provide a dramatic effect by going from a tall plant to a low one—perhaps from the plumleaf azalea (*Rhododendron prunifolium*) to the crested iris, or from the tall bugbane (*Cimicifuga racemosa*) to the dewdrop. These abrupt changes in height can be quite startling, and they are an effective way to draw attention to a special plant such as a clump of *Arisaema sikokianum,* an Asian species of Jack-in-the-pulpit, or double bloodroot. This technique is also particularly effective when it is used to capture attention in a large area where a number of beds of wildflowers, nearly all of the same height, are spotted along lengthy paths.

Island beds will be viewed from all sides and need careful planning. The taller plants are placed along the central line as a ridge around which the others swirl down and away, decreasing in height toward the edge of the bed.

❧ ❧ ❧

These are just some of the basics of good garden design. In addition, I suggest you look again at the individual wildflower gardens described in Part I of this book, keeping in mind the points raised in this chapter. These should help you plan an effective design for whatever type of wildflower garden you choose to create.

16
Building
a Wildflower
Garden

ONCE YOU HAVE A CLEAR IDEA of the type of wild-flower garden you want, its location and overall design, you are ready to prepare the site and soil.

Ideally, you should not acquire plants until the bed preparations have been completed, but I know from experience that plants are often gathered over a period of time. Sometimes friends give me unexpected gifts, and sometimes plants ordered by mail arrive earlier than expected. It is important, therefore, to have an easily accessible staging area where they can be gathered and taken care of either in their pots or by heeling them in until the beds are ready. By "heeling in," I mean planting quickly in a temporary home— perhaps at the edge of a well-decomposed compost pile, into the corner of a vegetable garden or in a cold frame. Dig a hole in good soil, set the plants into it, and firm the soil back around them.

Each type of garden will require different methods and amounts of preparation, from the simple job of obtaining suitable containers for a container garden to major tree work for a woodland garden. And the construction and acquisition of materials for a rock garden will obviously require more skill, effort and time than the renovation of a shady border. (See the discussion of these topics under each garden heading in Part I.)

General Preparation

The natural diversity of plants found in an area will depend largely on geographic location, with the greatest variety occurring in this country in the southeast and the Pacific Northwest. Also those regions that have not been subjected to drastic disturbances from lumbering and farming will still have a significant selection of wildflowers. The farther away your property is from large centers of population, the less likely the land is to have suffered from recent disturbance. And there may well be a number of wildflowers already growing on your property that you want to include in the wildflower garden(s) you are planning.

Generally speaking, with the exception of a woodland, where the trees and some of the understory plants are an integral part of the garden, much (if not all) of the existing vegetation will need to be removed. In a bed that is slated for renovation or enlarging, any existing plantings will need to be dug out. If they are not suitable for the new planting, they will have to be placed in another location or discarded; or, if they are to be part of the new design, they can be heeled in while the bed is being readied. Small plants can be potted up into suitable containers.

The specific details of site preparation for each type of wildflower garden are discussed under the garden headings further on in this chapter. No matter what sort of garden you are creating, however, there are a few guidelines and cautions that unfailingly apply:

Always do any major work first. If this involves heavy machinery, chain saws and lots of tramping back and forth over the ground, do this *before* you lay out and dig the beds, mix the soil or set out plants.

This way, you will avoid compacting the newly mixed soil and damaging the plants.

Refer often to your planting plan and notes, but be flexible. And when you do make changes during the building process, make notes so you will remember what you changed and why! This will be helpful later when you are doing similar work on this or any other garden. There may be more groundwater than you expected in a certain area, or what you thought was sandy subsoil may turn out to be hardpan 12 to 18 inches down, meaning water will not drain as well as you expected. Surprises like these may mean you might have to revise your original goal—but they may also present you with pleasant and unexpected opportunities.

Don't attempt to undertake more than you can comfortably and enjoyably handle. It is better to complete thorough preparations for a small site than to cut corners on a large garden. If you discover, midway through, that you've overestimated your time, energy or financial resources, scale your plans down to fit the resources you do have, and plan to complete the rest during the next season or year. Remember, one of the primary requirements of a good gardener is patience!

Paths

Once the major clearing has been done, it's time to lay out the paths. Since many wildflower gardens are by their very nature informal, the paths should have gentle curves to them—no matter how short the path or how small the area. The idea is to entice people to walk into a meadow or woodland garden or through a large border to savor and explore it, not merely to view it from a distance or walk around its perimeter. Consider also the general accessibility of the area and what equipment will need to be brought in and out for planting and maintenance. The paths will have to accommodate these needs as well.

Although we most often think of constructing paths in woodland or meadow gardens, the following general guidelines can be used for paths in other types of gardens as well.

In a woodland, I begin laying out a path by raking away the leaves where I envision it will go, to see how the lines will look, and then I play with the lines until I get them to where I am satisfied. If the path doesn't look right, I simply rake the leaves back into place and try again.

For a meadow garden, I experiment with paths by first marking them out with stakes or a garden hose. Once they look right, I mow the proposed path to get a better idea of how my chosen layout will appear.

Some paths, especially those in woodlands, will benefit from having an edging. Apart from its aesthetic value, this barrier also defines the utilitarian area and separates it from the planted area. The edging will keep the path mulch in the paths, and the plants, soil and garden mulch in the beds. It also helps keep people from stepping into the planted area and onto the plants. I like to use small trees or saplings (perhaps those that were thinned out earlier) for edging. Those 6 to 7 feet long and no more than 4 inches in diameter are the most suitable; anything larger will appear out of place and too prominent. Sinking them into the ground to about a third or a half

Placing a choice plant such as oconee bells (Shortia galacifolia) *beside steps will soften them and act as a highlight.*

of their diameter will stabilize them so they are not dislodged.

Remember that a path works best if it is wide enough for two people to walk comfortably side by side—perhaps two friends strolling hand-in-hand, a grandchild holding the hand of a grandparent or (more likely) two gardeners deep in conversation! The general rule of thumb is to allow 2 feet of width per person. If a 4-foot-wide path appears too large for a small garden, 3 feet is acceptable, but anything less is rarely satisfactory. It is far easier to make the path wide enough at the start than to go back a few years later and move all the plants and good garden soil to widen it.

Once the paths have been laid out, it is time to scoop any good topsoil—however shallow it is—from them to add to the soil mix that is being readied for the beds. This soil is too valuable to waste in a utilitarian area.

After the topsoil has been removed, you can put down your choice of mulch. This gives good definition to the path and creates a firm surface for working and walking on, especially when the ground is saturated. A cover 2 to 4 inches deep helps excess water drain away after heavy rain. Mulch also inhibits the growth of weeds and prevents soil from splashing onto the plants or being eroded in heavy rains.

There are many materials that can be used for a path cover, and different areas of the country will have different materials locally available. I prefer wood chips, as they blend into the natural look of a wood and, for me, are plentiful and inexpensive. (They may also be right at hand, left after the initial tree work in your woodland has been completed). Care must be taken, however, with fresh wood chips: they should not be placed near any plants. The soil microorganisms responsible for breaking down organic matter utilize nitrogen during this process and will deplete the soil of it, which can lead to nitrogen deficiency in surrounding plants. I let the wood chips age for several months before using them; by then, their color is more pleasing, also. If you do use chips when they are still fresh, it's a good idea to add a little nitrogen fertilizer both to the chips and to the surrounding soil to offset this problem.

You can also place black plastic on the ground under the cover material, but be sure to poke some holes in it to let water drain through. (Weed-barrier cloth is also available, but it is an expensive alternative for a path.)

A meadow garden or borders set into grassy areas will usually have grass paths, which will need regular mowing.

The Beds

After the paths have been created, I am ready to mark out the beds. Working from my plans, I create shapes of a size that is in scale with the garden area. In an informal garden, these are free-form in design; in a more formal border, they might be rectangular.

I prefer to locate and stake out all of the beds initially, even if I plan to prepare just one or two each season. Marking them all out at the beginning gives me a good sense of the scale of the entire garden, and I can determine if the beds are appropriate in size, location and planting density.

With a woodland garden, these beds will usually be set along the paths and rarely more than 10 or 15 feet back from them. Sometimes

I have created them in combination with larger shrubs, using a few of the taller perennials (those that may reach 36 inches or more in height) 10 to 12 feet back from a path, to create an intermediate screen and background. I will want to be sure these plantings make a good visual impact from a path or other vantage point. Beyond this distance, the flowers and overall effects of most plants are lost, except for the very largest shrubs—which are used as backgrounds in a big area.

If shrubs are to be included in the garden, I place stakes where they will go. Next, I create the outlines of the beds by raking away any leaves until I have the shape and size I am looking for, just as I did for the paths; then I put in stakes to show clearly the configuration of the beds.

How big should the beds be? This depends on how large an area you have and on how intensively you want it planted. The need to decide these points is another good reason to make the plan a long-range one to include your vision of the completed area. It allows for growth in stages, as you gradually add beds or enlarge existing ones over time. As you build the garden over the years, you may find that the original plan was too ambitious: you may want to do less, preferring the look of a less heavily planted area. Or you may decide to expand beyond your original boundaries as you learn more about your garden and discover new plants you want to grow.

After all the areas are marked, I decide which beds I want to do first. My personal preference is to work on the major ones first, as they will be in strategic locations and will help give me a good sense of the overall effect early in the garden's development. This, of course, is a personal choice, and some people prefer to begin by preparing all the beds in one section of a garden or along the paths before moving on to the next section.

I follow the same philosophy for a meadow garden. If the proposed location for my garden has an abundance of existing vegetation, and I am planning to create beds without clearing it all out and starting with bare ground, I try to lay the beds out when the weeds and grasses are low (in the dormant season, or after a mowing)—not only so I can see my stakes clearly but also so I can get a better idea of the shapes and sizes of the beds and a clear overview of the whole area.

When I am setting a border into a grassy area in a lawn or along a driveway, I mark it out with stakes or a garden hose to outline its shape. It is just as important with a border as it is with the other gardens to create beds that are in scale with the dimensions of the overall area: too large, and the garden will be overpowering and the plants will tend to look ungainly; too small, and the garden design and individual features of each plant will be lost.

Once the vegetation has been eradicated (manually or chemically), the soil additives can be mixed into the remaining soil: compost and other organic matter, and some drainage material if necessary. This should all be dug in deeply, to a foot or more in depth. After the soil preparations are completed, the level of the bed should be slightly raised and mounded above the adjacent ground. Once this has had time to settle (seven to ten days), the plants can go in.

These beds can easily be enlarged at a later date, if desired. Shrubs can be added later also, to complement the main display or to give it a backdrop.

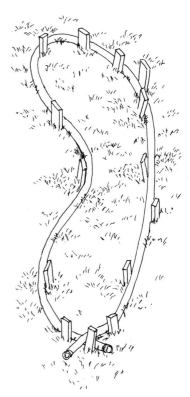

To lay out a free-form garden bed, use stakes to show its general outline and size. Then, use a garden hose or tape to show the actual curving line of the bed.

Soils

There is no single "perfect soil" for wildflowers, but there are general soil types for each habitat. Soil varies greatly from place to place, and it can be characterized by the proportions of its basic components (clay, sand, loam and the amount and quality of organic matter it contains), its ability to retain moisture, and the amount of nutrients and other compounds present in it. It is the proportion of these factors that creates the particular soil composition preferred by individual plants. And what works well for you with certain plants may not necessarily work as well for another gardener.

Whatever your soil type and its consistency, however, it is not enough just to scrape out a shallow depression and jam a fine plant down into it, pat the soil back around it and then expect it to grow well. You must dig the soil deeply, improve it by adding organic matter that you mix in well, and create a hole of adequate size for each plant. Well-prepared soil not only provides plants with the nutrients they need, but it also allows for good root penetration, air and water circulation—and it is easy to work with. The important point to remember is that wildflowers, like all other plants, are not going to thrive or reach their full potential if their soil is impoverished, compacted or not the right blend for them.

The pH Factor

Different plants have different pH requirements. The term "pH" is used to define the degree of acidity or alkalinity of a soil. In gardens, the range is generally from 4.0 (very acidic) to 7.5 (very alkaline); beyond either of these extremes, few plants will thrive. "Acid soils" have a pH of 4.5 to 5.5, while a soil with a pH above 6.5–7.0 is considered alkaline. Most garden soils fall between 5.0 and 7.0. Checking for pH can be done with home testing kits, or a soil sample can be sent to the local county agricultural extension service for a comprehensive analysis, which will include the pH factor along with a summary of soil components such as clay, nutrients and minerals. Extension service recommendations for enhancements, however, will be geared toward typical garden soils for vegetables and lawns and will not take into consideration the soil requirements for wildflowers.

Organic Matter

Organic matter is decomposed plant material and animal manure that adds nutrients to the soil and aids in the retention of moisture. It also gives a soil "structure," allowing air and water to circulate, and roots to penetrate easily.

Because different plants have different needs, various types of gardens require different amounts of organic matter in the soils. The soil for a meadow, for instance, should be "lean," which means it should be relatively low in organic matter and nutrients (but still well prepared and deeply worked).

The soil for a rock garden is made up mostly of organic matter and drainage material (usually sand). It must be well drained but not too fertile. The soil for a woodland garden needs to be rich in humus—that marvelous dark earth that is high in fibrous organic matter and retains moisture well. And the soil for a sunny border needs to have a high loam content, with enough organic matter to retain moisture during dry spells.

So how does a gardener get organic matter? Manure is a good source of it, but it *must* be well aged, as should any organic matter that is used to improve and build the soil. Otherwise, as discussed above, you may deplete the soil of nitrogen. Well-aged manure from a farm is as wonderful for humus-loving wildflowers as it is for any other cultivated plants. The largest Japanese primroses (*Primula japonica*) and bloodroot (*Sanguinaria canadensis*) I have ever seen were top dressed every year with a thick layer of well-aged sheep manure.

You can also purchase dried manure and various other kinds of organic matter from a garden center, but that can be expensive if you need a large quantity.

Decomposed leaves (leaf mold) are also a good source of organic matter for any garden; they provide a humus that is very close to what a mature wood creates through natural processes. Some towns collect the leaves in fall and make the decomposing piles available to the townspeople for gardening. (As with other forms of organic matter, the leaves should be aged for a season or two, or ground up in a shredder for best results.)

When I am preparing a niche for very special plants, I add to the soil rotted wood gathered from old decayed logs and tree stumps I find out in the woods. Woodland plants, in particular, love this, and I have had many successes with difficult plants by using decaying wood. Unfortunately, there is never as much of it available as I would like, so I save it just for very special or difficult plants such as bunchberry (*Cornus canadensis*) and twinflower (*Linnaea borealis*). I also use it for building the artificial hummocks in a bog garden. (See pages 180–181.)

For my garden in the South, I was able to get ten-year-old sawdust, which was wonderful, but because the native red-clay soil was so heavy, I also added fine bark mulch (also several years old) to help lighten it and improve the water and air circulation. (Regarding clay soils: do not fall into the trap of trying to improve and break up clay with lots of sand. This only creates something on the line of cement. It is organic matter that heavy clay soils need, with perhaps a little sand mixed in.)

My personal preference is to stay well away from peat moss. What is sold today as peat moss is little more than dust and has no fibrous properties whatsoever, which is one of the primary benefits of organic matter. If peat becomes dried out, it tends to wick moisture away from the surrounding soil and plants, and it is incredibly hard to remoisten. And never use it as a mulch, because it forms an impenetrable crust. It is far better to stay with one of the other forms of organic matter such as those already discussed, and use peat moss only sparingly.

Compost All gardeners should (and probably do) have their own compost piles. The basic ingredients of a good compost pile are: leaves, general garden refuse (but don't include weeds with seed heads, and avoid diseased material also), depleted garden soil, old potting compost, kitchen refuse (but no meat products), wood ashes and grass clippings—all of which will produce the dark humus so beneficial to plants.

Pine duff (the decomposed litter from pine needles) is extremely acidic and makes a good additive to a compost pile for acid-loving plants. However, it is best used sparingly and well mixed with the other ingredients, as it has little nutritional value and retains little moisture. The pine needles themselves make a good mulch for acid-loving wildflowers.

To convert these raw ingredients to compost, decomposition must take place. The microorganisms that are responsible for breaking down the organic matter use nitrogen in this process, which is why fresh, unaged organic matter can cause nitrogen deficiency in the soil if it is used as a mulch or mixed into the soil before it has thoroughly aged. There are several methods of hastening this process, but even a well-managed compost pile can take the better part of a year before it is ready to be added to a soil mixture. The time will vary depending on your climate, however: the warmer it is, the faster the decomposition will be.

There are many formulas for creating good compost, all basically consisting of alternating layers (4 to 6 inches deep) of the various ingredients. Every two months or so, add a good sprinkling of fertilizer (10-10-10 or 5-10-5) to enhance decomposition. If you are composting oak leaves or any other acidic material, add a sprinkling of lime occasionally to "sweeten" the mix. Moisture will also help speed the conversion of raw vegetation into a friable humus. I like to soak the layers down as I am building them, and if there has been no rain for a while, I will often water down the entire pile.

For best results and to hasten the process, the whole pile should be turned over every three months or so. The easiest method to accomplish this is to simply fork off the top layer and use it to create a new bottom layer, building the pile up again in the new site so that the bottom layers will then be on the top. This essentially turns the original pile upside down.

If you have a leaf shredder, you can run everything through it instead of turning the pile over; this will mix and chop everything at the same time, speeding up the whole process and thoroughly blending the mix. Shredded leaves are also, by far, the best mulch.

Mixing Soils

Remember that a wildflower garden will probably be planted more intensively, and with a greater variety of plants, than would occur naturally. The soil in a garden, therefore, usually needs to contain more nutrients than would be found in most natural-habitat soils.

Once I have all the ingredients for a basic wildflower soil mix—well-decomposed leaf mold, aged manure, good loam, coarse sand and any topsoil saved from the paths and the areas being prepared—I mix them together in the right proportions for the various garden types. (Different mixes for different gardens are discussed in detail later in this chapter.)

The quality and coarseness of the sand are important, as you do not want round granules that look and act like cement when wet. (To be sure I get the right sand, I visit the sand-and-gravel yard ahead of time to select the coarsest sand available.) The sand improves drainage, while loam helps to maintain the structure of the soil and give it body.

No fertilizers are necessary for these mixes, as the ingredients themselves (except the sand) are rich in nutrients and trace elements.

These trace elements are very important for healthy plant growth, and they are not contained in standard fertilizers.

Try to develop a feel for the right soil texture. In a woodland garden, for example, the mix should feel similar to the humus that makes up the topsoil layer in a mature wooded area—but with more of a gritty feel from the added sand. The soil mix for a rock garden, on the other hand, should have a very coarse, gritty, gravelly feel to it.

You can add various other "specialty" ingredients to your basic soil mix to meet the specific needs of various plants. For instance, for plants needing increased drainage, add coarse sand or gravel chips. To provide an alkaline soil for plants that love lime, there are several possible approaches. You can add ground limestone (dolomitic, not hydrated lime). Or you might add commercial chick grit, which is made from limestone; it is excellent for a small area, but it may prove too expensive for a large garden.

If you want to grow lime-loving plants, and your soil is not naturally alkaline, it is best to prepare a special bed by excavating to a depth of 12 inches or more, if possible. Cover the bottom of this area with limestone or mortar rubble (I have even seen bags of cement used to line the bottom of such a hole), and then backfill the area with a limy soil mix. If you can acquire some limestone rocks, bury them in the bed near the plants so lime is constantly being leached into the surrounding soil, where it will help to maintain the general alkalinity; otherwise you will need to add lime every year. This additional lime must be worked well into the soil. If an alkaline area such as this is planned as part of an acid-soil garden that is located on a slope, the alkaline area should be placed below the acid area so that the lime does not leach down into the acidic soil and contaminate it.

Planting

Plant Acquisition

Where do wildflowers for a garden come from? Contrary to what many people might believe, the answer should not be "from the wild." It is vital to protect our native flora in their natural habitats, and—in all but a few special situations—we must not even consider digging them from the wild. In some areas, so many native plants have been taken from the wild that their survival is in serious doubt. There are also unscrupulous commercial collectors who habitually obtain their plants by this method, and any gardeners who knowingly purchase plants from these nurseries are contributing, through their financial support, to the continued and unnecessary destruction of our native flora.

There are situations that do call for the rescue of wild plants, and they are discussed in Appendix A. Such an undertaking should be carefully planned and thought through before it is attempted.

Some plants will probably be acquired as gifts from friends. This is the nicest way to get a plant, as it then carries with it memories of the giver. Until you meet other wildflower gardeners, however, and before your own wildflower garden is well enough established to provide divisions and seedlings, you may not have many contacts who are in a position to trade or give you the plants you desire. Remember that there are a number of plant societies and groups that have annual or seasonal sales. They offer a marvelous way to acquire plants and meet other wildflower enthusiasts at the same time.

For many wildflower gardeners, the most common method of obtaining plants initially is to purchase them through a reputable nursery. In Appendix C, I have listed the addresses of Garden in the Woods and the Botanical Garden of the University of North Carolina, both of which sell plants and provide written information about wildflowers. They also publish source lists of nurseries that do not collect wildflowers from the wild but, instead, propagate the plants they offer for sale.

As wildflower nurseries that grow their own plants are located in many different parts of the country, most gardeners will find it necessary to buy plants through the mail. This has worked well for me. I have always been pleased with the size, condition and packing of the plants, and I have found the nursery owners very helpful with any questions or problems I have had.

If there is a sizable nursery or garden center near where you live, you may find that they do carry a small selection of wildflowers. I suggest that you make it a habit, before you buy, to ask where the plants come from. So often, unfortunately, a local nursery that does not specialize in wildflowers will purchase their plants from someone who has collected them from the wild and then pot them up for local sale. (If this is the case, you can explain why you do not choose to buy plants from them, and you can also let them know of the nurseries that propagate their own wildflowers.)

Care of Newly Bought Plants

Plants in Containers If the wildflowers you purchase are in containers, check them for dryness as soon as you receive them, especially if they have been sent through the mail. Soak them well if they are dry, and remove any damaged or broken parts. Let the plants recuperate for a few days by setting them in a lightly shaded area with good air circulation. After this, they can be planted out into the garden. It is a bad practice to plant anything that is dry, as this will only further stress the plant and hinder it from getting established.

Plants in containers that have been picked up at a local nursery can be planted immediately if the soil in the containers is moist.

If the new plants are healthy and large enough, and you have some experience in dividing plants, there is no reason not to make two or more divisions of them, either to enlarge an existing planting or begin a new one in a different spot.

Bare-Root Plants Sometimes plants are sent through the mail "bare-root." As soon as you receive the parcel, take it to a cool, shaded place such as a garage, basement or tool shed. (It is also a good idea to let the post office and UPS know that you would like to have any packages marked "perishable" or "live plants" left in a shady place.) Remove the plants from the box as soon as you can, or at least open it and stand them up in the box so they receive some light and air.

It is important to make the care of these plants a high priority. My recommendation is to unpack them and trim the roots, removing any broken or damaged ones that might rot and create an avenue for disease to enter. (Often these plants will arrive dormant, without foliage or visible signs of growth.) The trimming also stimulates the plant to grow new roots more rapidly. How much of the root system should be trimmed? This really depends on how the roots look and how

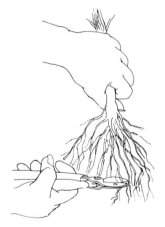

Use a sharp knife or secateurs to trim damaged roots or those that are too long.

much of a root system there is, but I will never remove more than one-third—generally less. Knowing how much to trim comes through experience, and it's a good idea to get some guidance from an experienced gardener at first, until you are comfortable making the decision. Next I set the new plants into shallow trays with tepid water covering the roots for several hours, or even overnight—but no longer, or they may rot—so the roots can soak up plenty of water. They should be planted the next day or heeled in somewhere until a permanent site is readied for them.

Occasionally, a plant will not fare well in the mail. In this case, it should be either kept in the pot or potted up, if it's bare-rooted, and placed in a special holding area (a cold frame or nursery bed) until it perks up. This may take as little as a few weeks or as long as an entire growing season.

A number of years ago, I saw a simple and very attractive display that was made from a small group of clay tile drains that had been set up on their ends, filled with soil and planted with wildflowers. A couple of the tile "planters" were set on bricks to give some variation in height. This idea was so simple, yet so effective, that I have used it in the years since not only for a display but to pot up newly acquired plants so I could watch them or pamper the few that I felt were not quite robust enough to put out into the garden right away. Later on, perhaps at the end of spring or even in the beginning of fall, I have planted them into the garden. This is a delightful way of "holding" new plants or divisions for a few weeks or months, and it also gives me the opportunity to watch closely and thoroughly examine a plant that is new to me.

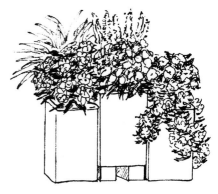

Tile drains make attractive containers for plants and are readily available at building supply stores.

Be sure to keep the labels with the plants so you will know which plants belong where and you do not have a miscellaneous collection of unknowns. It is also important to note where your various plants come from, so you will know whose plants did the best for you and where to order from in the future. As labels do have a tendency to get lost, I also keep a written record.

In most cases, mail-order plants arrive during the week, and therefore will probably need to be heeled in for a couple of days or planted in the evening. This is a good time for planting, as it will be cool and the plants will have a full night to begin settling in before the sun comes up. (See full planting instructions later in this chapter.)

Gifts and Cuttings Occasionally, I have been given a small clump of a treasured wildflower that has been out of the ground too long or may have been dug without sufficient roots. This goes into my special liqueur box (described on page 183) or a cold frame and nurtured along, much as I would do for a newly rooted cutting before it goes out into the garden. This way, I set out a vigorous plant with a good root system that will have the best chance to do well. A frail plant needs special care, and it cannot be expected to recover and thrive in an open garden situation.

Planting Time

When all the preparations are finally done and it is time to plant, try to minimize the stress on the plants as much as possible so they will be able to put all their energies into getting established. Plants will only grow well when they do not have to struggle unnecessarily to overcome the shock of transplanting or unfavorable conditions.

The two most important factors in planting (aside from having the right environment and the correct soil) are *timing* and *condition.* If you choose the optimum time to plant, and if the plants are in the best condition possible, there is little reason for them not to thrive.

A simple and rather general rule of thumb regarding planting time is to plant spring-flowering plants in the fall, and plant fall-flowering plants in the spring. In other words, do not move or otherwise disturb plants when they are just about to flower, are in flower or are full of flower buds. During these times, a plant needs a lot of water to support itself and, if it is moved or its roots disturbed at this time, it will undergo a great deal of extra stress, no matter how carefully this is done. If you must move a plant at this time, remove all of the flowers or flower buds to minimize the shock of transplanting.

The ideal transplanting times are just as a plant breaking dormancy and beginning vigorous growth, and when it is approaching dormancy, whether this is in late spring, early summer or fall. When a plant is approaching dormancy, it will still be able to initiate some new root growth and begin to establish itself in new surroundings before going completely dormant, and I have found that this is an excellent time to transplant. In both spring and fall, the soil is generally moist throughout the rooting area, and in the fall it is still warm. Both moisture and warmth will encourage the establishment process.

Another good time to transplant is just after the plant has finished blooming (providing this is not during the summer season). At this time, in the majority of cases, the flowering stems and much of the foliage can be cut back to lessen the plant's need for water and reduce transpiration, which uses up precious water when the plant does not have an established root system to replenish water readily. Plants such as iris, lilies, the taller phloxes and the ferns can have their foliage reduced by one-third or even one-half with no adverse effects. Most meadow and sun-loving plants naturally lend themselves to this treatment.

Certain plants, however, such as trillium, bloodroot, hepatica and Jack-in-the-pulpit (*Arisaema triphyllum*) cannot have their foliage cut back, because this removes all of their top growth. If you cut off the leaves, the plant has no way to make the food necessary to establish itself and grow new roots.

Transplants should have their roots and, where appropriate, their foliage trimmed in order to help them get established more readily.

The spring ephemerals, like Dutchman's-breeches (*Dicentra cucullaria*), squirrel corn (*Dicentra canadensis*), trout lily (*Erythronium americanum*), Virginia bluebell (*Mertensia virginica*) and shooting-star (*Dodecatheon meadia*), go dormant after they have dispersed their seeds, quite early in the growing season. These plants are best moved or divided when they are in a semidormant stage, which is indicated when their foliage turns yellow and begins withering. With plants in this category, care should also be taken so that the resting underground portions are not misplaced, inadvertently dug up or overplanted with something else.

Dividing Established Plants

If your plants have gone into well-prepared soil and are growing under good conditions, many will have put on enough growth to be divided after three or four years—perhaps even sooner with some plants and in areas with long growing seasons. Some plants, like the crested iris (*Iris cristata*) and rue anemone (*Anemonella thalictroides*), generally do better if they are divided every third year or so. It peps them up, maintains their vigor and stimulates flower production.

A few plants are quite fussy about when they are transplanted and divided. (See the individual plant portraits in Part II for specific information on dividing and transplanting.) Although they can be successfully moved at other times, it is not recommended, as the plants usually take a long time to recover and may not bloom for several years as a result. Sometimes they will not recover at all. Yellow lady's-slipper (*Cypripedium calceolus*), bloodroot and Virginia bluebells, for example, are best moved or divided just as they are going dormant. At this time they can be handled very successfully. Trillium and bloodroot tend to go dormant during the summer in response to drought, and they should *not* be moved during this drought-induced dormancy. In bloodroot, the red juice from the roots (from which it acquires its name) will bleed profusely if the root system is broken when it is actively growing, and this can severely weaken the plant. But good husbandry and close attention to the plant's time of dormancy can overcome these problems.

Transplants should be carefully knocked out of their pots. Hold the potted plant upside down and gently tap bottom of pot so plant slips out and rests safely in your hand.

Some plants such as the wild indigo (*Baptisia australis*) and butterfly weed (*Asclepias tuberosa*) have a deep taproot and resent being moved except when they are very young. After they are well established, they should be left to grow happily without being disturbed. Young plants of either species can be transplanted easily if they have been grown in containers where the roots have been undisturbed.

No matter which plants you are dividing and transplanting, good aftercare is vital. It is very important to keep transplants well watered and well shaded while they are getting established, to compensate for the major disturbances to their root systems. They need the best possible growing conditions to accomplish this quickly.

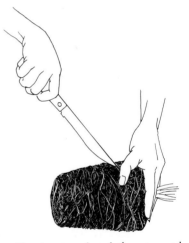

If a plant is rootbound, the roots must be broken up to allow new roots to develop and spread out into the soil.

Planting

The ideal day for planting is a cool, overcast one, and if the day is sunny and hot I will wait until evening. In either case, I always make sure the plants are well watered and the soil in their new home thoroughly moistened the evening or day before I intend to plant.

I bring all the plants to the site and, if they are in containers, set them out in the patterns I have selected. (Often, at this point, I move things around to revise my design somewhat, and I am careful to note on my plan any changes I make.)

If the plants are in pots, I check to see that they are not rootbound when I knock them out of their containers. If they are, the mass of roots must be broken up by tearing down the sides of the mass (as shown in the illustration), and some roots will probably need to be trimmed off. This encourages the formation of new feeder roots. If the root mass has formed a circle around the bottom of the pot, it is often better just to cut it all away by slicing through the whole circle as shown in the illustration. If this is not done, the plant will not grow out of the circular pattern that was formed in the pot, and it will never do well because it is unable to form a strong network of roots that move out into the surrounding soil.

Once the plants have been removed from their pots, I make sure not to leave the roots exposed to the desiccating effects of sun and wind, and I work quickly but thoroughly to get them planted as soon

With severely rootbound plants, be sure to slice off the bottom mass of circling roots.

Planting at the correct depth is essential for healthy growth. One method to insure this is to place a small bamboo cane across the hole. With bare-root plants care must be taken to spread out the roots and work soil gently around them.

as possible. I generally remove only one plant at a time from its container, moving on to the next only when the first has been properly planted. And I always have at least one plant in a group labeled. It's amazing how quickly I can forget where something was set and what it was, especially if it was dormant at the time. I'm careful to update my design sketch, also, so I will know just what was put in, where, and in what numbers. Labels may disappear as the result of activity by rodents, birds, children or a heavy-handed leaf raker.

After digging a generous hole in the newly prepared soil, I set the plant at the proper depth—that is, the depth at which it was growing in the pot—so that the top of the soil from the pot is even with the level of the surrounding ground. Plants often do poorly because they are planted too deep or too shallow. If a plant is set too deep, the crown may rot or the plant may flower poorly. If it is planted too high, its roots will be exposed and they will dry up and die. It is simple to raise or lower the plants to correct this as you set them out; it is much harder to change the planting depth after they have begun to establish themselves. This mistake can cause you to lose several months or seasons of productive plant growth in the meantime.

The best way to set a plant properly is to hold it at the correct depth with one hand while filling in the soil around it with the other. Once the plant is firmed in at the right depth, fill the rest of the soil in around it and smooth the soil to finish off the planting before going on to the next one. With a large shrub you may need another pair of hands to hold the plant while you fill in the soil.

If you are planting bare-rooted material, use a little extra care. Keep the plants in the shade and cover the roots with damp soil or moistened newspaper until you are ready to plant them. Be sure to spread the roots out in the hole so they are not packed into a tight bundle, which will only hamper their progress in becoming established. As with a pot-grown plant, hold it at the correct level and gently fill in around it with soil. Shake the plant gently to settle the soil down between the roots. Then work soil among them with your fingers, firming it securely but gently to be sure it is well set at the right height. If the soil has not been firmed properly, not only will the plant settle deeper when it is watered, it will also tend to fall over if it has much top growth. If the soil is too loose, it will not have good contact with the roots, which is essential for the plant to draw up moisture and nutrients to begin the growing process. Once you have finished planting, smooth the soil around the area before going on to the next plant.

How far apart should the plants be set? This can vary considerably and depends on several factors. You need to know what the ultimate width of the plant will be, and its rate of growth in your climate. You must also decide what sort of look you want in your garden. If you want a very full look from the beginning, you can set your plants quite close together and thin them in a couple of years. This can provide you with plants for a new area, but it can also be a big undertaking to move, for example, well-established shrubs that have been growing for a number of years in one location. You may decide instead to plant more sparsely at first, and allow the plants to fill in over the years.

With careful planning, it is possible to develop a happy medium between the dense and sparse planting methods, by using the larger or faster-growing perennials as filler plants in the early stages, and then removing this extra material in a few years before it becomes too full and cumbersome to handle. This works particularly well with shrubs, as they generally take more time to fill in. With this method, you might choose goatsbeard (*Aruncus dioicus*) and tall bugbane (*Cimicifuga racemosa*), for example, as fillers in a shady garden, or the narrow-leaved sunflower (*Helianthus angustifolius*) and boltonia (*Boltonia asteroides*) in a sunny one. If you use these plants in small groups, they will give the effect of a shrub without the bulk of a woody plant. Perennials can still be moved readily at the end of few growing seasons, and this is a good opportunity to divide them so they can be used to start a new area or to fill in another sparse planting.

Whatever method you choose, it is important that each plant be given sufficient room to fill out to its full proportions and have good air circulation around it.

Once the planting process is finished, water everything in well. To do this, don't drench the area with a heavy volume of water; instead, use a sprinkler or water breaker on the end of the hose so you apply a thorough but gentle soaking. If you are planting a large area, don't wait until all the planting is completed before you water; instead, water each bed or planting group as you complete it so the plants don't wilt. And no matter how tempting it might be, don't go off to lunch or walk the dog without watering in the plants you put in during the morning. (If you want to plant in an adjacent area later in the day, however, try not to let that area receive a soaking. The water won't have time to drain off before you begin to work with the new area. You will end up with a soggy mess that easily becomes compacted. And much of the soil will be caked on you.)

After the planting is finished, spread a mulch around everything to help retain soil moisture and shade the roots. Mulch also reduces weed growth, and as it breaks down it becomes mixed into the soil, improving it with organic matter. (See below.)

If it is a sunny day and the plants show some growth (and are not dormant), shade them right after they have received their watering. Do this in any way possible, with sheets of newspaper, an old screen from a window or a wooden lath structure made especially for the job. (See the accompanying illustration.) The shading should be left in place for several days unless the weather is overcast or rainy, when the newspaper cover, at least, should come off.

If the new plantings do not get watered naturally at least once a week, you will have to water them for the first few weeks. A long, gentle soaking is all that's needed, and as the plants become established, you should reduce the amount and the frequency of the watering, but never allow them to suffer from lack of water—especially during their first year. This applies to everything you plant, from trees to the smallest wildflower. A paucity of water will set them back, at the very least, and it may even kill them.

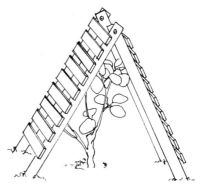

Lath shading device.

Mulch

I am always amazed at how few people use mulches. They are not only aesthetically attractive but also horticulturally sound, particularly with newly planted areas. The type you use is up to you and depends largely on what is available in your area. Some favorite choices for mulch are chopped leaves (which can be produced on a small scale by running a lawn mower over low piles), cocoa or buckwheat hulls, or finely shredded pine bark. Whatever mulch you use, I strongly advise you to select material that is small in size (not the big pine nuggets or wood chips), not only because the larger materials are out of scale and look ugly around wildflowers, but also because they do not form a cover dense enough to keep the weeds down and soil moisture in. Wood chips (providing they are aged, not fresh) are fine to use around the larger shrubs and trees, and they also work well for a path cover, as mentioned earlier.

If the natural layer of leaves in a woodland area is to remain as the mulch, it should always be thinned out, otherwise it will be so thick that plants will have difficulty growing through it, and they may be smothered. This layer of leaves should be thinned out considerably or cleared away early in the spring, well before the plants break dormancy and begin to emerge, so their growth is not impeded and you are not stepping on tender new growth at or just below ground level while you rake.

Even if you mulch with other material, you need to remove each year's collection of fallen leaves that gather on the garden before the plants come up in the spring. If you have placed a covering of evergreen boughs over the beds for winter protection, these should also be taken off early so the soil can warm and the plants are exposed to sunlight as soon as they emerge.

Considerations for Different Gardens
Woodland Gardens
Site Preparation A woodland garden will require some initial tree work and preparatory clearing of the woody growth before the beds can be laid out. Perhaps it will be enough to remove a few high branches and "limb up" the trees by removing their lower limbs (along with any damaged or diseased branches), but you may need to fell some trees, also. Some judicious pruning and shaping of trees and shrubs will very likely be necessary, especially in a small suburban woodland garden. Any brambles, honeysuckle, or other generally undesirable growths will have to be removed, along with their root systems.

I can hear the gasps at the very notion of cutting down a tree, but if the small understory trees, shrubs and herbaceous wildflowers are to grow well in woodland areas, you must expect to do at least some thinning. This will open up the wood floor to allow for good light penetration and air circulation, and it will reduce some of the root competition in the soil so that more nutrients and water will be available to the remaining plants—in particular the herbaceous ones.

The remaining trees will also grow more vigorously, be stronger and fill out to their full proportions so they can ultimately create the desired umbrellalike canopy. This shade cover is vital because it diffuses the sun's rays, which would otherwise sear the more delicate shade-loving wildflowers. A shade canopy also keeps the woodland floor cool and moist by reducing the effects of evaporation caused by both sun and wind on soil and plant tissue. At the same time, however, the canopy must allow enough light through for the plants below to flourish.

In addition, you will create spacious areas among the remaining

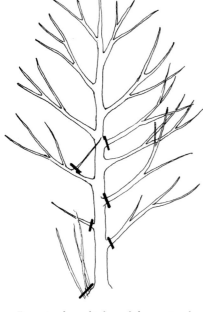

Removing lower limbs and the occasional branch from a tall tree will allow better light penetration onto the plants below the shade canopy. Suckers growing from the base of the tree divert energy from the main trunk and should also be removed.

trees for other plantings. Thus, the judicious removal of a few trees will make a great deal of difference in the overall quality of plant growth and flowering, and determine—at least in part—the success of the whole endeavor.

Winter is a particularly good time to look objectively at any garden, especially a wooded area. Without leaves on the trees, it is easier to get a clear picture of the area and to make decisions about which trees and understory shrubs should be removed.

Look at the growth in a crowded woodland site. These trees tend to have sparse, spindly lower growth and tufts at the top that have stretched into the sunlight. Reduced light penetration causes weak, thin growth at the lower levels, and lack of space results in a poor distribution of branches and unbalanced shapes. If the soil is poor and shallow, the problems become even more pronounced.

For comparison, look at a group of trees that have been properly thinned. Given space and time, they will have become healthy and vigorous, filling out to their natural shape and proportions.

Once this woodland preparation is done, little additional work will be needed to maintain the improved state over the years that follow—perhaps no more than the occasional removal of a branch or two that has been damaged in a storm.

Creating a woodland garden is a large undertaking—even in a small area—but it can be done in stages. Start with the largest jobs first by taking down whole trees where necessary, and follow this by pruning any dead or broken limbs and removing the lower branches of the trees to let in more light. By doing the heavy tree work *before* you create the beds and plant the wildflowers, you will not have the worry of dropping a tree or branch on top of one of the expensive newly planted shrubs and smashing it to pieces.

Ideally, the stumps and root systems of the felled trees and shrubs should be removed or killed, as they may continually sprout and create a recurring nuisance, while still taking water and nutrients from the desirable plants. (This is a particular problem with maples.) Likewise, any underbrush, brambles, poison ivy and the like should also be entirely removed and their roots grubbed out.

Soil and Beds My basic woodland and shade garden soil mixture for wildflowers is made up of three parts organic matter, two parts average garden loam and two parts coarse sand.

By using the right soil mix and preparing the beds correctly, you will provide the plants with the best soil conditions possible so they will establish readily and grow vigorously for many years. In a season or two, they will have blended into their surroundings. The ground covers, especially, will have spread out to form ribbons around and through the other plantings, and soon you will no longer see the manmade impressions in your woodland.

When soil preparation is done correctly, it won't be necessary to do patch-up improvements later, as always happens if inadequate initial work is done. When the soil is well prepared, it will be buoyant and full of nutrients, so little else except routine maintenance will be needed after the plantings have been mulched and watered in.

Before you begin work on the beds near the paths, try to plant the larger woody material, the understory trees and shrubs. Give priority to the background plants at this point, not only because they set the stage for the foreground plantings, but also because this system avoids having anyone walking back and forth over the foreground beds, compacting the prepared soil and running the risk of stepping on one of the carefully planted treasures while heavy plants, soil and equipment are carried into the background areas. Also, the woody plants need additional time to grow and fill out—so the longer they are growing in the garden, the sooner their display will become noticeable. The herbaceous plants, by contrast, will fill out quite rapidly.

Over the years, I have used two different methods of preparing the planting beds in a woodland garden, and both have given me very satisfactory results.

The first is to clear away the fallen leaves and existing vegetation, and then to spread a 4- to 6-inch-thick layer of prepared soil mix over the beds that have been marked out and work it in thoroughly—at least to the depth of the spade, and deeper if possible. A soil depth of 9 to 12 inches is a good goal to aim for. Most of the roots of both wildflowers and trees will be in the top 6 to 12 inches of soil, so it is vital that this top layer be properly prepared. As I dig the soil in, I remove and discard any rocks, roots or other debris I find.

I realize that in some areas this kind of bed preparation is almost impossible because of rocks, tree roots or other obstacles, but you should try to go as deep as you can. It is also perfectly acceptable to mound the bed a few inches above the surrounding soil level to create the needed depth; mounding the soil will ensure good drainage. This does expose the peripheral areas of soil and roots to greater temperature changes, as the plants in a mounded bed are not insulated by surrounding soil. Such a bed will warm up quickly in spring and summer and cool off quickly in autumn and winter. These problems can be counteracted by a slightly deeper mulch to protect the plants.

The second method—which is both more difficult and more time-consuming but infinitely more satisfactory—is to dig all of the soil out of the bed to at least 9 to 12 inches in depth, separating and saving the top layer of rich black humus. This humus (and the topsoil I've removed from my paths) will be combined with the prepared soil mix and used to fill the bed in again. I may also save the subsoil (the layer just under the topsoil) to mix into my compost pile. The lowest level of soil from the excavation will probably consist mostly of rocks and gravel. This material can be laid in the paths to replace the humus, or—most likely—it will need to be discarded altogether.

If a planting of several well-spaced shrubs is going into a large area, it is not necessary to dig an entire large bed for them. Each shrub can go into its own hole, providing it is generous in size and properly prepared.

If I'm not sure there will be sufficient drainage at the bottom of the beds or holes—if, for instance, there's a hardpan—I will break up the bottom of the excavation with a digging fork or maybe even a pick, then put down a 2- to 3-inch layer of coarse drainage material (stone, traprock or rubble) before I add the soil mix. I will also be sure that the beds are slightly mounded to encourage good drainage.

It is always best to wait until the beds have settled before planting, or if the preparations have been done in the summer, the ground can lie fallow until fall—which is an excellent time to plant, and a season greatly underutilized for planting by many gardeners. In areas that have warm or even hot, short springs that quickly develop into hot, dry summers, fall is an especially good time to plant, because it lets the plants have the winter to become established so they will be better able to withstand the onslaught of the next summer.

Borders

Site Preparation A border is an easy garden to create and maintain. If it replaces an earlier planting, you can take advantage of having a previously prepared bed and improve its soil simply by adding organic matter and working it deeply into the original soil. If you are starting an entirely new bed, the existing soil may be poor and may need considerable improvement—perhaps even with purchased topsoil.

If the border is to be set in front of a building, wall or hedge, any existing foundation plantings and all grass will need to be removed, as neither belongs in this type of garden.

Also be sure to leave enough space (at least 18 to 24 inches) along the back to allow for good air circulation and light penetration, and for access to maintain the back portion. Frequent walking over the bed itself to perform maintenance tasks will soon compact the soil and restrict the circulation of air and water through the soil, which adversely affects root growth and the general health of the plants, leading to poor growth and flowering.

The greatest effort involved in maintaining a bed set into grass is the need to edge it several times during the growing season, cutting back the grass that always intrudes into it. This has to be done regularly; otherwise the grass can become so entangled with the plants that they can only be separated by digging them up and painstakingly teasing out all the grass.

The scale of a border will be dictated by the size of the house, wall or fence or dimensions of the immediate garden area and, as always, by the ambitions of the gardener.

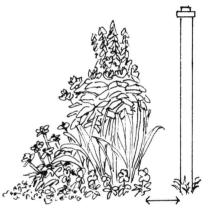

Side view of a border showing the space at back to allow for maintenance, good air circulation, and light penetration.

Fern Gardens

Site Preparation As with the woodland garden, some tree work and brush clearing will be necessary to provide good light conditions. This will also reduce the number of roots in the soil if the fern garden is to be set in a wooded area. And, to enjoy the garden to its fullest, I recommend that you include a path to meander through this changing sea of green.

Soil For ferns to prosper and attain their full size, deep soil preparations are essential. Plenty of humus must be added to create a rich, buoyant, moisture-retentive medium providing them with optimum growing conditions. One to 2 inches of mulch will also help keep the soil cool and moist, which is important to the well-being of most ferns.

Some ferns require a limy soil in which to grow. You can provide for this either by mixing lime chips into the soil mix (described under "Mixing Soils," pp. 162–163), and giving the entire area an annual top dressing of lime to maintain alkalinity, or you can create a small rock garden, setting limestone rocks into the basic lime soil mixture. (See the discussion of pH earlier in this chapter.) Since a number of lime-loving ferns like ebony spleenwort (*Asplenium platyneuron*), purple cliff brake (*Pellaea atropurpurea*), and bulblet (*Cystopteris bulbifera*), are quite small and are found naturally growing in conjunction with limestone rocks and outcroppings, this latter method can be a very effective way of handling them.

Once the plants are well established, a fern garden requires little maintenance. However, in hot, dry weather a good deep soaking once every seven to ten days will help greatly to keep them vigorous and lush, as few ferns take kindly to drought. An occasional overhead sprinkling also helps to cool the air and foliage.

Waterside Gardens

Obviously, this is a garden that will require quite a bit of initial work, whether it is artificially built or created from an existing wild area. No matter what your final design, thoughtful planning is vital. Creating a waterside garden can be a major undertaking, and you may want to think of developing this garden in stages spread over a span of several seasons or even years. This will make it far more manageable.

Site Preparation: Artificial Construction Designing and siting an artificial stream and pool will require a lot of thought on your part, but the contrived garden is really easier to create than the natural one, because you are free to select the location, size and layout for the water—and you won't have to deal with the taming of a wild area. With either approach, however, after a few seasons the end result will be very lovely. If your waterside garden is going to be artificially constructed, you must first have a reliable year-round source of water. Should your plan include a stream, excavate a shallow channel for this. If a pool is to be part of this feature, it should also be dug out at this time. You will then need to set a liner of some sort into place. This can be of heavy-gauge (4–6 mil) plastic, fiberglass or concrete reinforced with chicken wire, or a combination of these, such as a fiberglass pool running into a narrow stream lined with plastic.

When any part of an artificial waterside garden is made from concrete, certain precautions need to be taken, especially if your garden is in an area that is subject to freezing. First, put a 3- to 6-inch bed of sand down into the excavation for the pool or streambed to keep the cement from cracking through cycles of freezing and thawing. Over this pour the cement to a depth of 1 to 2 inches. While the cement is still wet, set into it a single layer of chicken wire that has been precut and molded to fit the bottom of the pool or stream. Then add another 1 to 2 inches of cement. It is important that the cement dries slowly, so if the weather is hot and dry during construction, cover the cement with moistened newspaper or an old sheet and rewet this periodically. Streams, pools and other features made of concrete must be well flushed out before planting, to wash away any residue of lime, which can be harmful to the plants in its raw state.

With plastic or fiberglass liners, a 3- to 6-inch layer of sand under the liner will also help it to settle well and remain undisturbed by frost heaves.

The edges of the stream and pool are finished by setting trailing plants beside the lip to drape over and conceal them, or by placing flat rocks at the edges to camouflage the artificial structures. A nice touch is to install a small recirculating pump to oxygenate the water and prevent it from becoming stagnant. This will require having a source of electricity to run the pump. The pump should be hidden—perhaps placed in a small hole in the ground or concealed by an ever-green shrub, or it can go into a rock formation that might be designed to simulate a spring or part of a waterfall. The pump should always be removed at the end of the season and stored in a tool shed or garage for the winter. This also allows it to be serviced yearly.

Although it isn't absolutely necessary, an overflow pipe will help to keep the water circulating at the correct level. If you do install one, it should be set at a height of 1 to 2 inches below the lip of the pool. The pipe should have a filter on it so it will not clog with debris. The water runs into the overflow pipe and is pumped to the top of the stream (or back into the pool if no stream is used).

When I wanted to have a bog garden in association with a water-side garden, I did not install an overflow pipe. Instead, I allowed the water to seep over the far end of the pool into the adjacent ground to keep it permanently moist—even wet—for the bog plants.

Circulating pump hidden behind an evergreen.

Site Preparation: Natural Construction If the pool or stream exists naturally, the biggest job will be cleaning out the weed growth in the general area. This is no mean feat, I realize, but if it is done in stages it will probably not be such an awesome undertaking, and it must be done to give the new plants a chance to gain a proper foothold without having to compete constantly for food and space. Any shrub or tree stumps that may resprout will have to be eradicated—otherwise, there will be a recurring maintenance prob-lem.

Having a few tall trees to give partial shade is a nice option (espe-cially in a climate with long, hot summers), but not essential. If there are no tall trees already in place, you can plant tall grasses or large, bushy perennials to create some shade quickly if this is desirable.

Soil The soil for a waterside garden needs sufficient organic matter to hold moisture, sand to let the water percolate through, and loam to maintain the soil structure. A recommended soil mix for this type of garden would be made of four parts organic matter and two parts each of loam and coarse sand.

In the area around the excavated pond in our illustrated garden, no full-scale soil preparation could be done because it was so swampy. I laid a thick layer of aged leaf mold across the area cleared for plant-ing, and worked it in with a garden fork wherever a plant was set in. In the sections farther back from the really wet edges—where the land is a little drier but the moisture-loving plants can still get their roots down into the wet soil—all the ground was forked over and the same aged leaf mold mixed in. The development of the entire garden was accomplished in stages, one section at a time.

Container Gardens
Soil To have your container-grown plants prosper, you need to keep several things in mind. First, it is important to prepare a light but moisture-retentive soil mix—one that has a high organic content to hold moisture, but enough drainage material to permit excess water to seep away. I use equal parts of a commercial soil-less mix, organic

matter and sand.

The drainage holes in the containers themselves must be adequate in size and number, also. The biggest problems with container-grown plants are caused by either too much water or too little water, problems a well-balanced soil mix can greatly ease.

Rock Gardens

Site Preparation and Construction For a rock garden, you can capitalize on existing rocky outcroppings or you can create the entire garden from scratch. In the first case, you will probably need to clean out some, if not all, of the existing vegetation. Where an outcropping occurs in a lawn, it will be necessary to peel the grass back from the rocks to provide planting areas and to separate the grass from the plants. (See the illustration on page 69.) This method also creates a more natural look.

You will also need to adapt the original soil around the rocks to meet the needs of the plants you choose to grow. Once you have made the proper soil mix, you can tuck it into crevices and work it into the soil around the ledge. You may also prefer to remove all the original soil and fill in the excavations with your rock garden soil to a depth of 9 to 12 inches.

If your garden is to be artificially constructed, chances are that rocks will have to be brought in to build the ledges and create planting pockets. The important thing here is to make the placement of the rocks look natural, simulating a ledge or rock formation found in the wild so the garden blends into its surroundings and does not look entirely artificial or out of place. The great rock garden expert and plantsman Lincoln Foster wrote in his book *Rock Gardening* that the "size, consistency and arrangement of the rocks and ledges should be pleasing *before* the plants are added to them," and I heartily agree.

The size of the plants to be used will depend on the overall size of the rock garden and the rocks it is made of. The smaller the area and the rocks, the smaller the plants will need to be, to remain in scale; conversely, the larger the garden, the bigger the plants can be.

The degree of difficulty in building a rock garden can vary greatly, depending on the existing features of your property and your ambitions. The goal should be to simulate a natural rock outcrop with ledges, pockets of soil and small crevices for the plants.

Soil Whether your rock garden is natural or contrived, soil is very important. It must be well drained, especially if you include plants that naturally occur in a desert or mountain habitat. The majority of plants that favor naturally rocky places do so not only because they prefer to have less competition from other plants but also because they need cool root zones, rapid drainage—especially at ground level around their crowns —and full sun for their upper parts. And because rock garden soil contains less organic matter than a typical woodland or garden soil, fewer soil-borne diseases can cause trouble for these plants. Therefore, my soil mixture for this garden consists of three parts coarse sand to two parts organic matter.

A true rock garden is always top dressed with small gravel of some kind to facilitate the rapid ground-level drainage these plants typically must have. The gravel is also in keeping with the natural look of a mountain rock outcropping and talus slope. (Talus consists of

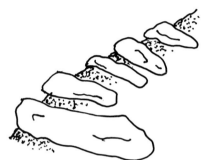

Theoretically, rocks should be set with two-thirds or more of their mass beneath the ground. In practice, if they are firmly set and look as though they are the top of a much larger subterranean mass, they will look fine and be far more doable. The bottom rock must always be the largest, as it must provide a stable base for the rocks and soil above it.

broken rocks fallen from mountain cliffs and rock faces.)

If your garden is not so much an alpine rock garden, but rather a garden that simply contains smaller plants and uses rocks for their aesthetic value (as described in Chapter 8, "A Rock Garden"), you may want to substitute for the gravel a mulch of some other material (buckwheat or cocoa hulls would be good choices) to reduce weeds and keep the soil cool.

Meadows

There are a number of ways to create a meadow garden. The two that have proved to be the most successful for me are outlined here. The first uses established plants while the second uses seeds. In a few years, either of the two methods described will give you a natural-looking meadow garden.

Creating a Meadow from Plantings The first method of creating a meadow is developed from a design that places the emphasis on color and bloom sequence rather than on a random mix of plants. In this design, the plants produce definite color bands that weave through the grasses and other greenery in predetermined patterns. Once the bed and soil preparations have been completed, plants are set out following the design, just as you would proceed in planting a traditional border. For best results, I suggest using plants established in 3-inch or larger pots, although smaller "starter" plants may be used, so long as they have a good root system.

An objection to using individual plants in a meadow garden may be that it can be quite expensive. Cost can vary greatly, however; it depends on how you plan the garden. The plants do not need to be massed in great swaths; a meadow, like any other kind of garden, can be made in stages. Also, an artificial meadow needs to have plenty of green woven through the flower colors, just as in a prairie or natural meadow. You can use only three or five of one kind of plant, amply spaced and mixed with native grasses to form a group; then continue to alternate these small groups throughout the area. This will give the impression of drifts of color. Then you can add to these small groups each season or year, until they are the size you want and give the impact you are looking for. In a few years (or less, in regions with long, warm summers), and given a well-prepared soil and conscientious aftercare, these young plants will have formed robust clumps which produce plenty of flowers.

This method can be supported, especially in the early stages (the first two to three years), by seeding the beds with wildflower seeds appropriate to your climate and design, to give an initial splash of color. If the annuals self-sow and the perennials become well established in the following year, then they complement and enhance the planned display. You can continue to use mixes composed primarily of annuals in subsequent years, if you desire, to augment the displays of the planted material.

The plants in these beds are initially treated much as they would be if planted in a traditional garden border. You will need to mulch the beds and remove the weeds, allowing the desirable plants to become well established and to spread so they are better able to compete with more aggressive plants later on. After about two years (depending on how well the plants are doing), you can remove the mulch—if it has not already broken down naturally—and allow the plants to settle completely into their surroundings. Your meadow will need only to be supported by annual maintenance from then on. (See Chapter 17, " Garden Maintenance.")

Concentrate on one or two areas at a time, expanding them each season, adding more plants until you have achieved the wonderful kaleidoscope of color that is the goal for most meadow gardeners.

In all meadows, one of the major objectives is to get a thick ground cover of desirable plants as soon as possible so that the undesirable ones are discouraged from gaining a foothold and are smothered out. With this method, the plants receive a good head start, the amount of time spent weeding is greatly reduced and the designs develop more quickly.

Creating a Meadow from Seed The other method of establishing a meadow—and the one most commonly favored, because it sounds like a simple, quick and easy way to have an instant meadow—is to use seeds. The biggest hurdle is providing a good seed bed where desirable seeds can germinate and thrive, without making conditions favorable for weed seeds.

There are two main schools of thought on how to go about this. The first recommends that the existing plant cover be removed entirely, either chemically or mechanically. In either case, the soil should be disturbed as little as possible to avoid inducing the dormant weed seeds in the lower soil levels to germinate. Wildflower seeds are then broadcast over this essentially unprepared ground.

The second school of thought believes it is best to thoroughly and deeply work the soil, encouraging the weed seeds to germinate and then dealing with them in a series of purges to dramatically reduce their presence, or—preferably—to eliminate them altogether. Then the wildflower seeds are sown on the well-prepared soil. If seeds are purchased by individual variety, rather than in a mix, it is possible to control the specific color patterns through the area, creating an effect very similar to that achieved by using the plants themselves. Sowing seeds will still produce a more random effect than setting out plants, however, and some gardeners will prefer this.

If you decide to purchase a mix of wildflower seeds to produce a random effect in your meadow, I strongly recommend that you have a reputable seed house (see Appendix C) make up a special mix for you that contains those plants most suited to your region of the country. If you purchase a nondescript assortment of seeds, many of them may not be right for your area or your needs. Most seed mixes contain annuals, and many of these are wildflowers that are not native to North America—a consideration which may or may not be important to you.

Regardless of the seeds you select, the seed beds will need to be prepared properly. (See below.)

Site Preparation Meadows are generally created either in an established lawn or in a wild area, perhaps an abandoned field. The disadvantage of creating a meadow garden in an existing lawn is that you will need to eliminate the lawn grasses. The advantage of replacing a lawn with a meadow—apart from retiring the lawn mower—is that there will probably not be many weed seeds in the soil that will germinate when the soil is disturbed.

The second fairly common meadow location is a place that is considered no-man's-land. Often wild and weedy, this may be a place you have pushed out of your consciousness and view because you didn't quite know what to do with it—until you thought of having a meadow. Or it may be far enough away from the house and main garden that it has been easy to ignore. It will need a major cleanup to remove the existing undesirable growth, which will include most of the plants on the site. This is the biggest problem whenever a meadow is developed from an existing wild area where all manner of rapacious seeds have been lying dormant and are just waiting for an opportunity to break into a frenzy of activity.

If reclaiming a wild area is too daunting a prospect, remember that it is not necessary to clear it all at once. Instead, select small sites for beds, prepare them thoroughly, and eliminate only the most noxious existing vegetation (poison ivy, Japanese honeysuckle, poke and so forth). The rest of the weeds can be gradually eliminated over time. The main drawback to leaving weeds in close proximity to the meadow garden is that, inevitably, the seeds from these undesirable plants will be carried into the new area.

I suggest you use whatever means is acceptable to you to clear the grasses and weeds growing on your meadow site. I have on occasion used chemicals with good success, and this is certainly a very simple and quick way to go about the job. Some of the newer herbicides now available break down on contact with the soil and do not create the lingering environmental damage caused by the harmful chemicals of years past.

Cosmos (Cosmos bipinnatus) and *Queen-Anne's-lace* (Daucus carota) *are good companions for a meadow garden.*

I have also tried digging out the original vegetation from meadow planting beds, but this is a long, arduous process, and much of the soil ends up in the compost pile, clinging to the roots of the vegetation you have dug out. This means more soil mix will be needed to replace the soil that is lost. But it is a great way to build up your muscles and work up an appetite!

Once the vegetation has been cleared, I deeply rototill the areas that are to be planted or sowed. Occasionally, I have asked a local farmer to bring his tractor with large tines mounted on the back to break up the soil really deeply. The tines are like a huge rake, and they dig down, crumbling the soil as they are pulled through it. This is followed by a good rototilling. (You can have it plowed, but this is not as effective and requires a lot more work on your part unless you also have a disk-harrow chop up the clods.)

After the area is tilled, it's time to mix in the various materials used to improve and enrich the soil. If it is a large area, I favor spreading the soil ingredients separately, one layer at a time (4 to 6 inches thick) and rototilling each layer in before going on to the next. You may have to go over the area a couple of times with the rototiller to get everything blended satisfactorily. Or, if the area is small, the prepared mix can be spread over the ground, in a layer about 6 inches thick, and tilled in.

After the soil has had a chance to settle for a week or two, I do the planting just as I would in the other gardens described. The immediate aftercare is also the same. There is one exception regarding mulch: As I mentioned earlier, I only keep a meadow bed mulched for two years, or until the plants have had ample time to get a head start. Then I let nature take its course, except that I do spot weeding to control any noxious plants that may appear.

Soil For a meadow, I use the existing soil but improve it by adding some loam and organic matter: about one part of each to three parts of the original soil. Then, if additional drainage seems necessary, I add one part of sand.

A meadow garden is not so much difficult as time-consuming. It requires that the gardener be patient and diligent. For me, however, it has always been worth the trouble, and the end results are always gratifying—even if getting there, at times, has been frustrating.

Bog Gardens
Site Preparation A bog garden must be located in full sun and can be of any size, although it is typically small—in the range of 4 to 5 feet at its widest part, 6 to 8 feet in length and 15 to 20 inches in depth. The most pleasing shapes are free-form outlines, perhaps in an oval or a kidney shape.

Initially, this garden requires some time to build and prepare, but this does not have to take too long. Once the basic work is done, it is not a hard place to keep up. The key is to maintain a high water level, especially in the summer when the area may have to be flooded periodically to keep it saturated. During the rest of the year, in all likelihood, nature will provide enough rain.

Construction of a bog garden is not difficult, but it does involve some serious earth moving. Once you have selected a suitable site (with full sun and easy access to water), excavate a hole of the desired proportions. Line it with heavy-gauge (4–6 mil) plastic just as you would an artificial pool. Leave a generous edge of plastic lying over the ground surrounding the hole. It is important to smooth the soil and remove any rocks or other sharp objects that might pierce the plastic liner. A sand base can also be used, as described for the construction of a waterside pool and stream.

Soil Fill the area with a half-and-half mixture of fine but sharp sand and sphagnum peat or peat humus. (Peat moss can be used as a last resort, if you cannot locate either of the other materials.) Fill the hole to within 1 or 2 inches of the top, and then flood the area with water until the mix is completely saturated. It is a good idea to wet the peat humus before mixing it with the sand and filling in the hole to be sure that it is totally saturated. Ideally, leave it overnight to absorb all the water it can, and check it the next day to be sure it is uniformly wet.

Next, trim the edges of the plastic to leave a 9- to 12-inch-wide rim lying on the ground surrounding the hole. This you can hide in one of two ways: by tucking it under the surrounding vegetation, or by mounding soil on it. To cover it with the existing plant material, peel back the plants in a mat, lay the plastic down, and roll the vegetation back over it. Or cover the plastic apron by mounding the soil excavated from the hole to form a low rim around the bog. The idea is to conceal the plastic so the artificially created bog blends into the surrounding landscape as well as possible. And nothing looks less attractive than glimpses of plastic—especially in a wildflower garden!

Next I create a hummock or two in the bog, depending on its size.

There are two methods I like to use. I may create a hummock by setting an old, rotten, lichen-covered stump into the peat-sand mix and then working crumbled, decayed wood and the peat-sand mix around and over the stump so there are ample places for the plants to grow in. Or I form a mound of rotting wood (gathered from decomposing logs and stumps) on top of the peat-sand mix. These hummocks give plants that prefer slightly elevated ground a place to grow.

The final (and very vital) step in creating an artificial bog is to cover the whole area with a 2- to 4-inch-thick mat of live sphagnum moss. To accomplish this, either set clumps of the live sphagnum over the peat-sand mixture or, if you have access to an extensive boggy place, roll up mats of it and lay them in place in your bog garden. (In most cases, the sphagnum will already have small seedlings of sundew and pitcher plant nestled down in it.) Water everything down well.

The bog is now ready to plant. Carefully tease the sphagnum apart just enough to tuck plants into it. Some will be happy settled into the sphagnum itself, while others will want to get their roots down into the special mix beneath it and lie sandwiched between the two layers. These plants include those that prefer to grow on the hummocks, such as the fringed orchids. Then gently pull the sphagnum back around the plants and water them lightly to settle them in.

Regularly check the wetness of the rooting mix, as neither it nor the sphagnum covering it must ever become dry.

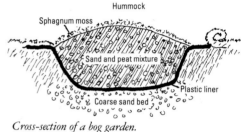

Cross-section of a bog garden.

Construction of a bog garden. The plastic liner is in place, its edges trimmed and held down temporarily by rocks. These will be removed as the surrounding vegetation is rolled over the liner to secure it. The excavation is ready to be backfilled with the sand and peat mixture.

17

Garden

Maintenance

THE BASIC MAINTENANCE FOR WILDFLOWERS and wild-flower gardens is very much like that required in any garden and involves securing the proper level of moisture and nutrients, removing undesirable weeds and protecting the desirable plants from pests and diseases. When plants grow too large, lose vigor and floriferousness or—in the case of container plants—become rootbound, they must be divided and transplanted. Some plants require protection from the harmful effects of weather or climate. All these things are vital for a successful garden.

While maintenance work is done primarily for the well-being of the plants and the attractiveness of the garden, there are many gardeners like me, who get tremendous pleasure and satisfaction from working with plants and simply being outside in the garden at every opportunity. We enjoy the maintenance "duties" nearly as much as the development of the garden itself.

As gardeners, we are acutely aware of the seasons of the year. The stages of rebirth, growth and dormancy are always fascinating and always slightly different from one year to the next. There are always decisions to make: When should the winter mulch be taken off the plants? Is now the time to mow the meadow? We consult almanacs, refer to books and notes from previous years, befriend the weather forecaster and call fellow gardeners. Through the years—and with a system of trial and error—we gradually gain the experience that tells us how best to maintain our wildflower gardens and care for the wildflowers in our particular climate.

There are many maintenance tasks that can be simplified through good garden management. The idea is to derive as much pleasure from your gardens as you can, without feeling that the work becomes a burden.

Differences in climate, altitude, exposure and local conditions always play a large role in garden maintenance. This guide, therefore, is a general one. You must rely on common sense and experience (your own and others') to decide what needs to be done to your garden, and when.

Early Spring

Early in the year, while the plants are still dormant, remove any vegetation that was left for winter interest. The tired evergreen foliage of the hellebores (*Helleborus* species), foamflower (*Tiarella cordifolia*) and marginal shield fern (*Dryopteris marginalis*), for instance, is of little use to the plants at this time, and it can look rather disheveled. The new foliage will push up early to replace the old. All these trimmings can be added to the compost pile. By now, there should be no fallen or broken tree limbs left (except for those from any recent storms) as this work is best done when the ground is still frozen, to avoid compacting the soil and damaging any plants.

Once winter is on the wane, clear away any winter mulches (evergreen boughs or salt hay—whatever was used to give extra protection to certain plants), and lightly rake off any fallen leaves that were not removed in the fall cleanup.

If your garden has a natural leaf cover, thin it somewhat (leaving a permanent cover of 1 to 2 inches), and fluff it up so new plant growth can easily push through. When you use a mulch of shredded leaves, try to develop the feel of lightly raking off the fallen leaves without greatly disturbing the plant labels or the mulch below. The removed leaves can be composted, or they can be put through a shredder and replaced around the plants as mulch.

If the leaves are to be shredded, it helps to make small piles in easily accessible places and shred them as you go. Areas where the mulch is thin should have their cover replaced first, and then the other places can be replenished after. Spring is such a busy time that this is one job often postponed, but if the mulch is sparse, you should try to make time to shred these leaves or bring in another kind of material to put on as a good thick cover. If you cannot get this done before the new growth appears, it is best to wait until later in the season when the plants are showing clearly so there will be less danger of treading on young tips or buds that were at or just below ground level earlier in the spring.

Maintaining the appearance of the plants and pulling weeds should be an ongoing process, as the key to avoiding major weed problems is to get them out of the garden area before they set seed, thus eliminating their potential to self-sow. I have found that if I mulch the beds properly and diligently remove all weeds soon after they appear, after a few years I have to do very little weeding at all. The few weeds that do appear are blown in from surrounding areas or brought in by birds or animals.

Once the frost is out of the ground, I get on with planting, being careful not to disturb those plants already in place. I like to get as early a start on this as possible so the plants have plenty of time to get established before the weather warms up and the sun becomes hot enough to harm the new transplants.

When Special Care Is Needed

If I have a plant that isn't quite ready to go right out into the garden because it is too small or has an insufficient root system, I will either pot it up and coddle it in a cold frame, or plant it out in a nursery bed until it is ready to go into the garden. The latter is simply a small bed of well-prepared soil in a shady area, easily accessible and close to the house and a source of water.

To pot up these plants, I like to use large, shallow bulb pans or—my favorites—the wooden boxes that expensive wines and liqueurs are packaged in. These boxes are usually available for the asking, and wine merchants have always been helpful in this regard.

When using these liqueur boxes, I place a layer of drainage material—pea gravel, broken pot shards or whatever else is suitable and available—in the bottom of the box, just as I would in any container, and then fill it with a mixture of equal parts compost (or leaf mold) and coarse sand, up to about 1 inch of the top. I firm this mix, then set the small plants into it, label them with their names and the date, water them well but lightly, and place the box in a well-aerated, shady place where I can keep a close eye on it.

The roots of some plants such as the fringed polygala (*Polygala paucifolia*) do take quite a while to regenerate after they have been disturbed. To facilitate this process, I have sometimes made a tent

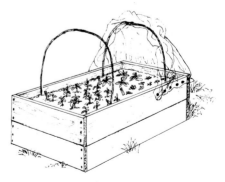

A minipropagation box is used to root cuttings or hold poorly rooted plants while they develop additional roots until they can be planted out into the garden.

over the box to reduce transpiration for the first few weeks, just as I do when I am rooting cuttings. I make this tent by bending two or three wire coat hangers (two are enough for my liqueur box) into hoops, setting the ends into the soil and then laying clear plastic over them and thumb-tacking it all around the edges of the box. I make sure the plastic doesn't rest on the foliage, because this would cause mildew and rotting. (See the illustration.) Once a day, I check the plants and open the plastic to exchange the air. (If the weather is cool and no sun is reaching this minipropagation box, it can go for a couple of days, if necessary, without being checked.)

The plastic cover can usually be taken off three to four weeks later if the roots are establishing well. I begin by untacking the plastic from the box, then I leave it off at night and finally I leave it off all the time. This slowly hardens off the plants and weans them away from this very nurturing and protective environment before the plastic is entirely removed. It usually takes the plants a few weeks to become thoroughly acclimatized, at which point they can be transplanted into the garden. Depending on the plants and how well they are developing roots, I may leave them in this container until the next season, when I will ease them out of it right at the planting site with as little disturbance to the roots and soil as possible.

For plants that don't seem to need this much coddling, but may still be on the small side or simply aren't quite ready to go into the garden, I will use my nursery area. Here, I can keep an eye on these small plants and, if necessary, give them some extra care. Later (perhaps after a few months, or during the next season), when they are larger and growing vigorously and have a good root system, they can go out into the garden itself.

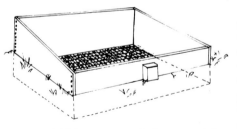

Fiberglass panel set into a lip created by a router. The wood strip placed on top gives a seal against moisture.

Cold Frames

I always have a cold frame or two, and these also work well as nursery areas for plants that need special care. I like to have one filled with sand, so I can easily plunge containerized plants into it and keep them under my eye until the time is more favorable for planting or until they are large enough for the garden—or until I have time to transplant them. The sand also insulates the roots from heat and cold, providing a situation that is similar to what the plants would find in the garden. And I keep another filled with equal parts of leaf mold or compost and sharp sand, so plants can be grown or seeds sown directly into this medium.

My cold frames are simple wooden structures made of treated wood so they will last a long time. (See the illustration.) I use 1- by 8-inch planks, placing them two high along the front and three high along the back, so when I place the tops on the frames they will slope forward, allowing the rain to run off. The low front also makes the frame easier to work with, as I can reach all the way to the back without difficulty on a frame 3 feet wide.

To construct a cold frame, first dig a hole as long and as wide as you plan to make the frame, to a depth of approximately 12 inches. Then spread 2 to 4 inches of drainage material (pea gravel, broken bricks or whatever is available) in the bottom. I've found that it is also a good idea to lay down hardware cloth over the drainage layer to prevent rodents from burrowing in from the bottom.

Set up the boards so the wood rests on the drainage material, and

Cold frame set up on drainage material with hardware cloth set in place to keep out rodents.

Completed cold frame. A brace holds the top open.

screw them together at the corners. (This is usually a two-person job.) If the length or width of the cold frame is more than 5 feet, stout stakes will need to be driven into the ground on the **outside** of the frame to prevent the boards from bowing. If it is a large cold frame, a board can be set on edge in the center to divide it into two sections, one of sand and one of soil mix.

After the boards are secured, backfill inside the frame to ground level with sand (if the area will be used to hold containerized plants) or a soil mixture. Any space on the outside of the wooden frame is packed with the soil from the original excavation, or with drainage material left over from the inside of the frame. In this way, the frame is partially set into the ground and the inside bed is level with the outside ground, which will give extra insulation to the plants' roots all year round.

The tops of these cold frames are more difficult to construct. Make wooden frames, or "sash" (as they are usually called), the same dimension as the bottom frame from front to back and approximately 2½ feet wide. (Any wider and the sash becomes too heavy and cumbersome to handle.) Glue and tack a sheet of fiberglass, purchased from a building or garden supply company, into the frame. (If this is done by someone with carpentry skills and tools, it is best to rout out a lip for the fiberglass to sit in and then place a strip of wood on top of the fiberglass to give it a better seal against moisture. See the illustration for details.) Heavy-gauge plastic can be used in place of the fiberglass, but its life span is quite short.

Many other kinds of cold frames can be created by inventive gardeners with good carpentry skills. They can be constructed from cinder blocks or bricks, and there are also premade ones that can be bought from garden supply companies.

A cold frame is by no means essential, but it is a useful piece of equipment and lots of fun.

The important thing is to manage it properly. The interior needs to be well aired, and the plants must be watched and kept watered, especially when the frame tops are kept closed or only opened a crack, as in winter. After a snowfall, I take off the tops, fill the cold frames full of snow and then put the tops back on. This gives the plants a good insulating blanket, and as the snow melts in the spring everything receives a good soaking.

Transplanting and Dividing

Spring is a good time to divide and transplant wildflowers. Those that flower early in spring can be moved now, right after they have finished flowering. However, once the weather starts to warm up—and especially if rain becomes infrequent—it is best to wait until fall to continue with this work.

It is very important to know something of how a plant grows before attempting to move or divide it, as this greatly influences how it should be handled.

Those with a central crown, such as wild bleeding heart (*Dicentra eximia*), cardinal flower (*Lobelia cardinalis*) and yellow lady's-slipper (*Cypripedium calceolus*), can be dug up and carefully divided by separating the new crown(s) from the parent plant by cutting down between the crowns with a sharp knife or spade.

Smaller plants with less massive crowns, such as hepatica (*Hepatica*

Crowns: After removing enough soil to expose the individual crowns, gently pull them apart. It may be necessary to aid this process by using a sharp knife.

species), shooting-star (*Dodecatheon meadia*) and bird's-foot violet (*Viola pedata*), can be separated by gently holding each crown and carefully pulling them apart. Often, a gentle twisting motion is needed to separate those roots that may be snagged together. With plants that require more careful handling, I wash all the soil off the roots so I can see the crowns and central parts more clearly; then it becomes easier to see how the plants can best be divided. Usually, several crowns or natural breaks are visible, so I know where to make the separation. After that, I remove any broken and damaged leaves or roots, then I trim the remaining roots and top growth (on the plants that are not dormant) if this is appropriate (as with the dwarf crested iris and merrybells). (See the illustrations on pages 164 and 166.)

Plants that carry their leaves at the tops of stems—such as twinleaf (*Jeffersonia diphylla*), heuchera and rue anemone (*Anemonella thalictroides*)—cannot have all their foliage trimmed in this fashion, because doing so would remove the plants' sole means of manufacturing food. To reduce stress on new divisions and transplants for this type of plant, a few leaves—no more than one-third—can be removed. This helps them establish more quickly, as it reduces the amount of foliage the plants have to support. I put these young divisions directly into beds, unless they are rather small or I want to give a few to friends later, in which case I will plant them in my nursery area or cold frame.

Ground-cover plants with a trailing growth habit, like partridgeberry (*Mitchella repens*), the gingers (*Asarum* species) and creeping phlox (*Phlox stolonifera*), are best moved in clumps. This keeps the central part of the clump intact with no root disturbance. Many of the plants in this category have their underground stems running just under the leaf litter or growing very shallowly in the soil. Along these stems, occasional fine roots occur, so it is important to get as many of these rooted stems in the clump as possible without disturbing them. The plant will not survive if these roots are badly damaged or are missing from the portion that is transplanted. When these trailing plants fail to reestablish after being divided, it is often because the gardener has taken too small a part of the plant, or dug too shallow a clump of earth and roots.

When this kind of wildflower is replanted, soil must be carefully worked in around the outside roots and firmed down all around the clump. On occasion, I may gently press a clump into the ground with my foot to ensure that it is firmly set! A good watering will also settle the soil down into any open pockets. This method ensures that even if some of the pieces around the edges of the clump fail to grow, the central part will do well.

In many cases, the small pieces of these trailing plants that are inevitably cut off during the transplanting and dividing process can be made into cuttings. Some may even have one or two fine, hairlike roots on them, which will give them a head start in the rooting process.

With plants that do not have a central crown, but form a strong, thick clump like that of many meadow plants including queen-of-the-prairie (*Filipendula rubra*), ironweed (*Vernonia noveboracensis*) and goldenrod (*Solidago* species), you can simply dig the plant up, shake off some of the soil, and divide it. The easiest way to do this is to set two garden forks back to back in the center of the clump and pull

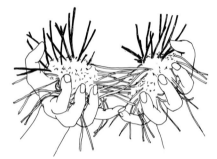

Small clump-forming plants that do not form crowns can be separated into desirable sizes by pulling them apart. A twisting motion will help separate snagged roots.

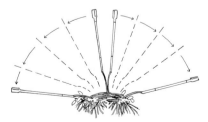

Large clumps are best divided by lifting them and then using two garden forks as shown to pull them apart.

them carefully apart, separating the two halves of the plant. This can be repeated a number of times, depending on the size of the clump, how many individual plants you want, and how big you want them. Before dividing them, trim back any top growth to about one-third of its height—not only to ease the job of dividing but also to lessen stress on the plant by reducing the amount of foliage and, therefore, its need for water. This leaves ample foliage for the plant to manufacture food.

Ferns, for the most part, have rather tough, wiry rootstocks that are frequently located at ground level. It may be necessary to use a sharp garden spade or a knife to cut through the rhizomes. The more soil you can leave around this rhizome when transplanting a fern, the more quickly it will become established. Because the new fronds are so brittle, I try to divide and transplant them either early in the spring before any new growth can be seen, or late in the fall as dormancy approaches, when no harm is done if the fronds are broken.

Ample water is vital to all plants after any kind of root disturbance, and it is important to avoid exposing the plants or their roots to sun and wind. I am especially diligent about watering bare-rooted divisions, as they will need a few days to get established well enough to enable them to take up water, and they can easily die if exposed to too much sun, heat or wind. Sprinkling them lightly with water every evening or morning for several days after they have been divided also helps to keep them turgid. Conversely, be careful not to overwater, as the roots will not be able to take up a lot of water. If the soil has been prepared properly, however, excess water should drain well.

If I have a large number of plants to divide and transplant, I will often take one large clump (or several midsized ones) of plants such as turtle-head (*Chelone* species), purple coneflower (*Echinacea purpurea*) or tall bugbane (*Cimicifuga racemosa*) into the garage or garden shed, so they will be sheltered from sun and wind during the process. I cover them with damp newspaper before and after I work with them, and I take the new divisions (still covered with the moist newspaper) back to the garden promptly to plant them. I am careful to water these plants thoroughly before I move on to the others or my next project.

Some plants grown in large containers can remain in them for one to three years—perhaps even longer—depending on how large they grow, how healthy they look, and how quickly they establish. Others may well need to be transplanted after twelve months, before they become rootbound.

If you have a container in which the ground covers have become too full, but you aren't ready to replant the other plants into the main garden, you can carefully dig out a clump or two of the ground cover (using a narrow trowel) and put these into the main garden or begin another container. Fill the hole that is left with compost, and in a short time the space will be covered over by the remaining plants.

Rhizomatous plants such as crested iris (Iris cristata) *and Solomon's seal* (Polygonatum biflorum) *are simply cut into sections, each with several buds (or leaves if the plants are not dormant).*

Late Spring and Early Summer

While early spring and fall are the times of greatest garden activity, late spring and early summer are busy, too. At these times, however, there always seems to be an opportunity to take a moment or two to savor our gardens and our plants, to enjoy and critique what we are working on, and to plan refinements and new projects.

There's certainly plenty to do. Many wildflowers (especially the early spring-blooming ones) can be transplanted and divided at this time of year. Staking and other routine maintenance not finished earlier can be completed now. Vines can be trained into place, and early-flowering shrubs that set next year's flower buds right after blooming such as rhododendron, Japanese andromeda (*Pieris japonica*), and mountain laurel (*Kalmia latifolia*) should be pruned right after flowering so new buds are not removed during this process.

Staking

Some of the taller-growing plants, like New England and New York asters (*Aster novae-angliae* and *A. novi-belgii*) and boltonia (*Boltonia asteroides*), may need staking in early spring. To avoid having to do this, I shear back by one-half or two-thirds those plants that flower in summer and fall. (This may be done in late spring or early summer, depending on where you live.) This still gives them plenty of time to set flower buds, but at the same time it keeps them shorter and bushier and frequently induces them to produce more flowers. Another method I use to avoid staking is to put the plants that need support near a shrub or stiff perennial upon which they can lean.

Fertilizing

A new wildflower garden will need little if any fertilizing, as there will be plenty of nourishment in the organic matter used in the soil mixes. One exception to this would be a garden with a great number of the more robust, larger perennials and woody plants. Sun-loving plants, in particular—which for the most part are larger and more vigorous than shade dwellers—will use the available nutrients faster than plants growing in shade. If the area is intensively planted, it may require fertilizing sooner and more frequently. In an area that is mulched annually, the mulch will also add nutrients as it breaks down and becomes mixed into the soil through the action of worms and small animals, and the general work performed by gardeners—weeding, transplanting and so forth. In an established garden, fertilizing may well have to become a regular part of maintenance.

In a garden's early years, I prefer to spot-fertilize when it is necessary, especially with woody plants. Whenever I see plants exhibiting foliage color that indicates a nutritional problem—generally paler than usual, or yellowish foliage—or if they don't appear to be as vigorous as I believe they should be, I will give them a sprinkling of a general garden fertilizer such as 5-10-5 or 10-10-10. If they are acid-loving plants I will use an acid fertilizer, being careful not to touch the foliage with any of it. Cottonseed meal is an excellent acidifying fertilizer, but it must be worked lightly into the soil or it will form a crust, which is not only unsightly, but of little value. Be careful that you do not tear the roots of shallow-rooted plants when you are working around them.

I fertilize my woody plants—the trees and shrubs—more often than the herbaceous ones, as they are larger with more top growth and tissue to support. Also, the woody plants cannot be lifted out to have their beds rejuvenated after a few years. If the soil is dry or the weather hot, I water the fertilizer in to prevent scorching the plants' tissues from too concentrated a dose. If I cannot water, I wait until it rains to fertilize.

I especially watch for yellowing, or chlorosis, of the leaves. This is often an indication of iron deficiency and is easily corrected by first spraying the foliage and drenching the soil with a spray of iron chelates and then following this with several applications of a granular or powdered form of nitrogen fertilizer. This treatment can be followed by one or two applications each year of slow-release nitrogen fertilizers. (If you are unsure of the cause of the problem, send some of the leaves to the county extension service for analysis, or take them to your local nursery or garden center.) Generally, regular feeding is all that is necessary to bring plants back to prime condition.

If a planting has been in place for five or more years, and little garden work has been done that adds nutrients—mulching or top dressing with leaf mold or compost—I would recommend an annual spring fertilizing.

Container-grown plants need more frequent feeding; how often depends on how long the plants will be in the container and what kind of plants they are—the more vigorous their growth, the more food they will need. For the short term, a liquid feed every seven to ten days will usually be sufficient. Or—to simplify matters—apply a granular fertilizer. (Remember to give the acid-loving plants an acid fertilizer.)

If the plants are to remain for several months or more in a container, then a slow-release fertilizer would be a good choice. With these long-term residents, it is important to keep an eye on their root growth so if they do outgrow the container and become rootbound, they can be transplanted into a larger one. At this time, a sizable specimen can be divided and the new plants either planted out into a garden, given to a friend or potted up to add to the display. The parent plant can then go back into the original container. This process will refresh the soils and invigorate the plants.

Summer maintenance is mostly a question of keeping an eye on watering and weeding. This is a good time to finish all those odd jobs that did not get done in the spring. I also find that summer is a good time for me to evaluate my planting design and decide what changes, if any, will need to be made in the autumn.

Weeding

I can never emphasize enough how important it is to keep on top of weeding, especially before the weeds have the opportunity to produce seeds. Be sure never to put weeds with seed heads into the compost pile, as they will germinate either there or in the beds when the compost is used later.

Some gardens require more weeding than others. A rock garden is usually more demanding in this regard—at least initially—than most of the other gardens in this book. Weeds seem to love this environment, where there is ample room between the plants, good air circulation, plenty of sun and perfect soil for seed germination.

A waterside garden that has been tamed from an existing wild area also needs extra attention to weed pulling for the first few seasons.

In a bog garden, it is important to keep an eagle eye out for the appearance of weeds, because—although this is an environment created for a specialized group of plants—weeds invariably find it to their liking, especially for seed germination. Any weed seedlings that are found must be carefully eased out of the sphagnum as quickly as possible before they become firmly established.

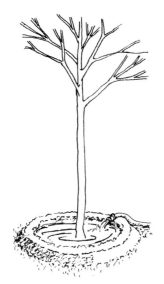

Water ring.

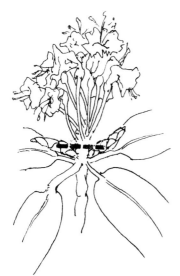

When deadheading a rhododendron, snap off the seed cluster as indicated.

Sun, Shade and Water

All plants must receive adequate amounts of water. How much is adequate depends on the needs of the plants, the composition of the soil and the climate.

Because of their size, newly planted trees and shrubs often need a great deal of water to help them overcome the trauma of transplanting and become established. Building "water rings" around these plants helps hold water in the soil directly around their roots.

A water ring is a low mound of soil (4 to 6 inches high) that circles a plant and works like a dam to retain water. After the planting has been finished and the soil firmed around the tree or shrub, create a low rim of earth around the plant at the edge of the hole. (This can be made from the excavated soil.) If it is located on sloping land, the water ring should be in the shape of a horseshoe with the opening on the higher side of the slope so water running down is caught inside. A water ring only needs to stay in place for the first twelve to eighteen months after planting, after which it can be removed. These rings also help hold mulch in place around new plantings.

Container-grown plants, especially, must be regularly watered. In warm weather, containers of all kinds dry out rather quickly, so they cannot be left untended for long periods of time. In the middle of summer, they will probably need daily watering.

Also, the root zones of the plants in containers are not insulated as they are in the ground, and consideration must be given to tempering the effects of the constant exposure of the roots to heat from the sun. It will benefit the plants if the containers themselves receive some shade each day, especially in the afternoon, to moderate the heating of the soil. This can be provided naturally by trees, other large plants or buildings, or by carefully siting the containers near a garden ornament or chairs. The spring wildflowers will happily sit in sun during the early part of the season, but when summer comes it is time for them to be put in the shade.

Deadheading

This is a rather strange but very descriptive term that simply means removing spent flowers. Deadheading can be performed for aesthetic reasons, as is sometimes done with woody plants, especially rhododendrons and mountain laurel, which begin developing next year's buds shortly after the flowers have gone by. It is most commonly done, however, to encourage flowering plants to channel all of their energy into growth and continued flower production rather than the production of unwanted seeds. In this case, it should be done right after flowering (especially in rhododendrons and mountain laurel), when the remains of the flower clusters will break easily. It is also best done in the morning, when the plant tissues are still full of water and are turgid, and the heads can be snapped off cleanly

Pinching off old flowers or cutting back the top of the spent flower stems on herbaceous plants frequently induces them to continue blooming, sometimes for many weeks longer than their usual bloom time—and then to rebloom.

Autumn

Fall, in a wildflower garden, is another busy season. This is a time to get everything cleaned and tidied up for winter. Plants need to be cut back as they go dormant, and mulches must be replenished. This is also a marvelous time to create new beds and to transplant and divide established plants.

I especially enjoy planting at this time of year because there always seems to be more time in the fall than in the spring, and most plants will reestablish well in the warm soil and mellow temperatures of autumn. In the South, late fall and winter are, without a doubt, *the* times to plant, as the autumns are long and the winters mild. When I lived in South Carolina, I found that everything I planted in the fall would be well established by the time the hot, dry summer months came along—and this also gave me the opportunity to be out in my garden during every free moment from September to June.

In areas with especially harsh winters, however, some evergreens such as conifers and rhododendrons are best moved in early spring, not fall. Antidesiccants may help avoid the damage caused by winter drying from sun and wind—known as "winter burn"—that is especially troublesome with newly planted evergreens. Antidesiccants can also be used during the growing season to help prevent water loss on all kinds of newly planted material.

Rejuvenating Beds

When I see a number of plants in an area exhibiting symptoms that indicate they require fertilizing, I am reminded that I should think about rejuvenating the soil in that general area—especially if it has been a number of years since the original soil work was completed. This rejuvenation is best done in spring or fall, just as for any transplanting.

Ideally, to rejuvenate a bed or an entire garden, I take the herbaceous plants out. (I often divide these before I replant the area.) Then I improve the soil by adding compost (or some other form of organic matter) or the same soil mix used originally, digging it in well before replanting the area. It is easy to make any changes to my original design during this rejuvenation process.

If the work is going to take more than a weekend to complete, I heel the plants into temporary homes in a cold frame, in another bed (if convenient), or—most often—in a well decomposed compost pile. As this transplanting is just for a short time—a couple of weeks at most—they are set into the ground in simple lines, if necessary, with no thought to aesthetics.

I leave the woody plants in place and work around them.

Meadow Mowing

The most important task in meadow garden maintenance is mowing. An annual cutting is essential to maintain the balance of a meadow and keep it vigorous. Mowing prevents any woody plants from getting a foothold, and the mowings will also act as a natural mulch and top dressing, replenishing the soil without making it too rich or wholesome. A rotary mower is the best tool for this, because it chops up the vegetation and disseminates the flower seeds.

If the layer of mowings is too thick to leave on the plantings, it can be taken away to a compost pile. But remember it will be full of seeds (ideally, desirable ones!), so it is better to leave it spread out in the meadow, at least for a while, and take advantage of this perfect way to reseed. Or you can make a separate compost pile of mowings which can be used later on to mix into a new bed within the meadow.

The best time to mow is late in the year when everything is dormant (or almost so) and the ground is quite hard. If this task is left until spring, the vegetation will have become matted down and difficult to cut, and it may need going over several times. At this time, the ground can also be wet and soggy from months of snow or rain, and then you'll be taking a chance of leaving deep wheel ruts.

If the winter aspect of the meadow appeals to you, and you prefer to leave the vegetation intact through the winter, then a sickle-type mower will do a better job in spring than the rotary type. If you use a sickle mower, however, the "hay" will have to be raked off, as it will leave too dense a cover for the plants to grow up through.

To give the meadow a neater appearance, you can cut it twice. Do a first, high mowing (with the blades set at 4 to 6 inches) in late spring, before the buds of the summer flowers develop, and the second in the early winter. With this method, the plants will be bushier and shorter.

Winter

Winter Protection and Mulch

A winter mulch is one that is only applied after the ground is frozen, to give added protection to either the dormant crowns and roots or the above-ground portions of plants that may be damaged by extreme cold, sun, drying winds or frost. A winter mulch usually consists of evergreen boughs and sometimes salt hay or extra leaves.

In areas that have extreme winter weather, new plants or those that might be borderline hardy may need an extra-thick mulch or other protective covering to lessen the effects of intense cold and frost heaving. Primroses (*Primula* species) are especially susceptible to this, as are cardinal flowers (*Lobelia cardinalis*) and other plants that like moist soils. Soils with a high moisture content are especially apt to heave, as wet soils freeze and thaw frequently and to a greater degree than drier soil, and this freezing/thawing action can push plants out of the ground, exposing their crowns and roots to desiccating sun and wind. Frost heaving can also tear the plants' roots.

Adequate winter protection is vital for container-grown plants. The most important thing is to protect the roots from being killed or damaged by the cold, and by the action of the soil when it freezes and thaws. A second concern is to protect the container from cracking or splitting.

In late fall, set on the ground any container that is standing on walls, blocks or tables. If there are several pots, group them close together, pack leaves, salt hay, straw or pine needles between the pots and then fill plastic garbage bags or feed sacks with leaves and stack them around the outside of the group. You can also use burlap to encircle the pots and pack leaves down inside, then lay evergreen boughs or leaves on the top. (Christmas tree branches work well.) Gardeners are imaginative people, and I am sure there are many other ways to insulate container-grown plants.

If leaves or boughs have been laid on top of the plants to protect the crowns, be sure to remove them early enough the following spring so the new growth is not smothered by this winter cover.

Plants in individual pots can also be plunged into a cold frame for the winter to protect their roots, or they can be set into a garden bed if you do not have a cold frame.

Check the containers once in a while throughout the winter to see if the soil has dried out and needs watering. This is especially important in warmer climates and on sunny days anywhere; if the temperature is high, the soil can dry out even in the middle of winter. Although the plants are dormant, the soil should never become dry, especially if they are evergreen. On the other hand, plants should not remain sodden, or they will rot.

A cool greenhouse (one kept below 50 degrees Fahrenheit) would be an ideal place for your container plants to winter over, but with careful monitoring an unheated garage can also be used. (In a garage, the containers can be grouped together in an out-of-the-way place and watched to keep the soil from drying out.) It takes some skill and experience to handle plants this way and to learn what works best for you.

Pruning

This is too complex a subject to address fully here, and there are a number of very good books already available on this subject. I do want to say, however, that pruning is too often sorely neglected in our gardens, and especially in wildflower gardens. Is that because we feel that "wild" flowers should be left to nature's rule?

To keep shrubs growing vigorously and flowering well, the old or damaged branches need to be removed. Judicious pruning encourages the production of strong new growth and flowers, while it opens up the plants to good light and air circulation. I have so often seen huge old rhododendrons and mountain laurels growing above the first-floor windows of a house—and working their way up to the second floor. The plants bloom poorly, paths and doorways disappear under their foliage, and their centers are completely filled with dead branches because all the light and air have been gradually eliminated over the years.

Good pruning benefits the entire garden. Some deciduous plants such as azaleas and viburnums, and the favored ornamentals from abroad like winterhazel (*Corylopsis pauciflora*) and beautybush (*Kolkwitzia amabilis*) will—if properly pruned—provide a wonderful haven for wildflowers to grow beneath them.

Some pruning should be done just for aesthetics, to accentuate the plant's overall form and beauty. The highbush blueberry (*Vaccinium corymbosum*) is almost Oriental in the way it grows, and this plant can be a spectacular specimen if it is pruned well to enhance its natural growth habit.

When should pruning be done?

The proper time to prune the majority of shrubs and trees is during the winter months when they are dormant. A sunny day in February is ideal. The exceptions to this are those woody plants like Japanese andromeda, redvein enkianthus (*Enkianthus campanulatus*), rhododendrons and mountain laurels that set next year's flower buds very soon after they have finished blooming. These must be pruned immediately after that time so as not to affect next year's flowering. Some, like the lovely native yellow wood (*Cladrastis lutea*), "bleed" profusely when they are actively growing, so they must only be pruned in winter when they are dormant and the sap does not run freely.

Spring to early summer is another popular pruning time, and it can

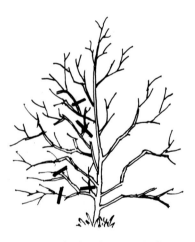

Pruning a shrub is done not only for aesthetic reasons but to open up the interior of the plant to light and air.

be helpful during the pruning process to see how the plants open up and look while in leaf. No pruning (except for the removal of a broken branch) should be done after August, as the new growth typically induced by pruning will not have time to harden before the onset of winter, and may be severely damaged by cold temperatures. An exception to this is in very warm climates where frosts do not occur.

If pruning is made a part of the continual maintenance of a wild-flower garden and kept up on a yearly basis, it never becomes an overwhelming chore. With regular, careful pruning, the plants do not have to be "butchered" and then allowed a year or two to recover, as so often happens when a gardener suddenly realizes a large plant is encroaching on a building or overwhelming a corner of the property or garden. Sometimes we inherit problems like this, and then we do have to perform aggressive pruning, but the sooner it is tackled the sooner the beneficial results will show.

There are two approaches to this need for drastic pruning. The first involves cutting all branches back to a height of 6 to 12 inches, which induces the dormant buds on the remaining branches to sprout. The best time for this is early spring, as the plant begins to grow.

The second method requires the removal of one-third of the plant each year to bring it back in stages. With this technique, you will not have to look at stumps with their unattractive tufts of growth for a year or two.

Whichever method you decide to use, it is important to keep drastically pruned plants well watered and give them a good fertilizing once new growth begins. In all likelihood, they have been neglected for a number of years, and the soil around them is depleted of nutrients and compacted. Remember that these are established plants, and they will have a substantial root system to encourage vigorous and ample new growth.

Showy trillium (Trillium grandiflorum)

AFTERWORD
Wild Places

SOME OF US HAVE COME TO APPRECIATE wildflowers through a love of the outdoors and a desire to enjoy its plant life, observed while walking, riding, picnicking or boating. The gardeners among us may have been struck by the simple beauty of wildflowers and wish to include them in their gardens, often with the idea of ensuring the plants' survival as their natural habitats are destroyed and incorporated into the human environment.

We have our favorite places to visit in the woods, meadows and mountains, and it is the wild aspects of these places that we want to bring into our gardens. Or, we may want to keep a place on our property essentially wild, and just make minor improvements so we can better enjoy its natural beauty.

My wild place is where, some years ago, all the trees were cut down, leaving a bleak, tortured-looking landscape. Now nature is slowly reasserting herself, casting a mantle over the bare, scarred and eroded ground. First to show were the birches and poplars, and then came the white pines and oaks. Finally, these trees are showing some height, and they promise one day to give me a wood to walk through. Where the desirable trees—oaks and pines—seeded in and grew too thickly, I have thinned them out so that those remaining will grow more vigorously and will fill out with a well-balanced branch structure. I also fertilize these trees every spring. I cut down and pull out the roots of the weed trees—cherries and maples—as these will resprout if their roots are left in the soil.

Beneath the trees that have sprung up during the intervening years, many naturally occurring wildflowers grow. Wintergreen (*Gaultheria procumbens*) forms thick carpets, while in moist places merrybells (*Uvularia grandiflora*) and early rue anemone (*Anemonella thalictroides*) are scattered beneath the witchhazel (*Hamamelis* species) and oak trees. At the edges of this sheltered area beneath large hickories that escaped the earlier lumbering gather wake robin (*Trillium erectum*) and Christmas fern (*Polystichum acrostichoides*).

This area will continue to evolve naturally and is a place for wildlife and quiet walks. Wild grapes clamber over shrubs and trees, their loose clusters of plump fruit hanging down in bundles each autumn. Here is a plant for a sunny, wild place where it can be encouraged, particularly because it is a favorite food of grouse. Old man's beard (*Clematis vitalba*) drapes itself over everything, creating a delicate, light shroud of white in summer as myriad small flowers put on their display. This is followed in fall by a gray haze of the familiar fluffy seed heads that are companions to the dried sedges and grasses of the winter landscape.

This fall display is continued by several of the small flowered clematis species that form small waterfalls of soft, feathery plumes. These clematis were planted to grow over a stone wall that separates this area from the main garden. In the main garden and in the wild area, the pods of milkweed (*Asclepias syriaca*) and butterfly weed (*Asclepias tuberosa*) split to expose the intricate, silky parachutes of the seed heads. Green leaves now change to their autumn mantle: shades of scarlet and red as seen in the three-toothed cinquefoil (*Potentilla tridentata*) and winterberry (*Ilex verticillata*), plum in the wintergreen and galax (*Galax aphylla*) and yellow in the sweet pepperbush

(*Clethra alnifolia*). The previously unassuming Indian cucumber root (*Medeola virginiana*) acquires conspicuous yellow foliage with striking red veins and shiny black berries. Now the ferns, those stalwarts of the spring and summer garden with their soft, rich greens and architectural lines, present to the fall landscape a mellow tapestry of rich hues of unsurpassed loveliness. They transform verdant woods into an extravaganza of color that blends with the crisp, spirited days of fall. And lingering to the last hard frost are the New England asters (*Aster novae-angliae*) in a variety of shades.

Winter brings constant reminders of the flower kingdom with frost patterns on glass so reminiscent of ferns. The dried seed heads of goldenrod (*Solidago* species) and sedges (*Carex* species) have their own charm. Icicles along a brook, snow caught amongst the pine needles, old wintered seed pods coated with ice—they all form "flowers" of their own. Such beauty can never be considered an ending, only a time of resting and transformation.

Throughout the year, there is always the incentive for the gardener to look ahead and prepare for the next growing season. Even as you plan and plant your gardens, try to keep your own images of wild places in your mind. Whenever I can successfully recreate a small corner of one of these habitats, I consider myself fortunate and pleased.

In winter, plants can still be ornamental, especially when coated with frost or snow.

APPENDIX A
Plant Rescues

WHEN WILDFLOWERS ARE THREATENED by "progress" (in the form of roadwork, construction or whatever else causes a bulldozer to scour the woods and fields), plants rescues are not only justified, but also an excellent way to acquire a collection of our native wildflowers while doing a good deed. A plant rescue might be a garden club project, a local conservation group endeavor, or part of an environmental exercise for Scout groups. Sometimes the staff and volunteers for a botanical institution or a wildflower preserve will spearhead these rescues.

There are several organizations around the country that have active plant rescue programs, which not only save our native flora, but also provide stock plants for their wildflower collections. (Several of these are listed in Appendix C.) The progeny from these plants can be sold at plant sales. Such sales provide a source of wildflowers for local people, encourage others to support the program and raise money that can be used for other environmental and preservation causes.

When a rescue is well planned and executed, it is an admirable undertaking, but it does require thought, preparation and cooperation among the participants. The key is to conduct a plant rescue with integrity and conscience, and to do it in a way that provides the best possible opportunity for the majority (if not all) of the plants to survive.

The first step in a rescue operation is to obtain permission of the landowner. Sadly, there can be times when permission to dig the plants may be refused for no apparent reason, and the plants will be destroyed. Fortunately, this is very rare, but it does happen, as not everybody values wildflowers and their habitats.

Ideally, the plants should be dug when the soil is moist and they are not suffering from the effects of drought. It is also preferable that they not be transplanted while they are in bloom. If they must be moved at this time, remove the flowers so all of the plants' energies will go into growing roots rather than into maintaining flowers and producing seed. In the case of those plants that have their only leaves just beneath the flowers, such as trilliums and rue anemones, be sure to remove only the flowers, not the foliage. Otherwise, you will be removing the plant's only means of producing food.

In most plant rescues there often simply isn't the opportunity to select the ideal time. You may just have to do the best you can to care for the plants and get them into a safe haven as quickly as possible.

Planning is critical to the success of a plant rescue, so everyone involved should meet a few times to review the operation. Chances are good that the group will be doing other rescues from time to time, so it will help to have a well-organized system. Write down the plan so you can discuss it, improve upon it, and share it with other groups. These are some of the things that need to be decided beforehand:

What equipment will be needed? Someone must be responsible for gathering tools, plastic bags and water containers. (Empty plastic milk jugs are perfect for this.)

Who will provide transportation, and what kind of vehicles are available? If an open truck is used, the plants will need to be covered

Plant stretcher.

to prevent them from drying out and having their tissue damaged from being buffeted by the wind during travel. If the site is not immediately adjacent to a road, how will the dug plants be brought to the vehicles? This is an important consideration, as the plants may be in an area inaccessible to vehicles, and sizable plants require sizable rootballs, which can be quite heavy to carry. I have seen people use everything from large wicker backpacks to an ingenious stretcherlike device developed by a friend of mine in New Jersey. This was made from two thick closet poles with a piece of plywood nailed across them. (See the illustration.) Two people were thus able to carry several plants at once with ease.

Who will take which plants, and how many? Where will they go? Be sure the place is prepared ahead of time so they can be slipped quickly into the ground.

Who will be in charge of listing the rescued plants and making labels for them? It's essential to visit the rescue site ahead of time to compile a list of what plants are growing there and decide which ones should be saved. At the same time, decide who will be responsible for vehicle access and transport.

Immediately after the plants have been dug, their roots must be covered in some way until they are replanted. Moist newspaper works well for plants going into a car trunk. Plants that will be transported in open truck beds should be placed in plastic bags or covered containers.

Large cardboard boxes and bushel baskets are also useful for carrying plants. My personal favorite carrier is the large two-handled metal feed tub often used for livestock. Feed and stable supply stores also sell lightweight fiberglass "muck baskets" that have plastic rope handles and are perfect for moving dug plants.

If you use containers, pack some soil or leaf mold around the roots after the plants are set in them. Dampen the soil, and water the plants if they are dry. Be sure to take along extra containers of water for this purpose. Do whatever you can to reduce the stressful effects of the rescue on the plants.

Last but by no means least, leave the rescue site in good shape: no litter or plastic lying around and no huge gaping holes, even if you are only a few days in front of a bulldozer. (If you are only a few *hours* in front of a bulldozer, then there is no need to worry about filling in the holes.) It is also a courteous gesture to send a thank-you note to the person who gave you permission to rescue the plants, and to anyone else who helped.

After the rescue has been completed, hold a final group meeting, both to celebrate and to review the results. Discuss what part of the operation went well, what could be improved upon, and what new measures might need to be considered for the next rescue.

APPENDIX B
Bibliography

Art, Henry W. 1987. *The Wildflower Gardener's Guide.* Pownal, VT: Garden Way Press.

Bailey, Liberty Hyde and Ethel Zoe Bailey. *Hortus Third.* Revised and expanded by the staff of the Liberty Hyde Bailey Hortorium. 1976. New York: Macmillan.

Barr, Claude A. 1983. *Jewels of the Plains.* Minneapolis: University of Minnesota Press.

Bell, Radford and Ahles Bell. 1964. *Manual of the Vascular Flora of the Carolinas.* Chapel Hill: University of North Carolina Press.

Berrisford, Judith. 1966. *The Wild Garden.* London: Faber and Faber, Ltd.

Birdseye, Clarence and Eleanor Birdseye. 1972. *Growing Woodland Plants.* New York: Dover.

Bradley, Jeff. 1985. *A Traveler's Guide to the Smoky Mountain Region.* Boston: The Harvard Common Press.

Brooklyn Botanic Garden Handbooks. Produced throughout the year on numerous subjects. 1000 Washington Avenue, Brooklyn, NY 11225.

Browse, Philip McMillan. 1978. *Plant Propagation.* New York: Simon & Schuster.

Bruce, Hal. 1982. *How to Grow Wildflowers and Wild Shrubs and Trees in Your Own Garden.* New York: Van Nostrand Reinhold.

Case, Jr., Frederick. W. 1964. *Orchids of the Great Lakes Region.* Bloomfield Hills, MI: Cranbrook Institute of Science.

Cobb, Boughton. 1963. *A Field Guide to the Ferns.* Boston: Houghton Mifflin.

Correll, Donovan S. 1950. *Native Orchids of North America North of Mexico.* Stanford, CA: Stanford University Press.

Dana, Mrs. William Starr. 1903. *How to Know the Wildflowers.* New York: Scribner. Reissued 1989. Houghton Mifflin.

Diekelmann, John. 1989. *Wildflower Gardening.* New York: McGraw-Hill.

Dirr, Michael. 1990. *Manual of Woody Landscape Plants,* 4th ed. Champaign, IL: Stipes.

Dormon, Caroline. 1965. *Natives Preferred.* Baton Rouge: Claitors.

Durand, Herbert. 1927. *My Wild Flower Garden.* New York: Putnam.

Farb, Peter. 1963. *The Face of North America.* New York: Harpter & Row.

Fernald, M. L. 1950. *Gray's Manual of Botany.* New York: American Book Company.

Foster, H. Lincoln. 1982. *Rock Gardening: A Guide to Growing Alpines and Other Wildflowers in the American Garden.* Portland, OR: Timber Press.

Gleason, Henry A. 1968. *The New Britton and Brown Illustrated Flora of the Northeastern United States and Adjacent Canada.* 3 vols. Riverside, NJ: Hafner Publishing.

Godfrey, Michael. 1980. *Sierra Club Naturalist's Guide, The Piedmont.* San Francisco: Sierra Club Books.

Harper, Pamela. 1990. *Designing with Perennials.* New York: Macmillan.

Isaacson, Richard T. (Updated yearly.) *Anderson Horticultural Library's Source List of Plants and Seeds.* New York: Garland Publishing.

Jekyll, Gertrude. 1983. *Color Schemes for the Flower Garden.* New York: American Book Co.

Jekyll, Gertrude. Edited by Penelope Hobhouse. 1985. *Gertrude Jekyll on Gardening.* New York: Random House.

Jekyll, Gertrude. 1989. *A Vision of Wood and Garden.* Sagaponack, NY: Sagapress.

Johnson, Charles W. 1985. *Bogs of the Northeast.* Hanover, NH: University Press of New England.

Jorgenson, Neil. 1971. *A Guide to New England's Landscape.* New York: Barre Publishers (distributed by Crown).

Korling, Torkel. 1972. *Prairies, Swell & Swale.* Dundee, IL: Torkel Korling.

Lacy, Stephen. 1990. *Scent in Your Garden.* Boston: Little, Brown & Co.

Lawrence, Elizabeth. 1984. *A Southern Garden: A Handbook for the Middle South.* Chapel Hill: University of North Carolina Press.

Mickel, John and Evelyn Flora. 1979. *The Home Gardener's Book of Ferns.* New York: Holt, Rinehart & Winston.

Miles, Bebe. 1970. *Bluebells and Bittersweet.* New York: Van Nostrand.

Miles, Bebe. 1976. *Wildflower Perennials for Your Garden.* New York: Hawthorn Books.

Mitchell, Alan. 1987. *The Trees of North America.* New York: Facts on File Publications.

Morris, Frank and Edward A. Eames. 1929. *Our Wild Orchids.* New York: Scribners.

Morse, Harriet. 1982. *Gardening in the Shade.* Portland, OR: Timber Press.

Neuse, Josephine. 1970. *The Country Garden.* New York: Scribners.

Newcomb, Lawrence. 1989. *Newcomb's Wildflower Guide. An Ingenious New Key System for Quick, Positive Field Identification of Wildflowers, Flowering Shrubs and Vines.* Boston: Little, Brown & Co.

Peterson, Roger Tory and Margaret McKenny. 1975. *A Field Guide to Wildflowers of Northeastern and North Central America.* Boston: Houghton Mifflin.

Phillips, Harry. 1985. *Growing and Propagating Wild Flowers.* Chapel Hill: University of North Carolina Press.

Preece, W.H.A. 1937. *North American Rock Plants.* New York: Macmillan.

Reader's Digest Illustrated Guide to Creative Gardening. 1987. New York: Reader's Digest Association (distributed by Random House).

Rickett, H.W. various dates (different volumes). *Wild Flowers of the United States.* New York: McGraw-Hill.

Roberts, A. Edith and Julia Lawrence. 1983. *American Ferns.* New York: Macmillan.

Robinson, William. 1983. *The Wild Garden.* Summit, MO: Century Publishing.

Rowntree, Lester, 1936. *Hardy Californians.* New York: Macmillan.

Rydberg, Per Axel. 1932. *Flora of the Prairies and Plains of Central North America.* New York: New York Botanical Garden.

Sackville-West, Vita. 1979. *Garden Book.* New York: Atheneum.

Schenk, George. 1984. *The Complete Shade Gardener.* Boston: Houghton Mifflin.

Schnell, Donald. 1976. *Carnivorous Plants of the United States & Canada.* Winston-Salem, NC: Blair.

Seymour, Frank C. 1969. *The Flora of New England.* Rutland, VT: C.E. Tuttle Co.

Smyser, A. and the editors of Rodale Press Books. 1982. *Nature's Design.* Emmaus, PA: Rodale Press.

Steyermack, Julian. 1975. *The Flora of Missouri.* Ames, IA: Iowa State University Press.

Thomas, Graham Stuart. 1967. *Color in the Winter Garden.* Boston: Charles T. Branford.

Watts, Mary Theilgaard. 1975. *Reading the Landscape of America.* New York: Macmillan.

Wherry, Edgar T. 1948. *Wild Flower Guide.* New York: Doubleday.

Wherry, Edgar T. 1961. *The Fern Guide.* New York: Doubleday.

Wilder, Louise Beebe. 1937. *The Wild Garden.* New York: Atlantic Monthly Press.

Wilder, Louise Beebe. 1990. *Color in My Garden.* New York: Atlantic Monthly Press. (Originally published in 1918. Garden City: Doubleday.)

Wiley, Leonard. 1968. *Rare Wild Flowers of North America.* Seattle: Wiley.

APPENDIX C
Plant Societies, Nurseries, Seed Houses and Other Resources

Plant Organizations and Societies

Both Garden in the Woods and the North Carolina Botanical Garden offer written information about wildflowers, and they also produce publications that list wildflower nurseries that propagate their own plants and do not collect from the wild.

Garden in the Woods, The New England Wildflower Society

Hemenway Road, Framingham, MA 01701.

Garden in the Woods is a 48-acre botanical garden owned and operated by the New England Wildflower Society. This beautiful property was purchased in 1930 by Will Curtis, who proceeded to develop it into an outstanding wildflower garden. He was subsequently joined by Howard O. Stiles, and together they continued to develop and maintain Garden in the Woods until they gave it in 1965 to the New England Wildflower Society.

North Carolina Botanical Garden

CB #3375, Totten Center
University of North Carolina, Chapel Hill
Chapel Hill, NC 27599-3375.

In addition to supplying written information about wildflowers, the North Carolina Botanical Garden contains five acres of native plants, featuring a collection of southeastern native carniverous plants and an area of native plants displayed in habitat simulations.

American Rock Garden Society

c/o Irma Market (Secretary)
102 Proctor Avenue, Ogdensburg, NY 13669.

The American Rock Garden Society provides an information-packed quarterly bulletin, holds regional meetings and offers an outstanding seed list.

Nurseries Offering Wildflowers

(Those marked with an asterisk specialize in wildflowers and do not collect from the wild.)

Andre Viettes Farm and Nursery, Route #1, Box 16, Fishersville, VA 22939.

*Boothe Hill Wildflowers, 23B Boothe Hill, Chapel Hill, NC 27514.

*Brookside Wildflowers, Route #3, Box 740, Boone, NC 28607.

Crownsville Nursery, P.O. Box 797, 1241 General's Highway, Crownsville, MD 21032.

*Don Jacobs, Eco Gardens, P.O. Box 1227, Decatur, GA 30031.

Fancy Fronds, 1911 4th Avenue West, Seattle, WA 98119.

Forest Farm, 990 Tetherow Row, Williams, OR 97544.

Garden Place, P.O. Box 388, 6780 Heisley Road, Mentor, OH 44061.

Goodness Grows, P.O. Box 311, Highway 77, Lexington, GA 30648.

Gossler Farms Nursery, 1200 Weaver Road, Springfield, OR 97478.

Holbrook Farm & Nursery, Route #2, Box 223B, Fletcher, NC 28732.

Montrose Nursery, P.O. Box, 957, Hillsborough, NC 27278.

*Native Gardens, Route #1, Box 494, Greenback, TN 37742.

*Niche Gardens, 1111 Dawson Road, Chapel Hill, NC 27516.

Northcreek Nursery, R.R. #2, Box 33, Landerberg, PA 19350.

*Orchid Gardens, 6700 Splithand Road, Grand Rapids, MI 55744.

Primrose Path, RD #1, Box 78, Scottsdale, PA 15683.

Rice Creek Gardens, 1315 66th Avenue NE, Minneapolis, MN 55432.

*Shooting Star Nursery, 444 Bates Road, Frankfort, KY 40601.

Siskiyou Rare Plant Nursery, 2824 Cummings Road, Medford, OR 97501.

*Sunlight Gardens, Route #3, Box 286-B, Loudon, TN 37774.

Tom Dodd Nurseries, Drawer 95, Semmes, AL 36575.

Transplant Nursery, Parkertown Road, Lavonia, GA 30553.

*We-Du Nurseries, Route #5, Box 724, Marion, NC 28752.

Weston Nurseries, P.O. Box 186, Hopkinton, MA 01745.

*Woodlanders, 1128 Colleton Avenue, Aiken, SC 29801.

Nurseries Offering Wildflower Seed

*Boothe Hill Wildflowers, 23B Boothe Hill, Chapel Hill, NC 27514.

Clyde Robin Seed Company, Box 2091, Castro Valley, CA 96546.

Environmental Seed Producers, P.O. Box 5904, El Monte, CA 91734.

Loft's Seed, Inc., P.O. Box 146, Bound Brook, NJ 08805.

Midwest Wildflowers, Rockton, IL 61072.

Natural Habitat Nursery, 4818 Terminal Road, McFarland, WI 53558.

Prairie Nursery, Box 365, Route #1, Westfield, WI 61072.

Prairie Restoration, Inc., P.O. Box 327, Princeton, MN 55371.

Prairie Seed Source, P.O. Box 11143, Palo Alto, CA 94306.

*Shooting Star Nursery, 444 Bates Road, Frankfort, KY 40601.

Stock Seed Farm, Box 112, Murdock, NE 68407.

The Vermont Wildflower Farm, Route 7, Charlotte, VT 05445.

Windrift Prairie Nursery, R.D. #2, Oregon, IL 61061.

Some Places to See Wildflowers

Arboretum of the Barnes Foundation, Marion, PA 19066.

Arnold Arboretum, The Arborway, Jamaica Plain, MA.

Audubon Sanctuaries

Bartholomew's Cobble, Ashley Falls, MA.

Bartlett Arboretum, Brookdale Rd., Stamford, CT 06903.

Bartram's Garden, 54th Street and Lindbergh Blvd., Philadelphia, PA.

Batstow Historic Site, near Hammonton in the Wharton Tract, Batstow, NJ.

Bear Mountain State Park, NY.

Bowman's Hill Wildflower Preserve, Washington Crossing State Park, Washington's Crossing, PA 18977.

Blue Ridge Parkway

Brandywine River Museum Gardens, P.O. Box 141, Rte. #100, Chadd's Ford, PA 10317.

Brooklyn Botanic Garden, 1000 Washington Ave., Brooklyn, NY.

Chicago Botanic Garden, P.O. Box 400, Glencoe, IL 60022.

Denver Botanic Garden, 909 York St., Denver, CO 80206.

George Lee Memorial Garden, Chichester Rd., New Canaan, CT 06480.

Greenbrook Sanctuary, The Palisades Nature Association, Box 155, Alpine, NJ 07620.

Holden Arboretum, Mentor, OH.

Leonard Buck Garden, Layton Rd., Far Hills, NJ 07931.

Longwood Gardens, Kennett Square, PA 19348.

Magnolia Plantation, Hwy. 61, Charleston, SC.

Mianus River Park, Merriebrook Lane, Stamford, CT 06903.

New York Botanical Garden, Bronx, NY 10458.

Norcross Wildlife Sanctuary, Tupperhill, Munson, MA 01507.

North Carolina Botanical Garden, Totten Center, University of North Carolina, Chapel Hill, Chapel Hill, NC 27599-3375.

Planting Fields Arboretum, Oyster Bay, Long Island, NY 11771.

Rancho Santa Ana Botanical Garden, 1500 N. College Ave., Claremont, CA 91711.

Rhododendron Species Foundation, P.O. Box 3798, 32nd Ave. S., Federal Way, WA 98063.

Scott Horticultural Foundation, Swarthmore College, Swarthmore, PA 19081.

Sieur La Monte Wildflower Garden, Acadia National Park, Mount Desert Island, ME.

Skylands Botanical Garden, Ringwood State Park, Ringwood, NJ 07456.

University of California Botanical Garden, Centennial Drive, Berkeley, CA 98063.

The Vermont Wildflower Farm, Rt. #7, Charlotte, VT 05445.

Winterthur, Route. 52, Wilmington, DE 29735.

✿ ✿ ✿

Most U.S. and Canadian national, provincial and state parks and forests feature a variety of native wild plants; check with park offices for information.

Acknowledgments

Author's Acknowledgments

I would like to thank all the people who over the years have given freely of their time, knowledge, plants and seeds. Their generosity and kindness have added greatly to my joy in gardening. I would especially like to thank:

Florence Roberts, with whom I have spent many a delightful day on trips to find, study and photograph wildflowers, and many a wonderful hour discussing them and how they might best be grown in cultivation.

Charles Moore, for giving me one of the most memorable days of my life trekking through the woods of North Carolina. Among the wonderful things he took me to see was a wooded hillside thick with *Trillium vasyi,* whose sweet fragrance permeated the warm spring day. And if that were not enough, we ended our visit by seeing a rare wild stand of my favorite plant, *Shortia galacifolia,* growing in great abundance.

Jo and Herb Breneman, whose lovely garden filled with rare and wonderful wildflowers grown to perfection, was not only an inspiration for me, but a place where I learned so much. During our quiet walks in their woods, they shared their knowledge freely with me.

My friends who have kindly allowed me to use the photographs I have taken of their gardens in this book. Their names and the location of the gardens have not been given to protect their privacy.

The sadness I feel at the loss of some of my other friends is eased whenever I see the plants they have given me growing in my garden, and I always feel a warm smile cross my face as I remember our shared love of plants. Through this book, I hope to be able to pass along some of the knowledge and the love of wildflowers my friends shared with me.

I also want to express my gratitude to those who have directly and indirectly contributed to the creation of this book.

My thanks and appreciation to Sarah Blanchard, whose editorial work on my manuscript and patience in typing my stream of horticultural consciousness made a very big undertaking easier. Her hard work helped ensure that the manuscript was finished and delivered to the publishers in time.

Special thanks to Dr. Richard Lighty, Director, Mount Cuba Center for the Study of Piedmont Flora and to Nicolas H. Ekstrom for reviewing the manuscript.

My thanks also to Sydney Eddison, who gave me support and encouragement when my spirits wilted before the task at hand. She kept me at the word processor when I would far rather have been out in my garden!

V.F.
Woodstock, Connecticut

Producer's Acknowledgments

This book has been a very special and demanding enterprise involving the joint efforts of some highly talented and committed people. I would like to offer my personal thanks to all of them:

To Carol Bolt for her beautiful paintings that bring the magic of gardens to paper; to Murray Belsky for his fine design sense that shows on every page; to Castle Freeman and Joan Rosenblatt for their meticulous care with the text; to Maggie Higgins who, as always, kept things moving ahead and under control; to Cathy Dorsey, for her wonderfully intelligent index; to Ellen Kagan for her sound advice and her exceptional ability with color-correcting; to Dan and Oscar Kantor of A & S Graphics for their quick and careful typesetting of a very complex manuscript; and to David Li and Rosy Zee of Oceanic Graphics, both of whom were extraordinarily helpful at every step of the way toward producing a beautifully printed book.

Thanks also to Dora Galitzki of the Plant Information Service of the New York Botanical Garden for her invaluable help on nomenclature and to Katherine Powis, Librarian of the New York Horticultural Society, for her equally valuable help on bibliographic matters.

And finally, special thanks to Jason Epstein of Random House for his understanding of the project and for his suggestions that were always right on target; and to Maryam Mohit of Random House for her keen eye, excellent editorial sense and amazing ability to get things done.

R.R.
New York City

Index

(Page numbers in *italic* refer to illustrations. Page numbers in **boldface** refer to main entries for wildflowers.)

About the author:

VIKI FERRENIEA is the former director of horticulture for the New England Wildflower Society. A graduate of Swanley Horticultural College in Kent, England, she received the National Diploma in Horticulture from the Royal Horticulture Society. She trained at the Royal Botanical Gardens at Kew, where she first began her love affair with North American wildflowers. The creator of the North American wildflower garden at the world-renowned Longwood Gardens in Kennett Square, Pennsylvania, she has lectured on and taught about wildflowers all over the country. Ferreniea has long taught a professional course on wildflowers at the New York Botanical Garden. Her articles have appeared in *Woman's Day, Horticulture, Fine Gardening,* and other professional gardening publications. She lives and gardens in Woodstock, Connecticut.

Notes

Notes